William Stubbs

ON THE

English Constitution

THE CROWELL HISTORICAL CLASSICS SERIES

UNDER THE EDITORSHIP OF *Herman Ausubel*

William Stubbs on the English Constitution
EDITED BY NORMAN F. CANTOR

Lord Beaconsfield by Georg Brandes
WITH AN INTRODUCTION BY SALO W. BARON

Queen Elizabeth by Mandell Creighton
WITH AN INTRODUCTION BY G. R. ELTON

Impressions of Russia by Georg Brandes
WITH AN INTRODUCTION BY RICHARD PIPES

IN PREPARATION

Americans of 1776 by James Schouler
WITH AN INTRODUCTION BY RICHARD B. MORRIS

The First Two Stuarts and the Puritan Revolution
by Samuel R. Gardiner
WITH AN INTRODUCTION BY WILLSON COATES

Hume by Thomas Henry Huxley
WITH AN INTRODUCTION BY ALBERT HOFSTADTER

Life of Andrew Jackson by William Cobbett
WITH AN INTRODUCTION BY MARCUS CUNLIFFE

꿏ꚏ ꚏꚏ ꚏꚏꚏ ꚏꚏ ꚏꚏ

William Stubbs

ON THE

English

Constitution

꿏ꚏ ꚏꚏ ꚏꚏꚏ ꚏꚏ ꚏꚏ

EDITED BY Norman F. Cantor

BRANDEIS UNIVERSITY

THOMAS Y. CROWELL COMPANY

Established 1834   New York

3-1303-00068-3178

CONTENTS

INTRODUCTION

᭤ The most celebrated and influential historians in any era are
not simply those who possess great erudition and strong powers of
literary exposition, but those whose presentation of the past re-
flects the dominant assumptions and critical intellectual problems
of the society in which they live. In our day, the most influential
historians are those who can organize the past according to the
concepts of the social and psychological sciences. In Victorian
England, the historians whose works were most avidly studied
were those who portrayed the rise and triumph of the English nation and who demonstrated the emergence and preservation of
those distinctive national parliamentary and legal institutions that
were universally assumed to be the foundations of England's greatness and power in the world. Parallel nationalist motifs dominated
nineteenth-century historiography in all countries, from Russia to
the United States.

The two greatest achievements of Victorian nationalist historiography were Thomas Babington Macaulay's five-volume *History of England from the Accession of James II* (published
1849–61 and dealing with the period 1685–1702) and William
Stubbs' three-volume *Constitutional History of England* (first edition published 1874–78 and dealing with the period c. 450–1485).
Both Macaulay and Stubbs received the enthusiastic applause of
educated society and were suitably rewarded by the Crown—
Macaulay with a peerage and Stubbs with a bishopric. Macaulay,
an experienced publicist and brilliant essayist, was eminently the
more effective and dramatic writer; the sales of his work during
his lifetime were phenomenal, far exceeding those of Stubbs in the
nineteenth century. But for the long run, Stubbs had two advantages over Macaulay—first, the broad scope of his subject, and

second, Stubbs' academic affiliation and respectability. As Regius Professor of Modern History at Oxford, he saw his *Constitutional History* and his *Select Charters*, a collection of medieval documents for undergraduate study, become the standard textbooks that they have since remained at all English universities. In 1948 Helen Cam, a leading English medievalist, announced that the history faculty of Cambridge University had placed Stubbs' work in a special category for students of medieval constitutional history, "a category," Miss Cam noted, "in which no other secondary book is to be found." Presumably the same exalted position for Stubbs' work existed at Harvard, where Miss Cam was professor of English constitutional history for several years in the 1950's. In 1952 the director of the Institute of Historical Research of the University of London, J. G. Edwards, defended Stubbs' interpretation of the emergence of the medieval English parliament as still substantially sound. And in 1960, in a textbook designed for American students, Bryce Lyon proclaimed that Stubbs' "insights into constitutional history will never be superseded."

While Macaulay gained a vast popular market, Stubbs became the paragon of the establishment in the academic world for the following hundred years, nor is this position likely to be soon undermined. A violent attack by G. O. Sayles and H. G. Richardson (*The Governance of Medieval England*, 1963) on Stubbs' interpretation of medieval English history has had a very qualified and generally unenthusiastic reception from scholars. The refusal of the establishment to abandon its shrines to Stubbs is not unwarranted, in view of the fact that Sayles' and Richardson's attack employs *ad hominem* arguments and highly controversial scholarship. They do not even seem to realize how close their own interpretation follows Stubbs at some crucial points. The movement away from Stubbs' interpretation will not be based on such frontal assaults but rather on the application of new assumptions and concepts to the study of medieval English government. This trend was in fact well inaugurated in F. W. Maitland's two-volume *History of English Law Before the Time of Edward I* (second edition, 1898; ostensibly but not actually, aside from the first chapter, written in collaboration with F. Pollock) but not carried very much further since Maitland's death in 1906.

William Stubbs (1825–1901) was the eldest child of a Yorkshire solicitor who died when William was a boy. His mother, to whom William was always deeply devoted, was left with a large family to take care of, but partly because of her own efforts, partly with the help of friendly clergymen, and partly because of William's precocious brilliance and skill in winning scholarships, he received an excellent public school and Oxford education. Stubbs was deeply committed to the Church of England—his position was rather high but not Anglo-Catholic—and on graduation from Oxford he was torn between service to the church and scholarly pursuits. He resolved the conflict by accepting a country parsonage in which he served from 1850 to 1866 with fervent dedication and at the same time began his studies in the documentary sources of medieval English history. His research was aided by appointment as librarian of Lambeth Palace, the archives of the archbishopric of Canterbury, and by assignment (after first being turned down a number of times by the incredibly obtuse directors of the project) as editor of several chronicles for the Rolls Series, the frequently inept series of volumes of sources of medieval English history carried out under Crown auspices in pale imitation of Germany's magnificent *Monumenta Germaniae Historica.*

Stubbs married, raised a family, gave hundreds of sermons, and arduously pursued the other duties of his parish. He also traveled up and down England and the continent, met and conferred with the great German medievalists, achieved a just celebrity for his splendid editions in the Rolls Series, and—most important— acquired a thorough knowledge of the sources of English history up to the death of King John (1216). Since after this date the sources were too voluminous for even Stubbs' Victorian perseverance and hard work to master, he settled for a much more superficial, but still impressively broad, knowledge of the following two and a half centuries. Consequently, one could say that his appointment in 1866 as Regius Professor of Modern History (in England, modern history is anything after A.D. 476) was completely justified

because of his fitness for the post. Yet it must be noted that since
the Regius professorship was a Crown appointment, Stubbs' strong
Tory convictions played their part in his appointment during the
few months of 1866–67 that the Tory party under the leadership
of Derby and Disraeli was in office.

During his nearly twenty years as Regius Professor, Stubbs
founded the first school of historical research in England, lectured
brilliantly—not only on English history but also along comparative
lines, on continental institutions—and produced his monumental
Constitutional History. Although there were several editions of the
work before his death, he made slight revisions after the first
edition of 1874–78. He was a somewhat dour, severe man who was
skilled in eliciting high payment for his scholarly services (and he
needed the money to carry out his research, in those days before
professors were blessed with research grants) and who vaunted his
Toryism, his Germanophilism, and his contempt for the French
and Italians. He announced with grim jocularity at one of his lectures that he had destroyed a book by Ernest Renan without reading it. But Stubbs' writings reveal that he accepted Darwinian
terms like "natural selection" very easily, and his Toryism did not
prevent him from being on very good terms with the liberal-Whig
historian E. A. Freeman and the radical publicist and historical
popularizer J. R. Green, both of whom he assisted in their research
and careers. Stubbs' ambience was generally that of a mid-
Victorian Anglican Tory, but he respected, even if he disagreed
with, many of the more radical opinions current in England in his
lifetime. His letters (ed. W. H. Hutton, 1904) reveal him as a
generous, kind, and extremely intelligent and perceptive man, a
fervent Christian, and a strong nationalist who firmly believed in
the innate superiority of English parliamentary, common law, and
ecclesiastical institutions. In 1884 Stubbs readily resigned his professorship to accept the bishopric of Chester, and in 1889 he was
appointed Bishop of Oxford, in which post he served with great
distinction until his death in 1901. After his elevation to the episcopate, he did very little in the way of historical scholarship.

The Victorian view of the English past was essentially not orig-

inal with nineteenth-century writers; it had already been deline-
ated by the early seventeenth-century legist and parliamentarian
Sir Edward Coke, and by left-wing democratic Levellers during
the Civil War of the 1640's; its outlines could even be perceived as
early as the opinions of the thirteenth-century monastic historian
Matthew Paris and the fifteenth-century political theorist Sir John
Fortescue. This view of English history presupposed that by the
thirteenth century the dimensions of the English constitution had
taken shape: the rule of law over executive authority and the legislative sovereignty of king-in-parliament. It was held that monarchy in medieval England was not absolutist, but subject to the
overriding authority of law, which meant that the law could not
be changed without the consent of parliament as the national legislature; finally the actions of the executive came to be subject to
parliamentary scrutiny, in order to prevent the executive from
transgressing the law.

In his *History*, Macaulay took up the story of English constitu-
tionalism late in its development. He contended that the Whig
revolutionaries of 1688 were right in saving England from James
II's anti-constitutional tyranny and in driving the king from the
country; this established the foundations for subsequent English
progress. The questions remained: How did the beneficent liberal
constitution develop in the first place? By what steps did Englishmen develop the common law and parliament which made them so
much more fortunate and prosperous than other peoples? (Many
scholars would say now that Victorian England's prosperity was
due to the simple fact that the Industrial Revolution occurred in
England a half century before other countries, and that the Industrial Revolution was at best an indirect consequence of England's
political institutions, and probably more the result of advances in
commerce and banking, coal and water resources, adequate food
supply, and capital gained from the empire—but Victorians did
not see it this way.) It was Stubbs' aim to answer these questions
and satisfy the curiosity of the educated public; given the assumptions and social concepts of the era, he succeeded magnificently.

Stubbs perpetuated the seventeenth-century belief that the

institutions of Anglo-Saxon England had a strongly popular nature and that the Norman Conquest of 1066 represented the coming of royal despotism to England. And he was inclined to regard the Church of England as being from the Anglo-Saxon period a distinct, virtually separate entity within the Latin Church. This view of medieval English ecclesiastical development had been a dogmatic truth for Anglicans since the Reformation of the 1530's and Stubbs did nothing to undermine the traditional Anglican interpretation. On the contrary, he made it a distinctive theme in his *Constitutional History*—nor are twentieth-century scholars unanimous in believing that Stubbs' view of the medieval English church was fundamentally wrong.

Besides earlier or long-held concepts, Stubbs had other aids in his study. He used the guide to the sources of medieval English history published by the brilliant antiquary T. Duffus Hardy. He was also indebted, perhaps more than he realized, to the pioneering research into Anglo-Saxon and Anglo-Norman history made by Sir Francis Palgrave. And Stubbs acknowledged his debt to the definitive study on the history of the jury made by the great German legal historian Heinrich Brunner (although Brunner's revisionist attribution of a French, rather than an Anglo-Saxon, origin to the jury was clearly disturbing to Stubbs—it was left to Maitland to perceive the significance of Brunner's discovery).

Stubbs' inheritance of earlier historiographical traditions and his debt to other scholars of his own, or slightly earlier, generation in no way detract from the magnitude of his achievement. We have to remember that he was entirely self-taught as a medievalist and that until he obtained the chair at Oxford he worked in his country parsonage for a decade and a half in isolation, broken only by trips to archives and libraries in England and on the continent (which he paid for out of his own pocket) and by a slowly increasing correspondence with scholars at home and in Germany. By the time he obtained his professorship, Stubbs had acquired a thorough knowledge of the sources of English history to 1216, and—because of the vastness of the material—a much more superficial but still impressively broad knowledge of the sources of the following two and a half centuries, and he was able to undertake and fully complete an original work of historical synthesis which remains one of the most astonishing achievements of the Victorian mind. On many particular points in his *History*, scholars would now say Stubbs has been superseded as more subtle and complex explanations have come into fashion, but on no point can it be said that Stubbs' judgment was completely without merit or that the thesis he propounded did not have a plausible basis in the contemporary documentation. And as a general interpretation of the significant trends in the history of medieval English government, the *Constitutional History* remains the holistic work to which all subsequent research has had to be related.

Since Stubbs did not doubt that the nature of political and legal institutions is organic, so that the ultimate form of an institution is already inherent in its pristine form centuries earlier, he believed that his task was to find the "origins" of English constitutional ideas and practices and to show how these "grew" into the recognizable English constitution based on the rule of law and parliamentary government. He could see no Roman contribution, no significant indebtedness of the common law to the Justinian code, nor any substantial English political heritage from Greek philosophy. The origin of the English constitution was for Stubbs entirely Germanic; consequently, he began his study by analyzing the *Germania* of Tacitus, written about A.D. 100. He concluded, along with the eminent German historians of the mid-nineteenth century, that there was a strongly popular element in pristine Germanic institutions—the ideal and practice of self-governing communities. Brought to Britain by the Anglo-Saxon invaders of the fifth century, these popular communities developed into the shire and hundred courts, and no subsequent political change or conflict succeeded in eradicating this popular communal principle from English life. The grand theme of the period from the fifth to the end of the thirteenth century—the formative era of the English constitution—was the development of a national community over and above these local communities. In this evolution the Norman Conquest was a significant and necessary departure,

Stubbs held, because while the Norman kings were vicious despots (a favorite theme among the seventeenth-century Levellers), they united the kingdom in a way the inept Anglo-Saxon monarchs were unable to do, and gave England the necessary "discipline" and effective central administration to go along with the Anglo-Saxon legacy of communal self-government. Stubbs believed that a national unity and a sort of national consciousness had come to exist in England by the end of the twelfth century, so that the baronial rebellions against the Crown—particularly the one of 1215, which resulted in Magna Carta, and that of 1297, which resulted in the confirmation of Magna Carta—were inspired by high constitutional ideals of the necessary legislative sanction of the community of the realm and the due process of the common law.

Stubbs claimed that the distinctive English constitution of limited monarchy made its appearance in the thirteenth century with the emergence of parliament, which owed its creation in part to the wisdom of two men, the baronial leader Simon de Montfort and King Edward I; that this parliament from the beginning was essentially a representative assembly of three estates, to which the middle class (that is, the knights and burgesses) were summoned to give consent to royal taxation, thereby laying the basis for a distinctive and powerful house of commons; and finally that the history of the fourteenth and fifteenth centuries in England was centered on the struggle to preserve the established constitutional system, already at least the embryo of the distinctive English form of government. Throughout the medieval period, according to Stubbs, developments on the national level were closely integrated with, and in part modeled on the structure of, local government, so that the community of the realm expressed institutionally in parliament found its background and partly its origins in the community of the shire court. Ecclesiastical leaders also made a contribution by standing as a bulwark against attempts at royal absolutism.

The fundamental assumption running through Stubbs' view of medieval English history was that the constitution was the product of the interaction of popular and royal forces and institutions, that by the time Magna Carta was drafted in 1215 these two agencies had meshed to form a national unit and a national constitution, and that in the thirteenth century a legislative parliament of three estates developed to implement the working of this constitution. The fourteenth and fifteenth centuries were merely postscripts to this story—an era in which the growing decadence of medieval civilization, marked by overripe chivalry and senseless aristocratic conflicts, did not fundamentally harm the national constitution fused in the earlier period, and particularly between 1066 and 1297, out of popular and royal elements.

An alternative view of medieval constitutional development was indicated (but not self-consciously proclaimed) in Maitland's *History of English Law*. While Maitland was a dedicated liberal, a turn-of-the-century secular Cambridge intellectual much further to the left than Stubbs, and in some ways a forerunner of the Bloomsbury group, he greatly accentuated the creative role of the royal government and attributed minor significance to the autonomous influence of the popular communities. In comparison with Stubbs, Maitland gave much less importance to the Anglo-Saxon juristic legacy and saw the common law as the pragmatic construction of royal administrators and lawyers in the Norman and Angevin periods. In his last work, Maitland similarly contradicted Stubbs' view of the thirteenth-century parliament and viewed it not as a national legislature but simply as the king's high court. Thus the Tory Stubbs could optimistically envisage English liberty as organically and securely based on medieval popular institutions; the liberal relativist Maitland could find no comfort in such deterministic assumptions.

Before Maitland's premature death in 1906, he was working toward a completely functional view of medieval English government as the empirical product of the interaction of social and cultural forces. This would have explicitly negated Stubbs' thesis that English institutions were the consequence of a dialectical conflict between despotism and freedom. Maitland found some able disciples in England—H. W. C. Davis, T. F. Tout, and G. O. Sayles—and also in the United States—C. H. Haskins, C. H. McIlwain, J. R. Strayer, and Sidney Painter—but the work done on medieval English government in the six decades since Maitland's death has been primarily in the direction of simply confirming his royal administrative-pragmatic view of the making of common law and parliament, and the holistic interpretation along the lines of social functionalism to which Maitland was working has not been forthcoming. It may indeed be said that Maitland's greatest disciple was the French historian of feudalism, Marc Bloch.

Thus although Maitland and his followers revealed the arbitrary schematization and lack of social realism in Stubbs' approach, they have not produced a synthetic work to supersede the *Constitutional History*. And since 1945, there has been a marked neo-Stubbsian trend among the historians of medieval England. Helen Cam has portrayed the local communities of medieval England markedly along the organic and quasi-autonomous lines envisaged by Stubbs. In his *Constitutional History of Medieval England* J. E. Jolliffe attempted, with moderate success, a new synthesis which fell much more in the tradition of Stubbs than Maitland; and Jolliffe's *Angevin Kingship* again has posited Magna Carta as the consequence of baronial reaction against royal absolutism. B. Wilkinson has produced a multi-volume history of the period 1216–1485 which stubbornly supports Stubbs' interpretation on almost every important issue; and J. G. Edwards has defended Stubbs' legislative view of the thirteenth-century parliament against the claims that it was merely a royal court and information center. Perhaps most significant of all, the brilliant Belgian scholar R. C. Van Caenegem has claimed to have rediscovered a popular element in the makeup of twelfth-century common law and to have traced the jury back to Anglo-Saxon origins. Van Caenegem sees the common law as the consequence of interaction between royal and popular institutions—which is precisely Stubbs' theme.

Furthermore, since the late 1930's there has been a marked shift back to Stubbs' opinion that the Anglo-Saxons had more to teach than to learn from the Normans, and ironically Richardson and

Sayles, in spite of their anti-Stubbs polemic, hold to this view. The attempt made by the American scholar Gaines Post to demonstrate that ideas of representation in England owed a great debt to Roman-canonical legal ideas of attorneyship, as against Stubbs' emphasis on the common law origins of representation, has been only mildly convincing. In fact, a careful reading of Stubbs shows he was not blind to the fact that the clerical training of many twelfth- and thirteenth-century English royal administrators allowed for some influence from ideas of representation prevalent in the Latin Church. While a general feeling of uneasiness over Stubbs' lugu-brious picture of the fourteenth and fifteenth centuries prevails, no scholar has come forward with any alternative general view. Stubbs' suggestion of a proto-modern fifteenth-century Lancas-trian constitution (responsibility of executive to parliament) has been condemned, but Stubbs was far more cautious in making this suggestion than his critics have allowed, nor has anyone yet made any alternative sense out of the constitutional experimentation of the fifteenth century.

What is most controversial in Stubbs' work is not his view on any particular institution but rather the whole organic, determin-istic, and teleological superstructure. Stubbs sensed that medieval government and law were "bundles of expedients" devised by "very fallible men." But this empirical decision-making always worked toward that goal of English liberty which had its "germ" in the "primitive instinct" of "the German races." He assumed that there is a definable "national" English constitution; that it had taken shape, in outline at least, by the end of the thirteenth century; and that the task of the historian of English government was to show how this constitution grew out of Germanic origins and how it was preserved and entrenched in English political life in the period after 1307. Stubbs was not completely unaware that this interpre-tation too easily assumed that the lay and ecclesiastical magnates of medieval England, in their political and legal practices, were acting with a clear consciousness of an overriding constitution. But he had to work within the context of this unproven assumption because it gave cohesion and form to the complexities of medieval institutions and the confusions of medieval politics. Historians now eschew Stubbs' blatant nationalist and organic terminology, but they still work on the assumption that there was an identifiable constitution, of which the leaders of medieval society had at least a vague understanding and hazy consciousness.

It is therefore much easier to point out the weakness of Stubbs' assumptions than to replace them with a framework which will give cohesion and significance to the turmoil of political life down to the end of the fifteenth century. And although we now find smug Victorian moralizing distasteful, it is hard not to agree that *something* came out of the development of medieval English government and law which *was* different from continental development. However awkwardly and unclearly, medieval politics and law do point the way to the liberal institutions of modern England and those ideals of rule of law and parliamentary government that are, as Stubbs and his contemporaries believed, the greatest things Englishmen have given to the world.

ᴇ§ NOTE ON THE TEXT: To provide a comprehensive view of Stubbs' interpretation of medieval history, I have drawn for the most part on his three-volume *Constitutional History of England* (Vol. I, 6th ed., 1903; Vol. II, 4th ed., 1896; Vol. III, 5th ed., 1903) and have chosen passages which give Stubbs' general conclusions on the course of constitutional development or which provide analyses, still well worth reading, of the nature of specific medieval institutions. Occasionally, I have combined these passages with excerpts from Stubbs' lectures at Oxford. In his lectures Stubbs frequently summarized for the novice his views on critical problems in English history, stating simply and directly interpretations which he presented at much greater length in the *Constitutional History*. The excerpts from the lectures are reprinted from *The Study of Medieval and Modern History* (third edition, 1903) and *Lectures on Early English History* (1900 edition, edited by A. Hassall). In the source references below, Stubbs' three works are abbreviated CHE, SMMH, and LEEH, respectively; citations appear at the end of each excerpt. The headings throughout are my invention, but I have tried in these headings to be loyal to Stubbs' terminology, and I have occasionally used phrases which appeared as marginal notations in the *Constitutional History*.

N.F.C.

I

HISTORIOGRAPHICAL ASSUMPTIONS
AND GENERAL VIEWS

ᴈᴤ The history of our country is in one way of looking at it the history of ourselves; it is the history of our mind and body—of our soul and spirit also—for it tells how our fathers before us became what they were, and how our ways depart from or resemble theirs—how they won the liberties in which we have grown to be what we are—how they received and modified and handed down to us the inheritance of the old times before them—how the true history of a people is the history of its laws and institutions, more especially of its manners: and manners, as we know, maketh man.

The knowledge of our own history is our memory, and so the recorded history of a nation is the memory of the nation: woe to the country and people that forget it; an infant people has no history, as a child has a short and transient memory: the strong man and the strong nation feel the pulsation of the past in the life of the present: their memory is vital, long and strong.   [LEEH, 1]

ᴈᴤ In my view . . . the modern and ancient world are divided, and ancient and modern history set one against the other: in the opinion of my critics they are continuous, one of the chief links being the influence of the imperial idea of Rome.

Now, I do not for a moment dispute the continuity of many important influences, such as are describable under the general term of civilisation, including Grecian ideas of art, and the language and even the law of Rome; but . . . firstly, the geographical area of modern history [which begins with the fall of the Roman Empire in the West] is for the most part outside of the geographical area of ancient history. Rome and Greece are secondary and insignificant in the ages in which the chief place is occupied by England, France, Spain, and Germany; and the Italy of modern Europe is a very different thing from the Italy of Roman times. Secondly, . . . the actors in the drama of modern history are different from the ancient; . . . the nations are new to history at the opening of the new period, and . . . the main influences of their historical life . . . inherent in their own condition are not derived from the continuous influences of the ancient world: the nations of modern history are new, and the chief characteristics of their history are their own, neither borrowed nor learned from the elder times. But thirdly, . . . the influence of Christianity, of the church, and Christian civilisation belongs far more to modern history than to ancient; and in modern history it is one of the chief, if not in all respects the chief, ingredient. In these three things, geographical area, national origin, and distinctive Christian civilisation, the world of modern history is self-contained, is divided from the old.   [LEEH, 195–196]

⁓§ In Modern History, . . . you are dealing with the living subject: your field of examination is the living, working, thinking, growing world of to-day; as distinguished from the dead world of Greece and Rome, by the life that is in it, as it is in geographical area and in the embarrassing abundance of the data from which only in their full integrity it is safe, or ever will be safe, to attempt to philosophize. England, France, Germany, the East, regions that have but a shadowy existence in the background of the pictures in which living Egypt, Rome, and Asia stand before us, after thousands of years of death, in the bright colouring and life-like grouping of yesterday; these are the areas in which the modern historian seeks and finds the interests of his pursuit. . . .

And in this new and modern and living world there has been since the era began, such a continuity of life and development that hardly one point in its earliest life can be touched without awakening some chord in the present. Scarcely a single movement now visible in the current of modern affairs but can be traced back with some distinctness to its origin in the early Middle Ages; scarcely a movement that has disturbed the world since the invasion of our barbarian ancestors but has its representative in the chart of law or thought or territory to this day. [SMMH, 16–17]

⊷§ The freedom of modern Europe is based not on the freedom of Greece or Rome, but on the ancient freedom of the Teutonic nations, civilised, organised, and reduced to system by agencies of which Christianity and the system of the church are far the greatest and most important, in which the civilisation of later Rome is a minor influence, and that an influence apparent in the way of restriction rather than of liberation; in which the ancient philosophic freedom such as is exemplified in ancient Greece is an influence too infinitesimally small and remote to be worth calculating. [LEEH, 197]

⊷§ It is to Ancient Germany that we must look for the earliest traces of our forefathers, for the best part of almost all of us is originally German: though we call ourselves Britons, the name has only a geographical significance. The blood that is in our veins comes from German ancestors. Our language, diversified as it is, is at the bottom a German language; our institutions have grown into what they are from the common basis of the ancient institutions of Germany. The Jutes, Angles, and Saxons were but different tribes of the great Teutonic household; the Danes and Norwegians, who subdued them in the north and east, were of the same origin; so were the Normans: the feudal system itself was of Frank, i.e. also German origin. Even if there is still in our blood a little mixture of Celtic ingredient derived from the captive wives of the first conquerors, there is no leaven of Celticism in our institutions.

[LEEH, 3–4]

⊷§ England . . . is the country in which the Teutonic genius has most freely developed, notwithstanding the intermixture of the blood and the disturbances of foreign influences. And here the proposition that I have to lay down is briefly this: that the main and paternal stock from which the English and their constitution spring is Teutonic: Teutonic in source, as from the Angles, Saxons, and Jutes of the first conquest; and Teutonic in the additional streams poured in from subsequent invasions by the Danes and Normans, who, although by their different history and discipline they were made at the time of their introduction into England to exhibit an antagonism in language and institutions to the earlier stock, showed by the ease with which they mingled with it, and the rapidity with which within a century and a half they returned to it, that they were originally closely akin. In intermixing with the English the Dane within a very few years cast off all that was Scandinavian, and the Norman retained in some few departments of language only what he had contracted during two centuries of a French home and apprenticeship to French institutions. The Teutonic is the paternal element in the English race, as shown in physique, in language, in law, and custom. This is my firm conclusion. I need not tell you that it is one which has been and is still fiercely contested.   [LEEH, 211]

The growth of the English Constitution . . . is the resultant of three forces, whose reciprocal influences are constant, subtle, and intricate. These are the national character, the external history, and the institutions of the people. The direct analysis of the combination forms no portion of our task, for it is not until a nation has arrived at a consciousness of its own identity that it can be said to have any constitutional existence, and long before that moment the three forces have become involved inextricably; the national character has been formed by the course of the national history quite as certainly as the national history has been developed by the working of the national character; and the institutions in which the newly conscious nation is clothed may be either the work of the constructive genius of the growing race, or simply the result of the discipline of its external history. It would then be very rash and unsafe to attempt to assign positively to any one of the three forces the causation of any particular movement or the origin of any particular measure, to the exclusion of the other two; or to argue back from result to cause without allowing for the operation of other co-ordinate and reciprocally acting factors.

But it does not follow that cautious speculation on matters of interest, which are in themselves prior to the starting-point, would be thrown away; and some such questions must necessarily be discussed in order to complete the examination of the subject in its integrity by a comparison of its development with the corresponding stages and contemporary phenomena of the life of other nations. Of these questions the most important, and perhaps the only necessary ones, for all minor matters may be comprehended under them, are those of nationality and geographical position;—who were our forefathers, whence did they come, what did they bring with them, what did they find on their arrival, how far did the process of migration and settlement affect their own development, and in what measure was it indebted to the character and previous history of the land they colonised?

Such a form of stating the questions suggests at least the character of the answer. The English are not aboriginal, that is, they are not identical with the race that occupied their home at the dawn of history. They are a people of German descent in the main constituents of blood, character, and language, but most especially, in connexion with our subject, in the possession of the elements of primitive German civilisation and the common germs of German institutions. This descent is not a matter of inference. It is a recorded fact of history, which these characteristics bear out to the fullest degree of certainty. The consensus of historians, placing the conquest and colonisation of Britain by nations of German origin between the middle of the fifth and the end of the sixth century, is confirmed by the evidence of a continuous series of monuments. These show the unbroken possession of the land thus occupied, and the growth of the language and institutions thus introduced, either in purity and unmolested integrity, or, where it has been modified by antagonism and by the admixture of alien forms, ultimately vindicating itself by eliminating the new and more strongly developing the genius of the old.

The four great states of Western Christendom—England, France, Spain, and Germany—owe the leading principles which are worked out in their constitutional history to the same source. In the regions which had been thoroughly incorporated with the

Roman empire, every vestige of primitive indigenous cultivation had been crushed out of existence. Roman civilisation in its turn fell before the Germanic races: in Britain it had perished slowly in the midst of a perishing people, who were able neither to maintain it nor to substitute for it anything of their own. In Gaul and Spain it died a somewhat nobler death, and left more lasting influences. In the greater part of Germany it had never made good its ground. In all four the constructive elements of new life are barbarian or Germanic, though its development is varied by the degrees in which the original stream of influence has been turned aside in its course, or affected in purity and consistency by the infusion of other elements and by the nature of the soil through which it flows.   [CHE, I: 1–3]

&c; The polity developed by the German races on British soil is the purest product of their primitive instinct. . . . England has inherited no portion of the Roman legislation except in the form of scientific or professional axioms, introduced at a late period, and through the ecclesiastical or scholastic or international university studies. Her common law is, to a far greater extent than is commonly recognised, based on usages anterior to the influx of feudality, that is, on strictly primitive custom; and what she has that is feudal may be traced through its Frank stage of development to the common Germanic sources.

. . . With the exception of the Gothic Bible of Ulfilas, the Anglo-Saxon remains are the earliest specimens of Germanic language as well as literature, and the development of modern English from the Anglo-Saxon is a fact of science as well as of history. The institutions of the Saxons of Germany long after the conquest of Britain were the most perfect exponent of the system which Tacitus saw and described in the Germania; and the polity of their kinsmen in England, though it may be not older in its monuments than the Lex Salica, is more entirely free from Roman influences. In England the common germs were developed and ripened with the smallest intermixture of foreign elements. Not only were all the successive invasions of Britain, which from the eighth to the eleventh century diversify the history of the island, conducted by nations of common extraction, but, with the exception of ecclesiastical influence, no foreign interference that was not German in origin was admitted at all. Language, law, custom and religion preserve their original conformation and colouring. The German element is the paternal element in our system, natural and political. Analogy, however, is not proof, but illustration: the chain of proof is to be found in the progressive persistent development of English constitutional history from the primeval polity of the common fatherland.   [CHE, I: 10–11]

◄§ What virtues were these [Anglo-Saxon] institutions the most likely to foster, and which to neglect? No doubt their general tendency was to produce independence of character: local self-government was especially the discipline of self-reliance: the Anglo-Saxon was always a brave man. But the discipline of self-reliance is not the same as that of self-restraint, and we are hardly surprised to learn that our fathers, brave as they were, were temperate neither in appetite nor passion. Then, again, too great independence is incompatible with obedience, and the Anglo-Saxons had but a very poor talent for obeying—for putting their own immediate views, likings, and interests out of sight for the common good. If they had been more disciplined they would have been more united—the battle of Hastings would not have decided the fate of the kingdom. That Harold, who possessed all the qualities needed for a great national leader, was unable to unite the nation, is a proof that something more was wanted to make them great: that discipline they got in the grinding despotism of the Norman kings and under the machinery of the feudal system. Happily the despotism did not grind their independence out of them; more happily still, the feudal system taught them loyalty and obedience. The admixture of the two is needed to make a great people. . . . Discipline England passed through, as grinding a despotism as ever depressed a nation; but in two hundred years from the Conquest it had arisen in might and liberty, strengthened by adversity, and begun that glorious course of self-reliance and self-restraint which is the true nobility of any land, and which we pray may be for ever the true character of our own. [LEEH, 16–17]

II

ANGLO-SAXON ORIGINS
(c. 450–1066)

The Nature of Anglo-Saxon Institutions

It is a very fortunate thing for the German races that we have from the pens of two such writers as Cæsar and Tacitus a sketch of the institutions of their fathers as they were flourishing 1800 years since: a sketch indeed fragmentary, meagre, and obscure, but all the better for that; those very faults are a proof of genuineness. They do not guarantee the accuracy, but they do guarantee the good faith of the writers: a man evolving history . . . out of his own consciousness would have drawn a much more complete and consistent and clear picture.

It is a very common thing to speak of Anglo-Saxon laws and institutions as if they were something definite and invariable for the time during which the race was independent and supreme. Just as foolish would it be to consider the Anglo-Saxon language to be as definite and fixed as classical Latin, or Anglo-Saxon architecture as regular and uniform as that of the most formal period of Italian or Greek art. . . . We will guard ourselves at the outset from this silly blunder, remembering that as to time the authentic history of Anglo-Saxon law reaches from Ethelbert to Harold, a space of 460 years: that as to origin, it is indeed all radically German, and the germs of much of it may be discovered in the German customs of the age of Cæsar and Tacitus, but that these germs had by the commencement of the historical period developed in different ways among different tribes: so that the laws of the different nations who conquered Britain might, if we possessed them, be found to possess only a family resemblance, as those of successors certainly do: further, that the conquerors came from different parts of Germany and at different periods, and brought some full-grown institutions with them, of which not even the germs can be traced in the earlier settlers. So far from being an age of uniform stagnation, it was a period of ever varying growth and development, scarcely a century passing that did not bring some new influence to bear on it, scarcely two divisions moving on at the same rate or in the same direction.

The earliest form of community of which we can find a trace is that described by Tacitus: a body of men living together in separate district dwellings with no several ownership in land, but cultivating the common estate in portions which were changed and redistributed every year. Cæsar describes the Suevi as having no several or private estates, and as not inhabiting the same lands for more than a year. This seems to be a sign of earlier customs than Tacitus found existing. Cæsar does indeed represent the Suevi as nomads. Tacitus says of the German agricultural races generally: 'The lands are held by the collective community, according to the number of cultivators, turn by turn: afterwards they divide them according to their estimation among themselves—the wide extent of the plains makes these constant partitions a matter of no difficulty—they change their cultivated lands every year, and there is land over.' I have translated the passage literally, and you see how involved it is. I will not lead you into the mazes which contradicting critics have woven round it. It seems to hint, however, at two descriptions of property—the actually divided and allotted property on the one hand, and that held in common by the community—private and public lands. Indeed, it seems almost impossible that a settled community could exist, inhabiting houses such as Tacitus describes, 'not,' he says, 'as in our fashion with buildings joined to and communicating with one another, but each house surrounded by an open space, either for the prevention of fires or owing to their ignorance in building;' it seems impossible that a community could exist in this way without private estate in land. Each cottage would demand a garden, a cornfield, a stableyard, an orchard. The race was no longer a nomad race that could dispense with such—settled habitations involve privacy, and every man's house is his castle. Imagine, then, a tract of land as extensive as a large English parish; surround it with a belt of wood a mile or two in breadth; dot little cottages or farms about it at consistent distances, each with its hide of land attached to it; mark out these hides or private properties from the rest of the land. This rest continues to be the property of the community—it will be divided into allotments as the increase of population requires it, or some one who requires rewarding for great services will have a slice cut from it for himself, or, perhaps, in the end, a king or duke may rise up and get it all. Now, however, in the state of primitive equality, some portion of it is arable and let out to the richer and larger families in consideration of bearing certain burdens and payments to the community; some remains in pasture, and each man has common pasture rights upon it. The woodland round the settlement is not divided nor divisible, but is sacred to the gods; it is called the mark, and the inhabitants of the settlement have a sort of right to turn out their swine to eat the mast and acorns it produces. The inhabitants of the settlement are probably all akin to one another: in this point of view they are called the *mægth* or kindred. Their land, as well as the boundary round it, is called the *mark*, and the name is applied to the community itself as a settled occupier of land. Several marks constitute a gau or ga, analogous in some measure to the hundreds of later times; several ga's make up a scyr; several scyrs in process of time make up a kingdom or county, governed by an ealdorman, earl, or count. Each of these divisions —the mark proper, the gau, the shire, the kingdom—has its proper belt of uninhabited land around it. . . .

Whenever I have occasion to speak of a mark . . . I shall mean the first or primary community, the village, the vicus. . . .

Britain was a conquered country, and the conquerors as soon as they were settled divided the lands. . . . Every free household had a hide of land of its own, an alod, an ethel: there was besides this the public land held in common now and to be divided in time.

On this common land possibly the old British proprietors were suffered to remain as tenants, or possibly it was cultivated by slaves, or still more probably the cultivation devolved on landless freemen, sons of allodial proprietors who had not yet got an alod for themselves. Of a state of things exactly like this we have, I believe, no direct record: it is not likely that we should, for the use of direct records was primarily to fix the ownership and tenure of lands; and as soon as direct records begin to exist, the division of land is not simply into allodial and public land, but into bocland and folcland, that is land held by title deeds as freehold of inheritance and land held of the community in consideration of certain services. But the division into bocland and folcland is not an exhaustive one. There were many allodial estates which had existed long before title deeds were invented; others that were conveyed by the gift of a horn or a clod of grass or some other token, and of these especially were grants for religious endowments. There were therefore three kinds of estates, allodial, and secondly the bocland, and in the third place the folcland. The allodial proprietor held his land of no one: he was bound of no homage: he was free, he owned no lord or king over his estate; but he was subject to what is called the *trinoda necessitas,* the duty of contributing to the building of bridges and castles, and of serving as a soldier in defence of the community, *pontis et arcis edificatio, et expeditio.* The tenants of folcland had, on the other hand, besides these duties, a liability to have strangers, messengers, horses, hawks, and hounds quartered on them by government; the duty of entertaining and sustaining the king and his officers and servants on their journeys, and of providing them with carriages and horses; and several others.

Proceeding from . . . the land to . . . the persons who hold it and cultivate it, we find . . . our first division into free and unfree. The unfree, slaves, theows or eones, were either the remains of the Ancient Britons, called also Wealas or Welshmen, or they were prisoners of war, or criminals condemned to penal servitude, or persons who had sold themselves into captivity for the purpose of raising a sum of money, or as the result of gambling transactions, which were not uncommon.

The free are divided exhaustively into *eorl* and *ceorl*, noble by birth and non-noble, but all originally possessed of land as the basis of freedom and citizenship. This simple and primary distinction is, however, early in historic times replaced by others; the churl, indeed, retains his title, but sinks in position into the villain of later times. The eorl, the noble by birth, ceases to be conspicuous in that dignity, and reappears as the ealdorman, or is revived as the Danish jarl or the Norman earl, or as the gesith, companion, comes or count, or thane and servant of the semi-feudalised court. This calls for an explanation at greater length, and we must look at the development of an aristocracy of blood into one of power, wealth, and preponderating influence in government.

We have seen the mark inhabited by its free settlers, friends and kinsmen. Among friends and kinsmen even in the patriarchal stage quarrels arise, and much more so when the lapse of a few generations has loosened the tie of kindred, and spread an increased population over a confined space. Every community had a judge —perhaps at first the eldest or wisest member of the kin, the ealdorman in its primary signification, later the elected magistrate, the reeve, graf, or graphio, the origin of whose name is unknown. The mark reeve presided in the courts of the mark; the gau-reeve, if there was such a person, in the courts of the gau; the shire-reeve or sheriff in the scyrmote or county court. These were originally all elective officers. In time of war each mark and scyr contributed its quota to the army—the command of the national army was entrusted to a heretoga, herzog, duke, or leader, who would probably choose his own officers. In this heretogaship or elective commandership originated the royalty of the German races. The kings were the elected generals in war, chosen from the nobles, mostly of the race of Woden. I need not describe the stages by which such an office becomes first perpetual, then hereditary in one family, then subject to the ordinary laws of succession by primogeniture or otherwise. The Anglo-Saxons had arrived at the hereditary stage when they came to Britain. They had kings—cyn-ing—the son or child of the kin or race. Although in a manner hereditary, the crown was not strictly so in our acceptation of the term. When the king died, his successor was chosen from his family, sometimes the eldest, sometimes the wisest or the richest or most able, not until later times necessarily the nearest in blood. The royal domain consisted, of course, of the original alod of the leader elected, of such portions of the folcland as were allotted to him in consideration of his services, and latterly at least the folcland itself, the duties and services payable by the tenants of it, such as sustenance etc., but it does not appear that the folcland was ever so vested in the king that he could alienate it or turn it into bocland without the consent of the community in the witenagemot or scyrgemot, parliament or county court.

Given a king, a new order of nobility was sure to arise—nobility by service. The ancient leaders of the Germans surrounded themselves with a court of brave men, the heroes and wise men of the nation. These are called the king's gesiths or companions, his servants or thanes; his comites or counts; his principes or princes. Of course many of these were noble by birth, but it was by no means necessary: they were enriched by the king with estates cut out of the folcland, they were the king's men, and so far forth were unfree. They were not feudal vassals, for the essence of that relation was in the tenure of land: there was no such in the character of the gesith—he was personally, and not by reason of his tenure, the king's man and creature. The king furnished him with a horse and armour to go to war in; and when he died the gift was returned to the king under the name of the heriot: his lands did not descend hereditarily unless under special deed.

Of the gesiths or thanes themselves there were two classes, the ealdorman, who owned forty hides of land, and the smaller thane, who owned five; but these distinctions seem to come in after the nobility by service had become hereditary and the gesithship to have been lost sight of. The thaneship was now even within reach of the churl who could scrape together the five hides of land, the merchant who had made three voyages on his own account, or the British unfree tenant who had acquired the requisite territory. Next in dignity to the king were the æthelings, his sons or near relations, then the ealdormen, then the simple thanes; next to them the churls. Of course the offices of the court were at first personal, not hereditary: there was the staller, that is the marshal or high constable; the discthegn, dapifer or high steward; the pincerna or cupbearer; the chamberlain or bower thane, who was also the high treasurer; the hræglthegn or keeper of the robes; traces of these offices subsist to this day. This was the court. But besides this there were numerous inferior officers, reeves of the king: for the king had his town reeve, and village reeve, and sheriffs to look after his interests, as the elective reeves represented the communities.

Before we proceed to take a view of the way in which the government was conducted, we must first give a glance at the church. The conversion of the Anglo-Saxons to Christianity followed immediately upon the establishment of their supremacy in Britain: placing their arrival about 450, 150 years may be allowed for the conquest. In 597 the conversion began, and the ecclesiastical organisation was completed by Theodore before 690. A comparison of these dates will show that as soon as the admitted supremacy of the invaders gave scope for their national institutions to work orderly, they are pervaded and modified by a new influence which had not been present in the land of their origin. The most ancient Anglo-Saxon laws that we possess are the laws of Ethelbert, the first Christian king. Another very important result of the introduction of Christianity and the organisation of the church by Archbishop Theodore in the south and Archbishop Egbert in the north, was this. There was no English state—no commonwealth, no kingdom of England as yet: there were the eight great kingdoms of the Heptarchy, there were the subkingships as of the East and West Kentings, the North and South Gyrvii, the Hwiccas, the Magasætas, and many others. Each of these was independent of his neighbour: they came from different parts of Germany, spoke different dialects, used different laws. There was occasionally a bretwalda, a sort of emperor over the whole, from time to time; but of his functions, if he had any, nothing at all is known. Every district was independent of every other. Mercia had no rights in Wessex, or Wessex in East Anglia: there was no bond, no unity in the land.

On the other hand, the church was one, well organised and regulated and closely united by every possible bond. There were eight kingdoms, but there were only two ecclesiastical provinces, York and Canterbury: the tribes that owned the political sway of six kings all obeyed spiritually the see of Canterbury. Every bishop had as a basis of his authority not the mere nomination or acceptance of the king within whose dominion his diocese lay, but the unity and fellowship of fifteen or sixteen other bishops under the archbishop, each precisely in the same circumstances, a unity and fellowship over which the royal power had no control. Now we might suppose that such a state of things was likely to lead to quarrels between church and state. But it was not so: whether it was that the kings were so pious as always to choose good bishops, or that the bishops were so strong that it was no use for the king to contest with them, or that the actual power and efficiency of the church machinery was less prolific of effects than we should expect, I cannot say; but it is clear that there were very few quarrels between the two powers before the Conquest, hardly any before the time of Egbert and the union of the Heptarchy, except the great one that exalted Lichfield for a few years into an archbishop's see, in the reign of Offa.

The result of this peaceable working of church and state side by side was twofold. In the first place, it promoted the gradual uniting of the kingdoms. The people were in all spiritual matters one nation already. When one king fell in battle, or one royal family became extinct, and Mercia or Wessex annexed the vacant dominion, there was no repulsion on the part of the people; it was easy for them to become one politically as they had long been religiously. The other result was this: that the bishops were not only ecclesiastical but civil functionaries. Every bishop sat with the king and his gesiths in the witenagemot or great council of the kingdoms; and in the shiremotes the bishop sat and judged with the ealdorman, or, in his absence, the king's shire-reeve or sheriff. Nor was their dignity in any respect less than that of their civil compeers. The life of an archbishop was estimated at the same rate of compensation with that of a prince of the blood; that of a bishop with that of an ealdorman; that of a priest who had an endowment of five hides, with that of a thane. . . .

The legislative functions of government were discharged by the witenagemot—the meeting of the wise men—the king and his bishops and abbots, the ealdormen of the shires, and such other councillors as they or the king summoned for the purpose. In these meetings laws were proposed and sanctioned, grants of folcland made and ratified, appeals heard in the last resort, and general measures consulted on and taken for the welfare of the kingdom. It was in a witenagemot of Northumbria that Christianity was nationally adopted; in a witenagemot of all England that Edward the Confessor was elected. Probably the elections of bishops and ealdormen were settled at these meetings, if not formally transacted through them. From the witenagemot we must carefully distinguish the ecclesiastical council, although constituted very much of the same persons and held at the same time and place. These assemblies were strictly confined to spiritual matters. Before the consolidation of the Heptarchy there were occasionally national or provincial councils, at which two or three kings were present; but these were purely religious assemblies, and could not interfere authoritatively in politics.

In a state of society so simple as that of the Anglo-Saxons a very remote court of appeal was hardly needed; and probably only a very small proportion of causes reached the appellate jurisdiction of the witenagemot. In general, they went no further than the county court. This, the shiremote or county court, was the great judicial resort of the people. We have seen how the mark was constituted, how a certain number of marks constituted a gau or a hundred, and how a number of gaus or hundreds made up the shire. We must now look at them in the reverse order, and describe the shire as divided into hundreds, and the hundreds into tithings. I do not mean to say that these divisions exactly correspond, for I believe the mark to have been the original unit of community, whereas the tithing does not appear before the age of Canute; but for most practical purposes they must have nearly coincided. A tithing contained probably ten free families; and a hundred, ten tithings, i.e. originally a hundred free families. You must know that there is a never-ending dispute among antiquaries as to the origin of hundreds; for they are of all sorts and sizes, and no theory will apply to account for all; some of the small shires having the largest number, and the largest counties the smallest. It appears to me probable that each hundred contained in the first instance ten tithings, or a hundred free families; and that as soon as the enumeration was made, the shire was divided into hundreds with local names and boundaries. In a few generations, the number of free families increasing, new tithings would be formed; but instead of forming new hundreds to take them in, and so necessitating a redivision of the whole shire, the most natural course would be to affiliate the new tithings to the hundred in which they locally were. So the institution of tithing remaining, the name of hundred would lose its original applicability, as we know it did in other cases, in the Roman civil centuriæ and military centuries especially. Now, each of these divisions had its court: the tithing court was probably little more than a modern vestry meeting—the tithing man, so far as his judicial functions went, was about on a par with a petty constable; and the court of the hundred and the shiremote were the real administrators of justice.

In the shiremote the ealdorman, or in his absence the sheriff, with the bishop presided; but all the thanes sat as assessors, and the inferior freemen also were summoned to attend. In it the civil and criminal causes of the county were investigated and decided. In its criminal jurisdiction it must be looked on as parallel to our courts of quarter session, and in its civil administration to the operation of the newly restored county courts. It moreover decided causes connected with land which come under neither of these tribunals. The part that the churls had in this jurisdiction was but small, for they did not constitute juries: trial by jury was not yet. Still they had duties: oaths of allegiance to take, frankpledges to enter into, and possibly arbitrations to decide among themselves. The judges were the bishop and ealdorman, with the thanes as assessors.

The hundredmote, or court of the hundred, was held under the writ of the sheriff, presided over by its hundred-man, and its power was restricted to its own hundred. It punished small offences and exercised view of frankpledge. The mention of frankpledge takes us down again to the tithing.

Every tithing contained ten freemen: every freeman must belong to a tithing; every ten freemen constituted a distinct tithing. The members of each tithing were responsible for each other's good behaviour: in this relation the tithing was called a frith-borh, or security for peace, and in later times frankpledge, which seems to be a corruption of the term. The members of the frith-borh were bound to produce in the court of justice any one of their number who was summoned. They were a sort of perpetual bail for one another. If one of them was accused and failed to appear, they might purge themselves by oath of being accessary to his flight; if they could not do so, they were obliged to make good the penalty of the offence of which he was accused. This institution is, as I said, of late growth: it was not until the time of Canute that it was made obligatory on every freeman. The obligation was examined into in the sheriff's hundred court. This examination or seeing into the frankpledges was called *visus franciplegii*, view of frankpledge. One of the ten was called a tithing-man, headborough, or constable, who represented his tithing in the courts and acted as a petty constable. In another point of view the tithing would often be coextensive with the township; and as a township sent a reeve and four freemen to represent it in the shiremote and hundred court, a tithing was in the north of England called a ten-man's-tale.

Besides the security of frankpledges every man was bound to have a lord or patron in whose protection or mund he was. As the frithborh secured his responsibility to justice, the protection of the mund was intended to secure justice for him. If he was slain or injured, the mund was said to be broken, and the culprit had to make a compensation to the lord as well as to the relations of the injured person. . . . The custom of the mund was one of the most efficient preparations for the reception of feudalism.

I have now glanced at most of the remarkable institutions of the Anglo-Saxon races: it remains to say a few words . . . on the leading Anglo-Saxon laws and customs. The most cursory view of the subject would be very incomplete without them.

The first of these is the wergild, the compensation that the criminal was bound to make to the family and protectors of the injured, especially of the slain. Capital punishment was inflicted only in cases of foul murder, arson, and theft: the exaction of the penalty was left to the will and execution of the injured party. But besides the capital penalty, and in cases where it was not exacted, there was a wergild to be paid. This differed according to a regular table of values. The life of a king was esteemed at 7,200 shillings, that of the ætheling or the archbishop at 3,600, that of a bishop or an ealdorman at 1,200 shillings, that of an inferior thane at 600, that of a simple ceorl at 200. There were other valuations for Britons and slaves. Besides the wergild, there were the following money penalties in case of murder: the king's mund, or fine for breach of his protection; healsfang, or commutation for the pillory; manbot, compensation to the lord or patron for the loss of his man; and frith-wite, a fine due to the crown for breach of peace. Besides capital punishment, there were banishment, outlawry, and mutilation for theft. Wergilds or *bots* were not payable only for murder; there was a regular tariff of wounds to be compensated by money payments. The piercing of the nose was estimated at 9 shillings, other wounds in it at 6 shillings apiece, 3 shillings a nostril; 50 shillings an eye; 12 for an ear—if one ear be deaf, 25; a thumb nail, 3; the thumb itself, 20; the shooting or forefinger, 8; the middle finger, 4; the gold or ring finger, 6; the little finger, 11. Even when the wergild was paid, the manslayer was not safe until he had paid a further bot, by which he redeemed himself from feud or enmity on the part of the relations of the slain.

The second point I have to remark on is process of trial. It used to be a favourite theory that trial by jury was a legacy of our early Anglo-Saxon forefathers. Modern lawyers have decided that the institution in its true character is not of so early a date. The error arose from a confusion between such trial and that which really took place. The real judges were the bishop and ealdorman or sheriff with the thanes as assessors. The number of twelve thanes was convenient and probably usual: it is fixed by a law of Ethelred II. Obviously it is a very different thing for a ceorl to be tried by twelve thanes and for every man to be tried as now by a jury of his equals.

There is another point that has lent assistance to the old theory. If a man denied that he was guilty of the act he was charged with, he was allowed to clear himself by producing twelve of his equals who were to swear with him that he was innocent. If he was under a lord, the lord or his reeve might come forward and swear that he had not failed in oath or ordeal since the last court day, after which the accused might clear himself by ordeal, or by his own oath and that of his companions. If the lord could not so swear, thrice the number of compurgators must be forthcoming. Each man's oath had a value proportioned to his rank, and if an accused thane could not find twelve thanes to swear for him, he might make up the number by supplying six ceorls for each. The accuser was obliged also to support his charge by the oaths of compurgators, but a smaller number was sufficient. The germ of the present system may possibly be traced in the number twelve, and in the assumed equality of the compurgators; it is difficult to find any nearer approach to the custom.

. . . Neither trial by combat nor ordeal by . . . hot water, hot iron, or otherwise, was in common use except in cases where the accused had forfeited his credit by some previous crime or was unable to produce compurgators.

Almost all the foregoing remarks, although primarily applicable to a country population, are true of the inhabitants of towns and cities: we ought further to notice the origin of municipal institutions during the same period. . . . The principal influences to be noticed are the ecclesiastical ones, the protection afforded by a great monastery to the town growing up under its walls, and the commercial ones. The latter, which are of course most apparent in maritime towns, are traceable in the frith-gilds, voluntary associations of trade, for mutual security, each governed by an ealdorman, the lineal predecessors of the aldermen of the present day. These gilds—and they were religious as well as commercial—acquired first a legal recognition and status, then endowments, subsequently a municipal unity, in consideration of which they were allowed to acquire the franchises of the city, soc and sac, etc., on paying a rent or farm to the lord of it, who in most instances was the king. . . .

These, then, are the laws under which our fathers grew for 450 years, and which have left their marks so conspicuous upon our map and statute book. Those of us who live in Essex live not in a department of the Chelmer and Thames, but in the ancient kingdom of Essex, the realm of the East Saxons; we have at the head of our magistracy not a prefect, but a lord lieutenant much in the same position as the ealdorman of old; the courts are held by the shirereeve in the shire hall. Our thanes are represented by county magistrates, the shiremoot by the quarter sessions, the hundred motes by the petty sessions and sheriffs' court of tourn and leet. The old names of hundreds and deaneries retain something of their meaning still. Our bishops and thanes represent us in the witenagemot; and our ruler is the cyn-ing, the child of the nation.

In other respects all is changed. We have a proper system of jurisprudence instead of partial and local statutes; trial by jury instead of compurgation and ordeal; local self-government is becoming less and less the rule among us. Still there is much unchanged and much unchangeable.

A slight knowledge of history is enough to show that these laws and customs grew up under difficulties, that nearly all the

Anglo-Saxon period was a time of war, sometimes internal, more generally against foreign invaders. These invaders were of the same original stock with the invaded. They conquered full half of England, the north and east; but owing to the system begun by Alfred and perfected by Canute they amalgamated with the Anglo-Saxons so entirely that before the Conquest they were one people. Some of the institutions that I have mentioned were perhaps Danish rather than Anglo-Saxon: they gave as well as received. Notwithstanding all this, the race was great in arms and art; the Anglo-Saxon merchants were found in all marts, the Anglo-Saxon manuscript painting is of the most refined and elegant description, their gold work was the astonishment of continental artificers. It was by Anglo-Saxon missionaries from the seventh to the eleventh centuries that Germany, Sweden, Denmark, Norway, and Iceland were converted to the gospel. The age of flourishing literature was over long before the Conquest; but there were still poets and prose writers in the monasteries who kept up the fame of the island of Bede and Alcuin. [LEEH, 4–16]

The Growth of the Anglo-Saxon Kingdom

◄§ Although the framework of Anglo-Saxon society was permanent, and its simple organisation easily adapted itself to the circumstances that fill the five centuries of its history, it was capable of development and liable to much internal modification, according to the variations of the balance of its parts and the character of its regulative or motive force. The exact chronological sequence of these variations it is difficult to determine, but as to the fact of the development there can be no question. A comparison of the state of affairs represented in Domesday book with the picture that can be drawn from Bede sufficiently proves it. The ages had been ages of struggle and of growth, although the struggle was often fruitless and the growth ended in weariness and vexation. But the transition is more distinctly apparent if we look back further than Bede, and rely on the analogies of the other Germanic nationalities in drawing our initial outline. And this we are justified in doing by the completeness and homogeneousness of the constitution when it first appears to us, and by the general character of the early laws. But the subject is not without its difficulties: the first and last terms of the development are as remote from each other in character as in date. There is a very great difference between the extreme and confusing minuteness of Domesday and the simplicity and elasticity of the ideal German system of the sixth century: whilst on the other hand the scantiness of our knowledge of the latter is compensated by its clearness, and the abundant information of the former is deprived of much of its value by the uncertainty of its terminology. For it is unquestionable that a great part of the Anglo-Saxon customary law, of which Domesday is the treasury, was unintelligible to the Norman lawyers of the next century, on whose interpretation of it the legal historian is wont to rely. The process of change too was very gradual: it is not marked by distinct steps of legal enactment; the charters afford only incidental illustrations, and the historians were, for the most part, too far removed in time from the events they described to have a distinct idea of it, even if it had been possible for the annalist to realise the working of causes in so slow and so constant action. But all the great changes in the early history of institutions are of this character, and can be realised only by the comparison of sufficiently distant epochs. There are no constitutional revolutions, no violent reversals of legislation; custom is far more potent than law, and custom is modified infinitesimally every day. An alteration of law is often the mere registration of a custom, when men have recognised its altered character. The names of offices and assemblies are permanent, whilst their character has imperceptibly undergone essential change.

The general tendency of the process may be described as a movement from the personal to the territorial organisation, from a state of things in which personal freedom and political right were the leading ideas, to one in which personal freedom and political right had become so much bound up with the relations created by the possession of land, as to be actually subservient to it: the Angel-cynn of Alfred becomes the Englalande of Canute. The main steps also are apparent. In the primitive German constitution the free man of pure blood is the fully qualified political unit; the king is the king of the race; the host is the people in arms; the peace is the national peace; the courts are the people in council; the land is the property of the race, and the free man has a right to his share. In the next stage the possession of land has become the badge of free-dom; the freeman is fully free because he possesses land, he does not possess the land because he is free; the host is the body of land-owners in arms; the courts are the courts of the landowners. But the personal basis is not lost sight of: the landless man may still select his lord; the hide is the provision of the family; the peace implies the maintenance of rights and duties between man and man; the full-free is the equal of the noble in all political respects. In a further stage the land becomes the sacramental tie of all public relations; the poor man depends on the rich, not as his chosen patron but as the owner of the land that he cultivates, the lord of the court to which he does suit and service, the leader whom he is bound to follow to the host: the administration of law depends on the peace of the land rather than on that of the people; the great landowner has his own peace and administers his own justice. The king still calls himself the king of the nation, but he has added to his old title new and cumbersome obligations towards all classes of his subjects, as lord and patron, supreme landowner, the representa-tive of all original, and the fountain of all derived, political right.

The first of these stages was passed when the conquest of Britain was completed; and only showed what it had been in the vestiges of the mark system, and in the permanence of the personal nomenclature. The village was the kindred settlement, the hide of land the allotment of the head of the family, the tribal divisions—the hundred, the mægth, the theod,—all personal. The tracing of the process of change under the second and third stages is the problem of Anglo-Saxon Constitutional History. The series is not fully worked out. The Anglo-Saxon king never ceases to be the king of the nation, but he has become its lord and patron rather than its father; and that in a state of society in which all lordship is bound up with landownership: he is the lord of the national land, and needs only one step to become the lord of the people by that title. This step was however taken by the Norman lawyers and not by the English king; and it was only because the transition seemed to them so easy, that they left the ancient local organisation unimpaired, out of which a system was to grow that would ultimately reduce the landownership to its proper dimensions and functions. If the system had in England ripened into feudalism, that feudalism would in all probability have been permanent. Happily the change that produced feudalism for a time, introduced with it the necessity of repulsion. The English, who might never have struggled against native lords, were roused by the fact that their lords were strangers as well as oppressors, and the Norman kings realised the certainty that if they would retain the land they must make common cause with the people.

Five historical events mark the periods within which these changes were working: the accretion of the small settlements in heptarchic kingdoms; the union of the heptarchic kingdoms under the house of Cerdic; the first struggle with the Danes; the pacification of England under Edgar; and the introduction of new forms and principles of government by Canute.

The development of constitutional life depends largely on the historical career of the nation, on the consolidation of its governmental machinery in equality and uniformity over all its area, on the expansion or limitation of the regulative power for the time being: in other words, on the general and external history marked by these eras; on the extension of the kingdom and on the condition of the royal power. England at the period of the Conversion, when for the first time we are able really to grasp an idea of its condition, was composed of a large number of small states or provinces bound in seven or eight kingdoms. The form of government was in each monarchical, and that of the same limited charac-

ter. By the middle of the tenth century it has become one kingdom, and the royal power is much more extensive in character.
During a great part of the intervening period the consolidation of
the kingdom and the power of the king have undergone many
variations. The tendency towards union has been developed first
under one tribal supremacy and then under another, and the royal
power, whose growth is of necessity greatly affected by the extension of its territory, and the presence or absence of rival royalties,
has fluctuated also. The two of course rise and fall together. But as
a rule, at the end of any fixed period, both manifest a decided
advance.

It can scarcely be said that the tendency towards territorial
union proceeded from any consciousness of national unity or from
any instinct of self-government. Nor can it be attributed solely to
the religious unity, which rather helped than originated such a
tendency. This tendency resulted not so much from the strivings
of the peoples as from the ambition of the kings. The task which
was accomplished by the West Saxon dynasty had been tried before by the rulers of Kent, Northumbria, and Mercia, and the
attempt in their hands failed. Nor would it have been more successful under the genius of Athelstan and Edgar, but for the
Danish invasions, the extinction of the old royal houses, and the
removal, to a certain extent, of the old tribal landmarks.

The ancient German spirit showed its tenacity in this. The land
had been settled by tribes of kinsmen, under rulers who as kings
acquired the headship of the kin as well as the command of the
host. Whilst the kin of the kings subsisted, and the original landmarks were preserved, neither religion nor common law, nor even
common subjection sufficed to weld the incoherent mass. And it
may have been the consciousness of this which hindered the victorious kings from suppressing royalty altogether in the kingdoms
they subdued: the vassal kings either became insignificant, sinking
into *eorls* and hereditary *ealdormen*, or gradually died out. But,
until after the Danish wars, provincial royalty remained, and the
cohesion of the mass was maintained only by the necessities of

common defence. When Ethelbert of Kent acquired the rule of
Essex, when Ethelred of Mercia annexed Hwiccia, when Egbert
conquered Mercia, the form of a separate kingdom was preserved;
and the royal house still reigned under the authority of the conquerors until it became extinct. Such a system gave of course occasion for frequent rebellions and rearrangements of territory; when
a weak king succeeded a strong one in the sovereign kingdom, or a
strong chief succeeded a weak one in the dependent realm. But the
continuance of such a system has the effect of gradually eliminating all the weaker elements.

The process of natural selection was in constant working; it is
best exemplified in the gradual formation of the seven kingdoms
and in their final union under Wessex: the heptarchic king was as
much stronger than the tribal king, as the king of united England
was stronger than the heptarchic king.   [CHE, I: 183–189]

⫷ The earliest legislation exhibits the king as already in a
position in which personal preeminence is secured and fortified by
legal provisions. In the laws of Ethelbert the king's *mundbyrd* is
fixed at fifty shillings, that of the *eorl* at twelve, and that of the
ceorl at six; and wrongs done to members of his household are punished in proportion. These laws mention no wergild for the king,
but it seems probable that if there were one it also would be cal-
culated on a like scale. A century later the laws of Wihtræd direct
that the king is to be prayed for without command, that is, that
intercession for him shall be part of the ordinary service of the
church; his word without oath is incontrovertible, and even his
thegn may clear himself by his own oath. The king's *mundbyrd* is
still fifty shillings. The laws of Ini king of Wessex, who was contemporary with Wihtræd, show that in that conquering and advancing kingdom the tendency was more strongly developed. If a
man fight in the king's house both his life and property lie at the
king's mercy; the king's *geneat* may 'swear for sixty hides;' his
burh-bryce is a hundred and twenty shillings. But in the reign of
Alfred the king's *borh-bryce* or *mundbyrd* was five pounds, his
burh-bryce a hundred and twenty shillings, whilst that of the *ceorl*

was only five. The value of the protection given by the higher classes rises in proportion to that given by the king, whilst that of the simple freeman remains as before, or is actually depressed. It is by the same code that the relation between the king and his subjects is defined as that between lord and dependent; 'if any one plot against the king's life, of himself or by harbouring of exiles, or of his men, let him be liable in his life and in all that he has. If he desire to prove himself true, let him do so according to the king's wergild. So also we ordain for all degrees whether *eorl* or *ceorl*. He who plots against his lord's life let him be liable in his life to him and in all that he has, or let him prove himself true according to his lord's *wer*.' The law of Edward the elder contains an exhortation to the *witan* for the maintenance of the public peace, in which it is proposed that they should 'be in that fellowship in which the king was, and love that which he loved, and shun that which he shunned, both on sea and land:' a clear reference to the relation between the lord and his dependent as expressed in the oath of fealty. The same king, in A.D. 921, received the submission of the East Anglian Danes on the same condition: 'they would observe peace towards all to whom the king should grant his peace, both by sea and land:' and the people of Northamptonshire and Cambridgeshire especially chose him 'to *hlaforde* and to *mundbora*,' so placing themselves under his personal protection. The principle is enunciated with greater clearness in the law of his son Edmund, in which the oath of fealty is generally imposed; all are to swear to be faithful to him as a man ought to be faithful to his lord, loving what he loves, shunning what he shuns. This series of enactments must be regarded as fixing the date of the change of relation, and may perhaps be interpreted as explaining it. The rapid consolidation of the Danish with the Angle and Saxon population involved the necessity of the uniform tie between them and the king: the Danes became the king's men and entered into the public peace; the native English could not be left in a less close connexion with their king: the commendation of the one involved the tightening of the cords that united the latter to their native ruler.

Something of the same kind must have taken place as each of the heptarchic kingdoms fell under West Saxon rule, but the principle is most strongly brought out in connexion with the Danish submission.

From this time accordingly the personal dignity of royalty becomes more strongly marked. Edmund and his successors take high sounding titles borrowed from the imperial court; to the real dignity of king of the English they add the shadowy claim to the empire of Britain which rested on the commendation of Welsh and Scottish princes. The tradition that Edgar was rowed by eight kings upon the Dee is the expression of this idea which it was left for far distant generations to realise.

Under Ethelred still higher claims are urged: again and again the witan resolve as a religious duty to adhere to one *cynehlaford:* and the king himself is declared to be Christ's vicegerent among Christian people, with the special duty of defending God's church and people, and with the consequent claim on their obedience; 'he who holds an outlaw of God in his power over the term that the king may have appointed, acts, at peril of himself and all his property, against Christ's vicegerent who preserves and holds sway over Christendom and kingdom as long as God grants it.' The unity of the kingdom, endangered by Sweyn and Canute, is now fenced about with sanctions which imply religious duty. Both state and church are in peril; Ethelred is regarded as the representative of both. A few years later Canute had made good his claim to be looked on as a Christian and national king. The first article of his laws, passed with the counsel of his witan, to the praise of God, and his own honour and behoof, is this: 'that above all other things, they should ever love and worship one God, and unanimously observe one Christianity, and love King Canute with strict fidelity.'

It is wrong to regard the influence of the clergy as one of the chief causes of the increase in the personal dignity of the kings. The rite of coronation substituted for the rude ceremony, whatever it may have been, which marked the inauguration of a heathen king, contained a distinct charge as to the nature of royal duties, but no words of adulation nor even any statement of the personal sacro-sanctity of the recipient. The enactments of the councils are directed, where they refer to royalty at all, rather to the enforcement of reforms than to the encouragement of despotic claims. The letters of the early Anglo-Saxon bishops are full of complaints of royal misbehaviour: the sins of the kings of the eighth century seem almost to cancel the memory of the benefits received from the nursing-fathers of the seventh. Far from maintaining either in theory or in practice the divine right of the anointed, the prelates seem to have joined in, or at least acquiesced in, the rapid series of displacements in Northumbria. Alcuin mourns over the fate of the national rulers, but grants that by their crimes they deserved all that fell on them. They are, like Saul, the anointed of the Lord, but they have no indefeasible status. In the preaching of peace and good-will, the maintenance of obedience to constituted powers is indeed insisted on, but the duty of obeying the powers that be is construed simply and equitably. It is only when, in the presence of the heathen foe, Christendom and kingdom seem for a moment to rest on the support of a single weak hand, that the duty of obedience to the king is made to outweigh the consideration of his demerits. And yet Dunstan had prophesied of Ethelred that the sword should not depart from his house until his kingdom should be transferred to a strange nation whose worship and tongue his people knew not.

Nor is it necessary to regard the growth of royal power, as distinct from personal pomp, among the Anglo-Saxons, as having been to any great extent affected by the precedents and model of the Frank empire. Although the theory of kingship was in Gaul perhaps scarcely less exalted than at Constantinople, the practice was very different, for the Merovingian puppets were set up and thrown down at pleasure. But during the eighth century the influence of England on the continent was greater than that of the continent on England. The great missionaries of Germany looked to their native land as the guide and pattern of the country of their adoption. It is only with the Karolingian dynasty that the imitation of foreign custom in England could begin; but . . . the circumstances that made it possible, the creation of national unity and the need of united defence, were much more important than a mere tendency to superficial imitation. The causes at work in Gaul and Britain were distinct and the results, in this point at least, widely different.

As the personal dignity of the king increased and the character of his relation to his people was modified, his official powers were developed, and his function as fountain of justice became more distinctly recognised. The germ of this attribute lay in the idea of royalty itself. The peace, as it was called, the primitive alliance for mutual good behaviour, for the performance and enforcement of rights and duties, the voluntary restraint of free society in its earliest form, was from the beginning of monarchy under the protection of the king. Of the three classes of offences that came under the view of the law, the minor infraction of right was atoned for by a compensation to the injured, the *bot* with which his individual good-will was redeemed, and by a payment of equal amount to the king by which the offender bought back his admission into the public peace. The greater breaches of the peace arising either from refusal to pay the fines, or from the commission of offences for which fines were inadequate, were punished by outlawry; the offender was a public enemy, set outside the law and the peace; his adversary might execute his own vengeance, and even common hospitality towards him was a breach of the law, until the king restored him to his place as a member of society. The third class of offences, which seemed beyond the scope of outlawry, and demanded strict, public, and direct rather than casual and private punishment, were yet like the former capable of composition, the acceptance of which to a certain extent depended on the king as representing the people. In all this the king is not only the executor of the peace, but a sharer in its authority and claims. But this position is far from that of the fountain of justice and source of jurisdiction. The king's guarantee was not the sole safeguard of the peace: the hundred had its peace as well as the king: the king too had a distinct peace which like that of the church was not that of the country at large, a special guarantee for those who were under special protection.

The *grith*, a term which comes into use in the Danish struggle, is a limited or localised peace, under the special guarantee of the individual, and differs little from the protection implied in the *mund* or personal guardianship which appears much earlier; although it may be regarded as another mark of territorial development. When the king becomes the lord, patron and *mundborh* of his whole people, they pass from the ancient national peace of which he is the guardian into the closer personal or territorial relation of which he is the source. The peace is now the king's peace, although the *grith* and the *mund* still retain their limited and local application, they entitle their possessor to no higher rights, they do but involve the transgressor in more special penalties; the *frith* is enforced by the national officers, the *grith* by the king's personal servants; the one is official, the other personal; the one the business of the country, the other that of the court. The special peace is further extended to places where the national peace is not fully provided for: the great highways, on which questions of local jurisdiction might arise to the delay of justice, are under the king's peace. But the process by which the national peace became the king's peace is almost imperceptible: and it is very gradually that we arrive at the time at which all peace and law are supposed to die with the old king, and rise again at the proclamation of the new. In Anglo-Saxon times the transition is mainly important as touching the organisation of jurisdiction. The national officers now execute their functions as the king's officers, and executors of his peace; the shire and hundred courts, although they still call the peace their own, act in his name; the idea gains ground and becomes a form of law. Offences against the law become offences against the king, and the crime of disobedience a crime of contempt to be expiated by a special sort of fine, the *oferhyrnesse*, to the outraged majesty of the lawgiver and judge. The first mention of the *oferhyrnesse* occurs in the laws of Edward the elder. It is probable that the reforms which Alfred, according to his biographer, introduced into the administration of justice had a similar tendency; and these two reigns may be accepted as the period at which the change of idea seems to have become permanent.

But, although it may be convenient to accept this approximation to a date, the influence of the idea may be traced much further back. The administration of the peace is inseparable from the exercise of jurisdiction; those who are in the national peace are subject only to the national courts; those who are in the church's *grith*, are also in the church's *socn;* those who are in the king's *mund*, are under his cognisance; those who are amenable to any jurisdiction, owe suit and service to the courts of the jurisdiction; when all are in the *mund* or *grith* or *frith* of the king, he is the supreme judge of all persons and over all causes, limited however by the counsel and consent of his *witan.*

In regard to the holders of *folkland*, the special royal jurisdiction must have been much older than the time of Alfred; as these tenants were liable to special burdens payable directly to the state, and as the profits of jurisdiction, which were counted among these burdens, were inseparable from jurisdiction itself, it is probable that the jurisdiction of these lands was administered by royal officers, not necessarily separate from the business of the hundred courts, but as a part of their work, having special reference to the king's interests. They would be from the first in the peace of the king rather than in that of the hundred. When, however, folklands were turned into booklands in favour of either churches or individuals, and all their obligations save the *trinoda necessitas* transferred with them, the profits of jurisdiction and jurisdiction itself followed too. Such jurisdiction as had been exercised on behalf of the king, in or out of the popular courts, was now vested in the recipient of the grant. This may have been a very early innovation. The terms *sac* and *soc*, which imply it, are not found until late in the period, but occur almost universally in Norman grants of confirmation, as describing definite immunities which may have been only implied, though necessarily implied, in the original grant, and customarily recognised under these names. The idea of jurisdiction accompanying the possession of the soil must be allowed to be thus ancient, although it may be questioned whether, except in the large territorial lordships, it was actually exercised, or whether the proprietor would not as a rule satisfy himself with the profits of jurisdiction, and transact the business of it through the ordinary courts. It is probable that, except in a very few special cases, the *sac* and *soc* thus granted were before the Conquest exemptions from the hundred courts only, and not from those of the shire; and that thus they are the basis of the manorial court-leet, as the mark-system is that of the court baron. There is no evidence of the existence of a domestic tribunal by which the lord tried the offences or settled the disputes of his servants, serfs, or free tenantry; he satisfied himself with arbitrating in the latter case, and producing the criminal in the public courts. But when grants of *sac* and *soc* became common, these questions would swell the business of his private courts, and his jurisdiction would apply as much to those who were under his personal, as to those who were in his territorial protection. By such grants then, indirectly as well as directly, large sections of jurisdiction which had been royal or national, fell into private hands, and as the tendency was for all land ultimately to become bookland, the national courts became more and more the courts of the landowners. The ancient process was retained, but exercised by men who derived their title from the new source of justice. Their jurisdiction was further modified by enactment: as the *thegn* had *socn* over his own men, the king had *socn* over his *thegns;* none but the king could exercise or have the profits of jurisdiction over a king's *thegn;* none but the king could have the fines arising from the offences of the owner of bookland. And, although this might practically be observed by recognising the popular courts as royal courts for the smaller owners of bookland, the king had a '*thening-manna*' court, in which his greater vassals settled their disputes. But the time came when the great local landowner was vested with the right of representing the king

as judge and *land-rica* in his whole district, and so exercised jurisdiction over minor landowners. This change, the bearing of which
on the history of the hundred courts, which also were placed in
private hands, is very uncertain, seems to have begun to operate in
the reign of Canute. It is at that date that the *land-rica* becomes
prominent in the laws; the further development of the practice, as
shown in large and almost exhaustive grants of immunity, must be
referred to the weak reign and feudal proclivities of Edward the
Confessor. Wherever it prevailed it must have brought the local
jurisdictions into close conformity with the feudalism of the continent, and may thus serve to explain some of the anomalies of the
system of tenure as it existed in the times reported in Domesday.

These immunities, tying the judicature, as it may be said, to the
land, and forming one of the most potent causes of the territorial
tendency, so far ousted the jurisdiction of the national courts,
whether held in the name of the king or of the people, that it
might be almost said that the theoretical character of the sovereign
rises as the scope for his action is limited. This, however, was to
some extent counteracted by the special retention of royal rights
in laws and charters. Accordingly, in the later laws, the king
specifies the pleas of criminal justice, which he retains for his own
administration and profit; such a list is given in the laws of Canute;
breach of the king's protection, house-breaking, assault, neglect of
the fyrd, and outlawry. These were the original pleas of the
crown, and for them special fines were received by the king's officers in the local courts. By a converse process, such small parts of
criminal process as still belonged to these courts, arising from the
offences of smaller freemen, together with the voluntary and
contentious jurisdiction for which the courts of the landowners
were not competent, came to be exercised in the king's name. He
interfered in suits which had not passed through the earlier stage
of the hundred and the shire, and asserted himself as supreme
judge in all causes, not in appeals only. All jurisdiction was thus
exercised either by the king through his officers, or by landowners
who had their title from him. The royal officers acted in the hundred courts with freemen of all classes that still owed suit to them;

and the shire courts were composed of all lords of land, *scir-thegns*, and others, including a representation of the humblest landowners.   [CHE, I: 193–206]

ᴈ§ Although the progress of the Anglo-Saxon system, from the condition in which its whole organisation depends on personal relations to that in which everything depends on territorial ones, is marked at each step by some change in the royal power, it is better described in this formula than as a progress from democracy to monarchy, or from a democratic to an aristocratic monarchy, or from allodialism to feudalism. The growth of the royal power was theoretical rather than practical; what it gained on one side, it lost on another. The king became the source of justice, the lord and patron of his people, the owner of the public lands; but he had almost immediately to part with the substantial exercise of the powers so appropriated. By the grants of land, constantly increasing in number, the royal demesne was continually diminished, and the diminution of royal demesne made the taxation of the people the only available means of meeting public emergencies. The immunities which, by grant or by prescription, were vested in the holders of bookland, actually withdrew the profits and powers of jurisdiction from the source from which they themselves emanated. The patronage or lordship which was to unite the king more closely than ever before with the people, was intercepted by a number of mesne lordships and superiorities, which kept them in reality further asunder.   [CHE, I: 227]

ᴈ§ Notwithstanding the series of developments which have been traced so far, the forms of primitive organisation still generally survived. The warriors of the shire, whether free men of full political right, or the church vassals, or the contingents of the great thegns, fought as men of the shire under the ealdorman or his officer. The local force of Devonshire and Somersetshire was beaten by the Danes at Penho; the East Anglians and the men of Cambridgeshire fought apart at Ringmere; the men of Dorset, Wilts and Devon at Sherstone. Even the political attitude of the province was determined by the ealdorman and the thegns. The Northumbrian earl Uhtred and the West Saxon earl Ethelmar made their separate agreements with Sweyn, and in doing so declared their independence of Ethelred. But still more certainly in the local courts the old spirit of freedom found room. The forms were the same whether the king's gerefa or the lord's steward called the suitors together: the hundred retained its peace, the township its customs: the very disruption of society preserved these things for the better days.

In the preservation of the old forms,—the compurgation by the kindred of the accused, the responsibility for the wergild, the representation of the township in the court of the hundred, and that of the hundred in the court of the shire; the choice of witnesses; the delegation to chosen committees of the common judicial rights of the suitors of the folkmoot; the need of witness for the transfer of chattels, and the evidence of the hundred or shire to the title to lands; the report of the hundred and shire as to criminals, and the duty of enforcing their production and punishment, and the countless diversity of customs in which the several committees went to work to fulfil the general injunctions of the law,—in these remained the seeds of future liberties; themselves perhaps the mere shakings of the olive tree, the scattered grains that royal and noble gleaners had scorned to gather, but destined for a new life after many days of burial. They were the humble discipline by which a downtrodden people were schooled to act together in small things, until the time came when they could act together for great ones.

The growth of national character under these changes is a matter of further interest. Although the national experience was not enough to produce a strong and thorough feeling of union, it had been equable and general. No part of England was far behind any other in civilisation. The several kingdoms had been Christianised in rapid succession, and the process of amalgamation, by which the Danes became incorporated with the English, had been so speedy as little to affect the comparative civilisation of the districts they occupied after it had once fairly begun. Northumbria had indeed never recovered the learning and cultivation of her early days, but Kent and Wessex had retrograded nearly as much during the dark century that preceded Alfred. The depression of national life under Ethelred was much the same everywhere. The free man learned that he had little beyond his own arm and the circle of his friends to trust to. The cohesion of the nation was greatest in the lowest ranges. Family, township, hundred, shire held together when ealdorman was struggling with ealdorman and the king was left in isolated dignity. Kent, Devonshire, Northumbria, had a corporate life which England had not, or which she could not bring to action in the greatest emergencies. The witenagemot represented the wisdom, but concentrated neither the power nor the will, of the nation.

The individual Englishman must have been formed under circumstances that called forth much self-reliance and little hearty patriotism. His sympathies must have run into very narrow and provincial channels. His own home and parish were much more to him than the house of Cerdic or the safety of the nation. As a Christian, too, he had more real, more appreciable social duties than as an Englishman. He could accept Sweyn or Canute, if he would be his good lord and not change the laws or customs that regulated his daily life. There was a strong sense of social freedom without much care about political power. It was inherent in the blood. Caesar had seen it in the ancient German, and the empire of Charles and Otto strove in vain to remodel it in the medieval aggregation of the German-speaking nationalities; Bavarian, Saxon, Franconian, Swabian, were even less inclined to recognise their unity than were the nations which now called themselves English.

[CHE, 1: 229–231]

The Role of the Church of England
in Constitutional History

⇜§ The Church of England is not only the agency by which Christianity is brought to a heathen people, a herald of spiritual blessings and glorious hopes in another life; it is not merely the tamer of cruel natures, the civiliser of the rude, the cultivator of the waste places, the educator, the guide and the protector, whose guardianship is the only safeguard of the woman, the child, and the slave against the tyranny of their lord and master. The church is this in many other countries besides Britain; but here it is much more. The unity of the church in England was the pattern of the unity of the state: the cohesion of the church was for ages the substitute for the cohesion which the divided nation was unable otherwise to realise. Strong in its own conformation, it was more than a match for the despotic rule of such kings as Offa, and was the guardian of liberties as well as the defence of the oppressed. It was to an extraordinary degree a national church: national in its comprehensiveness as well as in its exclusiveness. Englishmen were in their lay aspect Mercians or West Saxons; only in their ecclesiastical relations could they feel themselves fellow-countrymen and fellow-subjects. And for a great part of the period under our view, the interference of foreign churches was scarcely if at all felt. There was no Roman legation from the days of Theodore to those of Offa, and there are only scanty vestiges of such interference for the next three centuries: the joint intercession of Leo III and Charles the Great effected the restoration of king Eardulf in Northumbria; an envoy of Eugenius II, bearing an English name, attests the acts of the council of Clovesho in 824; the action of pope Formosus appears, in a legendary way, in the final division of the West Saxon dioceses. But there are few other traces of Roman influence. Dunstan boldly refused to obey a papal sentence. Until the eve of the Conquest, therefore, the development of the system was free and spontaneous, although its sphere was a small one. The use of the native tongue in prayers and sermons is continuous; the observance of native festivals also, and the reverence paid to native saints. If the stimulating force of foreign intercourse was wanting, the intensity with which the church threw itself into the interest of the nation more than made up what was lacking. The ecclesiastical and the national spirit thus growing into one another supplied something at least of that strong passive power which the Norman despotism was unable to break. The churches were schools and nurseries of patriots; depositories of old traditional glories and the refuge of the persecuted. The English clergy supplied the basis of the strength of Anselm when the Norman bishops sided with the king. They trained the English people for the time when the kings should court their support and purchase their adherence by the restoration of liberties that would otherwise have been forgotten. The unity of the church was in the early period the only working unity; and this liberty, in the evil days that followed, the only form in which the traditions of the ancient freedom lingered. It was again to be the tie between the conquered and the conquerors; to give to the oppressed a hold on the conscience of the despot; to win new liberties and revive the old; to unite Norman and Englishman in the resistance to tyrants, and educate the growing nation for its distant destiny as the teacher and herald of freedom to all the world.   [CHE, I: 266–268]

III

THE NORMAN DESPOTISM
(1066–1154)

The Impact of the Norman Conquest

◄§ [In 1066] the domestic civilization of England, with all its drawbacks, was far beyond that of France. The Norman knights despised, undervalued and destroyed much that they could not comprehend. England was behind Europe in some of the arts which they had in common, but she had much that was her own, and developed what she had in common by her own genius. She might be behind in architecture, although that remains to be proved, for much that we know as the work of Northern architects was imitated from Roman models; an imitation which, although it later developed into systems far freer and nobler than anything that had existed before, was still only advancing from its rudest stage in France and Germany. England was slow in following the architecture as she was in following the politics of the continent. It is seldom remembered in comparing Norman and Anglo-Saxon in point of civilisation, how very little the Norman brought in comparison with what he destroyed, and how very little he brought that was his own. His law was Frank or Lombard, his general cultivation that of Lanfranc and Anselm, far more Italian than native: in civilisation—taken in the truer sense of the word,—in the organisation of the social life, in the means of obtaining speedy and equal justice, in the whole domain of national jurisprudence, he was far behind those whom he despised with the insolence of a barbarian: he had forgotten his own language, he had no literature, his art was foreign and purchased. But he was a splendid soldier, he had seen the great world east and west, he knew the balance of power between popes and emperors; and he was a conqueror: he held the rod of discipline which was to school England to the knowledge of her own strength and power of freedom: he was to drag her into the general network of the spiritual and temporal politics of the world, rousing her thereby to a consciousness of unsuspected, undeveloped powers: he was to give a new direction to her energies, to widen and unite and consolidate her sympathies: to train her to loyalty and patriotism; and in the process to impart so much, and to cast away so much, that when the time of awakening came, the conqueror and the conquered, the race of the oppressor and the race of the oppressed, were to find themselves one people.

[CHE, I: 235–236]

⚮ The effect of the Norman Conquest on the character and constitution of the English was threefold. The Norman rule invigorated the whole national system; it stimulated the growth of freedom and the sense of unity, and it supplied, partly from its own stock of jurisprudence, and partly under the pressure of the circumstances in which the conquerors found themselves, a formative power which helped to develop and concentrate the wasted energies of the native race. In the first place it brought the nation at once and permanently within the circle of European interests, and the Crusades, which followed within a few years, and which were recruited largely from the Normans and the English, prevented a relapse into isolation. The adventurous and highly-strung energy of the ruling race communicated itself to the people whom it ruled; its restless activity and strong political instinct roused the dormant spirit and disciplined even while it oppressed it. For, in the second place, the powers which it called forth were largely exercised in counteracting its own influence. The Normans so far as they became English added nerve and force to the system with which they identified themselves; so far as they continued Norman they provoked and stimulated by opposition and oppression the latent energies of the English. The Norman kings fostered, and the Norman nobility forced out the new growth of life. In the third place, however, the importation of new systems of administration,

and the development of new expedients, in every department of
government, by men who had a genius not only for jurisprudence
but for every branch of organisation, furnished a disciplinary and
formative machinery in which the new and revived powers might
be trained:—a system which through oppression prepared the way
for order, and by routine educated men for the dominion of law:
law and order which when completed should attest by the
pertinacious retention and development of primitive institutions,
that the discipline which had called them forth and trained men
for them, was a discipline only, not the imposition of a new and
adventitious polity. For the Norman polity had very little substantial organisation of its own; and what it brought with it to England
was soon worn out or merged in that of the nation with which it
united. Only the vigour and vitality which it had called forth was
permanent.   [CHE, I: 269–270]

    ◆§ The merely tyrannical rule of the Norman and Plantage-
net kings was not enough to bring out of the nature of the people the
self-restraint which, added to their already acquired self-reliance,
was to help them on to and make them worthy of greatness.
Tyrannical government might force them to unity and drill them
to obedience, but could never make them orderly, loyal, or patriotic. The feudal system, with all its tyranny and all its faults and
shortcomings, was based upon the requirements of mutual help and
service, and was maintained by the obligations of honour and
fealty. Regular subordination, mutual obligation, social unity were
the pillars of the fabric. The whole state was one: the king representing the unity of the nation. The great barons held their estates
of him, the minor nobles of the great barons, the gentry of these
vassals, the poorer freemen of the gentry, the serfs themselves
were not without rights and protectors as well as duties and service. Each gradation, and every man in each, owed service, fixed
definite service, to the next above him, and expected and received
protection and security in return. Each was bound by fealty to his
immediate superior, and the oath of the one implies the pledged
honour and troth of the other. Doubtless there were many hard-

ships, more in theory perhaps than in reality. It would seem hard to the allodial landowner who until now had held his land of no earthly lord, as free as heart might wish or eye might see, to be obliged to own a superior of whom he should hold his land, subject to exactions, fines, reliefs, escheats, forfeitures, without whose consent he could not part with an inch of ground, or raise a sum of money, or even leave his children as he wished at his death. Doubtless it seems a hard thing for necessary military service to be taken and exercised under the command of a foreign nobleman, instead of the leisurely and desultory exercise of the old militia, in which every man was very much like his own master—to exchange the theoretical equality of all freemen for the theoretical bondage of feudal subjection. But if . . . the reality of Saxon equality was fast disappearing, and the security of allodial possession coming already to require the maintenance of the superior lord, as the military service was becoming a perpetual grievance instead of an occasional duty, and the protection of law universally required almost as much as its restraints, we may not be far from the truth if we conclude that a well-administered feudalism was better for the people than a continuance in their old state.   [LEEH, 18–19]

⋙ William the Bastard claimed the crown of England as heir of Edward the Confessor, and as soon as the alarm and confusion that followed the battle of Hastings had in a measure subsided, the English nation acquiesced in the claim.   [LEEH, 28]

⋙ A general view of the reign of the Conqueror suggests the conclusion that, notwithstanding the strength of his personal character, and his maintenance of his right as king of the English and patron of the people both in church and in state;—notwithstanding the clearness of his political designs and the definiteness and solidity of his principles of action, there was very much in the state system which he initiated that still lay in solution. So much depended on the personal relations between himself and Lanfranc in church matters, that after their deaths the whole ecclesiastical fabric narrowly escaped destruction; and in temporal matters also, Lanfranc's influence excepted, the king had no constitutional adviser, no personal friend whose authority contained any element of independence. William is his own minister. His policy, so far as it is his own, owes its stability to his will. His witan are of his own creation,—feudatories powerful in enmity, no source of strength even when they are friends and allies,—with a policy of their own which he is determined to combat. His people fear him even when and where they trust him: he is under no real constraint, whether of law or conscience, to rule them well. His rule is despotic therefore, in spite of the old national and constitutional forms which he suffers to exist: it is the rule of a wise and wary, a strong and resolute, not a wanton and arbitrary despot; it avoids the evils of irresponsible tyranny, because he who exercises it has learned to command himself as well as other men. But a change of sovereign can turn the severe and wary rule into savage licence; and the people, who have grown up and have been educated under a loose, disorganised polity, see no difference between discipline and oppression. The constitutional effects of the Conquest are not worked out in William's reign, but in that of Henry I. The moral training of the nation does not as yet go beyond castigation: the lowest depth of humiliation has yet to be reached, but even that yields necessary lessons of its own. It is useless to ask what the result would have been if the first Norman king had been such a man as William Rufus: but it was most fortunate for the English that in the hour of their great peril, when they had neither ruler, counsel, nor system, they fell under the rule of one who was a law to himself, who saw the coincidence of duty and policy, and preferred the forms of ancient royalty to the more ostentatious position of a feudal conqueror. He was a hard man, austere, exacting, oppressive: his heavy hand made the English themselves comprehend their own national unity through a community of suffering. Yet in the suffering they were able to discern that there might be still worse things to bear: one strong master was better than many weak ones, general oppression than actual anarchy. The king made and kept good peace. The Danegeld and the Forest-law were not too much to pay for the escape from private war and feudal disruption. [CHE, 1: 313–314]

ﺳ Terrible as the tyranny of the Conqueror was, it was gentle compared with that of his sons. He was a great man, though covetous and unscrupulous: they were monsters of rapine, cruelty, and lust. As long as Lanfranc lived he exercised a salutary power over the mind of William Rufus, who had been his pupil, but on his death he gave rein to his ambition and avarice. . . .

The reign of Henry I lasted thirty-five years; these were comparatively speaking years of peace to the English; his only wars were foreign wars. His absences from England were long and frequent, and the tendency of his cruel and unscrupulous nature was checked by the influences of his queen, the Anglo-Saxon princess Matilda, whom the grateful people remembered for many years as the good Queen Molde. He also began his reign with good promises—he made a promise to God and all the people before the altar at Westminster that he would abolish the injustice that prevailed in his brother's time, and observe the most equitable of the laws established in the days of any of the kings before him; and the charter in which he embodied his promises is the basis of English liberties and the foundation stone of the structure on which was raised the noble fabric of the Magna Carta. . . . If the terms of this engagement had been kept, obviously the worst evils of the feudal system in its pressure on all but the very lowest classes of society would have been remedied. We have no warrant in believing that they were. The iron hand pressed as heavily, although perhaps more evenly, as it had done during the reigns of the father and brother of Henry. . . . The sum of his goodness seems to have been that he oppressed Norman and Saxon alike, a system that was not incompatible with the administration of strict justice between them or with a considerable measure of personal security.

Stephen, as his uncle had done before him, purchased the adhesion of the people by the grant of liberties: the church lands seized by William Rufus and Henry are restored; the forests made by Henry are disforested; ecclesiastics are allowed to make wills, and the other engagements made by Henry are enlarged and confirmed. But if Stephen had the will, he had not the power to keep his promises, and his reign was one continuous civil war.

[LEEH, 30–32]

Anglo-Norman Institutions

THE KING AND HIS MINISTERS

◄§ The Norman period . . . was the epoch of the growth of a new administrative system, having the source of its strength in the royal power. The constitution of this system distinguishes it from that of earlier and later times. In the earlier history, constitutional life seems to show itself first in the lower ranges of society, and to rise by slow degrees and unequal impulses towards the higher; in the later history, the equilibrium of the governmental system is maintained by regulating the balance between popular liberty and administrative pressure. The foundation of the administrative system marks the period that intervenes: and this foundation was the work of these four reigns. . . .

The Norman idea of royalty was very comprehensive; it practically combined all the powers of the national sovereignty, as they had been exercised by Edgar and Canute, with those of the feudal theory of monarchy, which was exemplified at the time in France and the Empire; and it discarded the limitations which had been placed on either system, in England by the constitutional action of the witan, and on the Continent by the usurpations or extorted immunities of the feudatories. The king is accordingly both the chosen head of the nation and the lord paramount of the whole of the land: he is the source of justice and the ultimate resource in appeal for such equity as he is pleased to dispense; the supreme judge of his own necessities and of the method to be taken to supply them. He is in fact despotic, for there is no force that can constitutionally control him, or force him to observe the conditions to which, for his own security or for the regular dispatch of business, he may have been pleased to pledge himself. If the descendants of the Conqueror had succeeded one another by the ordinary rule of inheritance, there can be no doubt but that the forms as well as the reality of ancient liberty would have perished. Owing however to the necessity under which each of them lay, of making for himself a title in default of hereditary right, the ancient framework was not set aside; and, perfunctory as to a great extent the forms of election and coronation were, they did not lose such real importance as they had possessed earlier, but furnished an important acknowledgment of the rights of the nation, as well as a recognition of the duties of the king. [CHE, I: 365–366]

⊷§ The chief minister of the Norman kings is the person to whom the historians and later constitutional writers give the name of *justiciarius*, with or without the prefix *summus* or *capitalis*. The growth of his functions was gradual, and even the history of the title is obscure; for it is often bestowed on officers who, although they discharged the functions which at a later period were attached to it, are not so styled by contemporaries or in formal documents. The office appears first as the lieutenancy of the kingdom or vice-royalty exercised during the king's absence from England. In this capacity William Fitz-Osbern, the steward of Normandy, and Odo of Bayeux, acted during the Conqueror's visit to the Continent in 1067; they were left, according to William of Poictiers, the former to govern the north of England, and the latter to hold rule in Kent, in the king's stead, 'vice sua;' Florence of Worcester describes them as 'custodes Angliae,' and Ordericus Vitalis gives to their office the name of 'praefectura.' It would seem most probable that William Fitz-Osbern, at least, was left in his character of steward, and that the Norman seneschalship was thus the origin of the English justiciarship. After the death of William Fitz-Osbern, Odo acted alone; William of Malmesbury describes him as 'totius Angliae vicedominus sub rege.' In 1074, when the king was again in Normandy, William of Warenne and Richard of Bienfaite were

left in charge of England; to these Ordericus, who lived a generation later, gives the title 'praecipui Angliae justitiarii;' but there is no
reason to suppose that the name as yet was definitely attached to a
particular post. On another occasion the office seems to have been
committed to Lanfranc, Gosfrid of Coutances, and Robert of
Mortain. In all these cases, although the function discharged was
one which belonged to the later justiciar, and they are accordingly
stages in the development of that office, it would seem safer to give
to the persons employed the more general name of lieutenant or
vicegerent. There is no evidence to show that they held any such
position during the king's presence in England, or that they exercised even in his absence supreme judicial functions to the exclusion of other great officers of the court. In the placitum held at
Pennenden in 1075 Gosfrid acted as president of the court, and in
similar trials touching the rights of Ely and Rochester Odo of
Bayeux appeared in the same position.

Under William Rufus the functions of the confidential minister
were largely extended; the office became a permanent one, and included the direction of the whole judicial and financial arrangements of the kingdom. It is probable that the king, who had no
great aptitude for any other business than that of war, was inclined
at first to throw the cares of government on his uncle Odo and the
bishop of Durham, William of S. Carileph; to these prelates later
writers give the title of justiciar. But their treason opened the
king's eyes to the imprudence of trusting so great authority to
such powerful and ambitious personages. Ranulf Flambard, who
succeeded to the place of chief adviser, seems to have earned his
master's confidence by his ingenious and unscrupulous devices for
increasing the royal revenue, and he may be looked on as the first
consolidator of the functions of the office. It is impossible not to
suspect that he had a share in the work of the Domesday Survey.
He was a native of the diocese of Bayeux, in which Caen, the seat of
the Norman treasury, was situated, and had been brought up
among the inferior officials of the ducal court. He had held, in the
days of Edward the Confessor, a small estate in Hampshire, possi-

bly acquired in the service of the Norman bishop William of London. He was afterwards attached to the household of Bishop Maurice, whom he left to become chaplain to the king, an office which he had held for some years before he came into prominent importance. As the annals of the Conqueror's reign furnish the names of no great lawyers or financiers, as Ranulf was employed at court during the later years of it, and as his subsequent career proves him to have possessed great ability, if not a systematic policy of administration, it is not unnatural to suppose that he rendered himself useful in the compilation of the great rate-book of the kingdom. And such a supposition almost answers the objection taken to the statement of Ordericus, that he made a new survey in the reign of William Rufus, of which there is no other evidence. The chronicler may have heard that he was employed in the registration of the revenue, and may have attributed it to him as a measure adopted during his term of high office.

However this may have been, and by whatever name the post was distinguished, it became in Flambard's hands all important. He is called by Florence of Worcester 'negotiorum totius regni exactor,' and 'placitator et totius regni exactor:' expressions which recall the ancient identity of the *gerefa* with the *exactor*, and suggest that one part of the royal policy was to entrust the functions which had belonged to the praefectus or high steward to a clerk or creature of the court. Robert Bloett, bishop of Lincoln, is called by Henry Huntingdon 'justitiarius totius Angliae:' he may have succeeded Ranulf, but of his administration nothing is known. The next holder of the office is Bishop Roger of Salisbury. He had a history somewhat like that of Ranulf Flambard. He also was a poor priest of the neighbourhood of Caen. He had attracted Henry's notice, long before he came to the throne, by his expeditious way of celebrating divine service, had been enlisted by him as a sort of chaplain steward, and by his economy and honesty had justified the confidence reposed in him. After Henry's accession he was at first employed as chancellor, and after the reconciliation of the king with Anselm was consecrated to the see of Salisbury, being the first prelate canonically elected since the dispute about investiture had arisen. He seems to have risen at the same time to the place of justiciar. Under his guidance, whether as chancellor or as justiciar, the whole administrative system was remodelled; the jurisdiction of the Curia Regis and Exchequer was carefully organised, and the peace of the country maintained in that theoretical perfection which earned for him the title of the Sword of Righteousness. He is the first justiciar who is called 'secundus a rege.' He retained the title of justiciar until his arrest by Stephen. His personal history need not be further pursued. Roger of Salisbury certainly bore the title of justiciar; whether he acted as the king's lieutenant during his absence is uncertain, and even yet it must be questioned whether the name possessed a precise official significance. Several other ministers receive the same name even during the time at which he was certainly in office: even the title of *capitalis justitiarius* is given to officers of the Curia Regis who were acting in subordination to him. We have, however, been tracing the development of the office rather than the history of the title. The latter, not improbably, gained definiteness of application as the functions of the office developed. The 'magister justitiarius' of the Norman kingdom of Sicily, who possibly took his name from the Norman chief minister of England, appears soon after the middle of the twelfth century. The title of *justiza* of Aragon, a minister not unlike the later chief justices of England, is first found in the twelfth century. The seneschal of Normandy receives the name of *justitiar* under Henry II. It is only in the same reign that the office in England acquires the exclusive right to the definite name of *summus* or *capitalis justitiarius*, or *justitiarius totius Angliae*, a title occasionally paraphrased or interpreted as '*praefectus Angliae.*'

For the office, the development of which is thus only obscurely traceable, it is easier to find analogies in foreign systems than to produce a consecutive history to connect it with known antecedents. A general view of the Norman policy suggests that the form taken by the institution on English ground arose partly from the king's desire to prevent the administration falling into the hands of a hereditary noble. In a small territory like Normandy, where the duke was always at home, and where very much of the judicial business was devolved on the courts of the feudatories, an officer like the seneschal might suffice for all necessary business of state. But in England, where the king could not be always resident, where the amount of public business was increasing rapidly in consequence of the political changes, and where it was of the utmost importance to avoid the creation of hereditary jurisdictions, it was absolutely necessary that a new system should be devised. The same need was felt in France; and the same tide of events which threw the administration here into the hands of Bishop Roger, brought the management of affairs there into the hands of the Abbot Suger. In each case we see an ecclesiastical mayor of the palace; a representative of the king in all capacities, lieutenant in his absence, chief agent in his presence; prime minister in legal, financial, and even military affairs; but prevented by his spiritual profession from founding a family of nobles or withdrawing from the crown the powers which he had been commissioned to sustain. The expedient was a transitional one; the clerical justiciars were superseded by baronial ones when Henry II felt himself strong enough to stand the risk, and occur again only under his sons, whose exigencies and whose policy compelled them to employ such ministers as they found trained to their hands, and as were otherwise qualified to act as mediators between themselves and their people.

The chancellor, who at a later period entered into many of the rights and dignities of the justiciar, appears in history very much earlier. The name, derived probably from the *cancelli*, or screen behind which the secretarial work of the royal household was carried on, claims a considerable antiquity; and the offices which it denotes are various in proportion. The chancellor of the Karolingian sovereigns, succeeding to the place of the more ancient *referendarius*, is simply the royal notary: the archi-cancellarius is the chief of a large body of such officers associated under the name of the chancery, and is the official keeper of the royal seal. It is from this minister that the English chancellor derives his name and function. Edward the Confessor, the first of our sovereigns who had a seal, is also the first who had a chancellor: from the reign of the Conqueror the office has descended in regular succession. It seems to have been to a comparatively late period, generally if not always, at least in England, held by an ecclesiastic, who was a member of the royal household, and on a footing with the great dignitaries. The chancellor was the most dignified of the royal chaplains, if not the actual head of that body; and he had the especial duty of securing and administering the royal revenue which accrued from vacant benefices. The whole of the secretarial work of the household and court fell on the chancellor and chaplains; the keeping of the royal accounts under the treasurer and justiciar, the drawing up and sealing of the royal writs, and the conducting of the king's correspondence. The chancellor was, in a manner, the secretary of state for all departments. He was generally rewarded for his service with a bishopric, and it was not regarded as fitting that the office should be retained by him after his consecration. Of the early chancellors none are of particular eminence, or perhaps they are overshadowed by the greatness of the justiciar. The office was however held by William Giffard, whose services were influential in procuring the election of Henry I; by Roger of Salisbury himself, before his promotion to episcopal rank and to the justiciarship; and by his son, also named Roger, who was one of the victims of Stephen.   [CHE, I: 374–381]

⮫§ The separation of the great functionaries of the household from those of the State is ultimately marked by the fact of the former becoming hereditary, while the latter continue to be ministerial. And this is further distinguished: the ministerial offices are saleable. The treasurer, the chancellor, even the justiciar, pays a sum of money for his office, or even renders an annual rent or ferm for it. This practice runs on to the thirteenth century, when, so many of the dignities having become hereditary, and the feeling of the nation being strongly expressed in favour of reform, the king was compelled to choose his subordinate ministers with some reference to their capacity for business. Such a history may account for much of the indefinite and complicated character of the offices of State.

The powers of these officers were very considerable, and were extended by continual encroachments. Each dignitary of the household was a member of the Curia Regis and Exchequer, and in that capacity exercised from time to time judicial functions. Each too had under him a staff of servants over whom he exercised judicature and discipline; and this was extended to the cognisance of all offences committed or disputes arising in the department which was nominally under his management. Hence the origin of the courts of the high steward, the constable, and the marshal, which are subjects of complaint down to a late period. These courts were naturally regarded as exceptions to the common law of the land which was administered by the justiciar or under his superintendence.

COUNCIL AND COURT

The witenagemot of the kingdom, now subsisting under the title of the great court or council, forms a second circle round the sovereign. Under the Conqueror this assembly retained very much of its earlier character: the bishops and abbots still attended in virtue of their official wisdom, and with them the great officers of State and the chief of the Norman baronage. It was however rather a court than an organised council. It cannot be certainly affirmed that the tenure of a particular estate of land, held by homage and fealty, either was an indispensable qualification or bestowed the privilege of membership: and before the reign of Henry II it would be rash to maintain that every tenant-in-chief of the crown was a member of the assembly, although every member of the assembly was, after the settlement of the question of investiture, obliged to hold his barony by homage and fealty. It is of course only to the bishops and abbots that that measure directly

applies, but its operation in their case necessarily involves the observance of the rule in all others. It is sufficiently obvious from the
Domesday record that the tenants-in-chief had long had their position and character defined. That the forcing of homage and fealty,
with the baronial tenure, upon the bishops had the effect of
annihilating their earlier title to appear in the witenagemot as
sapientes can scarcely be maintained. It completed however the
symmetry of the baronage, and gave a basis of uniformity to the
court in which they were assembled. The kings no doubt exercised
the right of associating in their deliberations such counsellors as it
might seem convenient to admit, as, for instance, a Roman legate, a
Norman prelate who would be unlikely to have lands in England,
or even lawyers, monks, or clergymen of special skill or sanctity;
but it does not follow that such strangers would be allowed to vote
in case of any difference of opinion. Except in the anomalous
period of Stephen's reign, there are no records of any such discus-
sions as might lead to divisions. In private perhaps the sovereign
listened to advice, but, so far as history goes, the counsellors who
took part in formal deliberations must have been unanimous or
subservient. An assembly of courtiers holding their lands of the
king, and brought together rather for pompous display than for
political business, may seem scarcely entitled to the name of a national council. Such as it was, however, this court of bishops,
abbots, earls, barons, and knights was the council by whose advice
and consent the kings condescended to act, or to declare that they
acted.

A council based on the principle that its members are qualified
by feudal tenure of land ought not to confine itself to an assembly
of magnates: it should include all freeholders of town or country
who are not under any mesne lord, and would thus be in theory a
much larger and more liberal representation of the nation than
anything that had existed since the days of the Heptarchy. On
some occasions, especially at the great councils of Salisbury in 1086
and 1116, it is probable that a general muster of the landowners of
the kingdom was held, at which all were expected either to be

present or to send their excuses by the sheriffs, who on the former occasion are especially said to have been summoned. But the number of persons who were really consulted on business, or to whom the show of such attention was paid, must have been always very limited. As both earlier and later was the case, only the highest class was called on to treat of the highest matters; the people, if they were called at all, would hear and obey. And thus the constituent parts of the assembly are reduced to the archbishops, bishops, abbots, earls, barons and knights. The sheriffs, who would come invariably under one of these heads, may be left out of consideration in this relation. The enumeration is however in no way based on a logical division; all the members were barons by tenure, greater or less, and all the earls and barons strictly so called were probably knights.

On the ecclesiastical members of the council it is unnecessary to dwell: their character is, except as affected by the acceptance of feudal baronies, exactly the same as it was before. The archbishop of Canterbury is still recognised as the first constitutional adviser of the crown. William Rufus acknowledges the right of Lanfranc as distinctly as Henry I does that of Anselm. And the importance of this position probably lay at the root of the claim made by the kings to decide which of two rival popes should be recognised in the country: the theory that it was by the acceptance of the pall from Rome that the metropolitical status was completed, might have exposed the king to the necessity of receiving his chief counsellor from a hostile power, unless limited by such a condition: and as the papal theory of appeals and legations was not yet applied to England, the power of the archbishop to further or retard the promotion of bishops was practically unlimited, except by means which it would have been highly dangerous for the king to adopt. Even at the best the relations of the archbishops to the Norman kings were hazardous, and depended far more on personal than on legal considerations. The fact that even William Rufus was obliged to except the primatial see of Canterbury from his unscrupulous misuse of patronage, is another proof of the strong constitutional hold of the archbishops; a hold which their consistent exertions for the protection of the people and the purification of the Church most amply justified. The whole of the episcopal body was until the middle of Henry I's reign sworn to obedience to Canterbury; and the archbishop of York, even after he had obtained recognition of his independence, had so small a body of suffragans as to make his position in fact subordinate. He was very powerful in Yorkshire, but of secondary importance at court. [CHE, I: 384-389]

&⸹ The idea of representation which was familiar enough in the local courts might be expected, in a constitution so entirely based on land tenure, to appear in the central council as well. But it is not to be traced in existing records, and, when it does appear later, it is in that intermittent, growing, and struggling form which shows it to be a novelty. Of any representation of the freeholders in general there is not even a suspicion. The sheriffs would, as being barons themselves, have their places in the council, and might report the needs and wishes of their neighbours, but, as royal nominees and farmers of the revenue, they could not be expected to sympathise deeply with the population which they had to assess and to oppress.

It is not to be supposed that the assemblies at which all, or even a large proportion, of the tenants-in-chief presented themselves were very frequent. The councils of Salisbury already referred to are perhaps the only occasion on which anything like a general assembly was brought together. These were for the special purpose of taking the oaths of fealty, and comprised other elements besides the tenants-in-chief. The ordinary courts or councils were of a much more limited character, seldom containing more than the bishops and 'proceres,' a term that would include only the earls and greater barons. These courts were held on the great Church festivals, Christmas, Easter, and Whitsuntide: generally at the great cities of southern England, London, Winchester, and Gloucester. The king appeared wearing his crown; a special peace was maintained, necessarily no doubt in consequence of the multitude of armed retainers who attended the barons; and magnificent hospitality was accorded to all comers. 'Thrice a year,' says the Chronicle, 'King William wore his crown every year that he was in England; at Easter he wore it at Winchester, at Pentecost at Westminster, and at Christmas at Gloucester. And at these times all the men of England were with him, archbishops, bishops and abbots, earls, thegns and knights.' A similar usage was observed by his sons, although neither he nor they regularly followed the rotation thus described; they called together their barons whenever and wherever they pleased; and many of their courts were held at their forest palaces in Wiltshire and Berkshire. Under Henry I the number of places of council was largely increased, and the enlarged accommodation afforded by the growing monasteries was utilised. Councils were held at Windsor, Rockingham, Woodstock, among the forest palaces; at Oxford, Northampton, and other midland towns. The cessation of the solemn courts under Stephen was regarded by Henry of Huntingdon as a fatal mark of national decline.

These assemblies must be regarded as legally possessed of the full powers of the old witenagemot: but the exercise of their powers depended on the will of the king, and under the Conqueror and his sons there are scarcely any traces of independent action in them. Their legislative authority is admitted: it is with their counsel and consent that William the Conqueror amends the laws of the Confessor, and divides the ecclesiastical from the secular courts. Henry I mentions in the preamble to the charter that he had received the crown by the counsel of the barons; with their consent he had retained the forests; and it was with the counsel of his barons that his father had amended the laws of S. Edward; Stephen, in the corresponding document, asserts his election by the clergy and the people; but neither of them distinctly declares the share of the council in the acts thus prefaced. The writs by which Henry I revived the action of the county courts and declared the penalties for false coining, are drawn in the form of edicts or charters, and contain no mention of counsel or consent. As, however, the historian Eadmer distinctly describes the latter piece of legislation as one of a series of edicts of reform issued by the advice of Anselm and the 'proceres,' the omission of the formal words is not conclusive.

The right of the council to join in taxation is nowhere distinctly stated: yet Henry I describes an aid as 'auxilium quod barones mihi dederunt;' and it must be supposed that the king would lay before his barons any plan for increasing the existing burdens, and that such announcement would be regarded as necessary for the validity of the exaction; the silence of the counsellors or their ready assent would be a matter of form.

The judicial proceedings which took place in the king's presence are frequently mentioned, but even here a question may be raised as to the freedom of debate. It was by a judicial sentence that Earls Waltheof and Roger were condemned; in a great session of the king's court the bishop of Durham was tried in 1088; in a council at Salisbury in A.D. 1096 William of Eu had his trial by battle and his cruel punishment; in the same council the king sentenced William of Alderi to be hanged, and the other conspirators to be imprisoned; in A.D. 1102 Henry I summoned Robert of Belesme before his court, and alleged forty-five articles of treason against him; in A.D. 1130 Geoffrey de Clinton was accused of treason in the Easter court at Woodstock. In all these, and numerous other cases which might be adduced, it is clearly the full national assembly, and not the mere justices, before whom the trial is conducted. The barons act as judges, the king apparently gives the sentence, although in this respect also he is open to advice. It was by the counsel of Hugh of Chester that William of Eu suffered mutilation; King David of Scotland, as earl of Huntingdon, took an active part in the trial of Geoffrey de Clinton. The mode of trial was probably the same as in the lower courts, the accusation by sworn witnesses, compurgation, ordeal and trial by battle. On one occasion, we are informed, the barons interfered so far as to recommend William Rufus to show mercy; it was by the advice of his wise men that he spared the minor criminals in A.D. 1096.

Matters of civil jurisdiction were also brought before these assemblies, although the determination in such cases would fall to the lot of the more experienced lawyers of the Curia Regis or Exchequer. A great council at Pedreda in the Conqueror's reign determined the suit between the churches of York and Worcester, and a similar quarrel between the bishops of Llandaff and S. David's came before the court more than once in the latter years of Henry I. In A.D. 1126 the king, by the advice of his barons, granted the custody of Rochester Castle to the archbishop of Canterbury. The proceedings of Stephen against the bishops, impolitic as they were, were conducted with a shadow of legality in a similar assembly.

Most, however, of the proceedings of the national council at this period, of which any record is preserved, come under the head of general business. The nominations of bishops were always made on these occasions until the right of canonical election was admitted by Henry I: and even then the election took place in the king's court, often at the great festivals when the majority of the barons were present, and when the consecration and the investiture could be celebrated with equal pomp. The ceremony of conferring earldoms and knighthood was a public business of the court, as well as the witnessing of the homages paid to the king or his presumptive successor. The foreign and ecclesiastical policy of the king was here canvassed without much jealousy or intimidation; war and peace, royal marriages, and the like. Henry I took the advice of his council on his negotiations with the see of Rome; and even on the choice of a second wife. The see of Ely was founded by the same king with the advice of the archbishop and other magnates. Of the share taken by the baronage in the election of the king enough has been said already: it was a right which each sovereign in turn was politic enough to acknowledge, and of the reality of which he was so far conscious that he took every means of escaping it. The election of Henry I and Stephen, the claim put forward to elect the empress, the acceptance of the heir of King

Henry and the rejection of the heir of Stephen, place this preroga-tive of the nation, however indifferently the council which exer-cised it represented the nation, upon an incontestable basis.

The power of the clergy was so strong during these reigns that we must not expect to find ecclesiastical questions treated in the secular councils except under the greatest reserve. It must however have been a very large gathering that accepted the conditions made by Henry I and Anselm in 1107: in the following year we find the canons of a Church council at London passed in the presence of the king, with the assent of all his barons; in A.D. 1127, after a sim-ilar council, Henry granted his assent to the statutes passed in it, and confirmed them 'by his royal power and authority,' on the principle of his father's policy. On this and some other occasions we find distinct traces of a usage which forms a peculiar mark of our ecclesiastical history; the king holds his court at Westminster, whilst the archbishop celebrates his council in the same city; the two assemblies together form a precedent for the coincident sum-moning of parliament and convocation in later days. The special significance however of the king's ratification of the canons of 1127 lies in the fact that the archbishop had just returned from Rome, invested with that legatine character which was so often a stumbling-block both in civil and ecclesiastical affairs. The king had succeeded in obtaining the office for the first time for the primate, with whom he was acting in concert; the canons of the council had thus the threefold sanction of the national Church, the King, and the Holy See, without any concession being made by either as to the necessity of confirmation by the other two. These proceedings completed the harmony of Church and State, which was one of the great objects of Henry's policy, and which was rudely broken by the quarrels of Stephen.

In the last reign of the period the ecclesiastical councils claim and exert more real power than could be decently claimed for such assemblies of the barons as either party could bring together. The assembly at Winchester in which Matilda was elected was a synod of the clergy, who were present in three bodies, bishops, abbots, and archdeacons, and were separately consulted; but it was largely attended by the barons of the party. The council of A.D. 1151, in which Stephen, Eustace, and the barons appeared, and in which both parties appealed to the pope for the settlement of their claims, was primarily an ecclesiastical council summoned by archbishop Theobald in his capacity as legate. It is in fact difficult to discover after the fourth year of Stephen any assembly to which the name of national council can be given, although, in the confused accounts of the final pacification, we may detect evidence that proves such assemblies to have been held. The abeyance however of all the constitutional machinery at this period, and the almost irreconcileable chronological difficulties which meet us in the annals, may well excuse some hesitation in forcing a general conclusion from these precedents.

The exact relation of the administrative system to the national council is not very easy to define; for the lawyers and historians gave no glimpse of a theory of government, and the documentary evidences of the Norman period are by no means abundant. It would be rash to affirm that the supreme courts of judicature and finance were committees of the national council, although the title of Curia belongs to both, and it is difficult to see where the functions of the one end and those of the other begin. And it would be scarcely less rash to regard the two great tribunals, the Curia Regis and Exchequer, as mere sessions of the king's household ministers, undertaking the administration of national business without reference to the action of the greater council of the kingdom. The historical development of the system is obscure in the extreme. The Conqueror, as Duke of Normandy, had no doubt a high court of judicature and a general assembly of his barons; Edward the Confessor had his national witenagemot, which likewise exercised the functions of judicature; he also, as we must infer from Domesday, had a centralised system of finance, a treasury with its staff of keepers and assessors. How much of the new administrative machinery was imported directly from Normandy, how much was English, how much derived its existence from the juxtaposition of the two, we have to decide on conjecture rather than on evidence; and the materials for answering the question, which concerns still wider generalisations, will be given further on. It may be enough here to note, that whereas under William the Conqueror and William Rufus the term *Curia* generally, if not invariably, refers to the solemn courts held thrice a year or on particular summons, at which all tenants-in-chief were supposed to attend, from the reign of Henry I we have distinct traces of a judicial system, a supreme court of justice, called the Curia Regis, presided over by the king or justiciar, and containing other judges also called justiciars, the chief being occasionally distinguished by the title of 'summus,' 'magnus,' or 'capitalis.' The same body also managed the assessment and collection of the revenue, and for this purpose had a separate and very elaborate organisation, through the history of which the character of their judicial work is chiefly made intelligible: and this may accordingly be stated first.

TAXATION

The Exchequer of the Norman kings was the court in which the whole financial business of the country was transacted, and as the whole administration of justice, and even the military organisation, was dependent upon the fiscal officers, the whole framework of society may be said to have passed annually under its review. It derived its name from the chequered cloth which covered the table at which the accounts were taken, a name which suggested to the spectator the idea of a game at chess between the receiver and the payer, the treasurer and the sheriff. As this name never occurs before the reign of Henry I, and as the tradition of the court preserved the remembrance of a time when the business which took place in it was transacted 'ad taleas,' 'at the tallies,' it seems certain that the date of complete organisation should be referred to this period. Under the Anglo-Saxon kings we may presume that the treasure or *hord* was under the management of a *gerefa* or *hordere*, but, although the mention of such an officer is not uncommon, there are no distinct traces of courts of account: the taxes were collected by the sheriffs and other reeves, and the treasure was preserved in the palace: some machinery for account and guardianship must be inferred. Under the Conqueror and William Rufus the word 'fiscus' or 'thesaurus' is commonly used: the word 'scaccarium' comes into use only under Henry I.

The officers of the Exchequer are the great officers of the household; the justiciar who is the president, the chancellor, the constable, two chamberlains, the marshal, and the treasurer, with such other great and experienced counsellors as the king directs to attend for the public service, and who share with the others the title of Barons of the Exchequer. Amongst these, if not identical with them, are the justices or ordinary judges of the Curia Regis, who appear to be called indiscriminately 'justitiarii' and 'barones scaccarii.'

Twice a year, at Easter and at Michaelmas, full sessions were held in the palace at Westminster, attended by all the barons, with their clerks, writers, and other servants, each of whom had his assigned place and regular duties. Two chambers were used for the transaction of business: the upper one, or exchequer of account, was that in which the reports were received, and all the legal negotiations carried on and recorded; and the lower one, or exchequer of receipt, in which the money was paid down, weighed, and otherwise tested. The record of the business was preserved in three great rolls; one kept by the treasurer, another by the chancellor, and a third by an officer nominated by the king, who registered the matters of legal and special importance. The rolls of the treasurer and chancellor were duplicates; that of the former was called from its shape the great roll of the Pipe, and that of the latter the roll of the Chancery. These documents are mostly still in existence. The Pipe Rolls are complete from the second year of Henry II, and the Chancellor's rolls nearly so. Of the preceding period only one roll, that of the thirty-first year of Henry I, is preserved, and this with Domesday-book is the most valuable store of information which exists for the administrative history of the age.

The financial reports were made to the barons by the sheriffs of the counties. At Easter and Michaelmas each of these magistrates produced his own accounts, and paid into the Exchequer such an instalment or *proffer* as he could afford, retaining in hand sufficient money for current expenses. In token of receipt a tally was made; a long piece of wood in which a number of notches were cut, marking the pounds, shillings and pence received; this stick was then split down the middle, each half contained exactly the same number of notches, and no alteration could of course be made without certain detection. At the Michaelmas audit these tallies were produced, and the remainder of the accounts made up. If the sheriff were able to acquit himself entirely, he began the new year without arrears; if not, a running account was kept by the same primitive method.

The particulars accounted for by the sheriffs afford us a complete view of the financial condition of the country. The first item is the 'firma' or ferm of the shire. This is a sort of composition for all the profits arising to the king from his ancient claims on the land and from the judicial proceedings of the shire-moot: the rent of detached pieces of demesne land, the remnants of the ancient folkland; the payments due from corporate bodies and individuals for the primitive gifts, the offerings made in kind, or the hospitality,—the *feorm-fultum,*—which the kings had a right to exact from their subjects, and which were before the time of Domesday generally commuted for money; the fines or a portion of the fines paid in the ordinary process of the county courts, and other small miscellaneous incidents. These had been, soon after the composition of Domesday, estimated at a fixed sum, which was regarded as a sort of rent or composition at which the county was let to the sheriff, and recorded in the *Rotulus Exactorius;* for this, under the name of ferm, he answered annually; if his receipts were in excess, he retained the balance as his lawful profit, the wages of his service; if the proceeds fell below the ferm, he had to pay the difference from his own purse. If land chargeable with these sums fell out of cultivation, he was excused a proportionate amount under the head of waste; if new land was brought under tillage, he had to account for the profit under the title of increment. Before rendering this account, the sheriff discharged the king's debts in the shire, paid the royal benefactions to religious houses, provided for the maintenance of stock on the crown lands, the expenses of public business, the cost of provisions supplied to the court, and the travelling expenses of the king and his visitors incurred within his district. The payments had been long made in kind, and even in the reign of Henry II old men remembered how corn and cattle had been once brought up to the court as the tribute of various shires; horses, hounds, and hawks were still received at a settled valuation, in payment of debt or fine.

The next item in point of importance is the Danegeld, a tax which had assumed in Norman times the character of ordinary revenue, and which, like the ferm, was compounded for by the sheriff at a fixed sum. This tax had been increased heavily by William the Conqueror: in A.D. 1084 it had been trebled; six shillings were exacted from each hide of geldable land, instead of two, the usual sum raised under the Anglo-Saxon king, and the accounts of the sum received from the Western counties on this occasion are preserved in the record known as the Domesday of Exeter. It may be reasonably inferred that the fixing of the sum of the Danegeld for each county was one of the results of the Domesday Survey; and it must not be understood that the sums accounted for under this head afford any clue to the extent of land in cultivation. Monasteries possessed in many cases immunity from Danegeld; in other cases they had special commutations; a large extent of land frequently 'defendit se,' that is, was held responsible, or rated, as one hide; and all persons employed in the king's service were excepted from the impost. The Danegeld was a very unpopular tax, probably because it was the plea on which the sheriffs made their greatest profit; it was believed that Henry I had made a vow to abolish it; and the abolition was accordingly made a point among the concessions won from Stephen at the beginning of his reign. It was really got rid of by Henry II, who however taxed the land in much the same way under other names; and it was in very nearly the same form reproduced under the title of carucage by the ministers of Richard I. With the Danegeld may be noticed another impost which fell in the time of Henry I on the towns chiefly, and which, although it bore the feudal name of auxilium or aid, and answers to the later tallage, was probably the tax which represented in the case of the towns the same demand as in the country was met by the Danegeld. It seems, like the Danegeld, to have been a fixed sum payable annually.

A third head of ordinary or ancient national revenue comprised the proceeds of the pleas of the crown; the fines and other profits arising from the trial of offences which had been severed from the ordinary operation of the shire and hundred, and which, although tried before the sheriff in his character as justice, were, so far as the fines were concerned, made to contribute directly to the income of the king. Of these the most important is the *murdrum*, the fine payable, as has been already stated, by the hundred in which a murder has taken place in case of its failing to prove the slain man to be an Englishman. The commixture of the populations had so far proceeded in the time of Henry II that it was impossible to decide the question of nationality, and all murders were punished alike. With these may be mentioned a wide class of amercements, some of which have their origin in Anglo-Saxon and some in feudal customs; of the former are fines for non-appearance in the hundred and shire courts, and of the latter penalties for breach of forest law.

Under the head of feudal income come all the items arising from the transfer of lands, reliefs, guardianship, marriage, escheat, and other incidents; the sale of public offices included. This was of course a large and comparatively permanent source of revenue. The arbitrary sums exacted under the name of reliefs by William Rufus were one of the grievances which Henry I in his coronation charter undertook to redress. We are not able to discover how this promise was fulfilled, for although in the reign of Henry II a regular arrangement appears to be in force by which the relief of the knight's fee was five pounds, and that of the barony one hundred, the corresponding payments in his grandfather's reign are not to be brought under so simple a principle. It is however probable that a record of the number of knights' fees in England had been made before the death of Henry I, and that it was the basis of the computation adopted by his grandson. Before this was done, the valuation, where the payment was not altogether arbitrary, must have been made according to the record of the hidage preserved in Domesday. And it may be observed, that whilst Henry I took, as an aid for the marriage of his daughter, three shillings on each hide, Henry II, on a like occasion, took one mark on the knight's fee. Whatever was the basis of rating, all the feudal incidents would be accounted for in the same way. Henry I may have taken an aid on the occasion of his son's knighthood, as he did on his daughter's marriage, but of this there is no record. The Pipe Roll of the thirty-first year of his reign contains several notices of sums paid for permission to determine suits connected with land, by covenant or by trial by battle; for leave to marry, to avoid answering the claim of another claimant, for cancelling agreements of exchange, and for other liberties which betray the existence of a good deal of legal oppression.

The forest law, which, heavy as it was under William the Conqueror, seems to have reached the extreme of severity and cruelty under Henry I, was also made a source of revenue. The fines exacted by the justices under this system form a considerable item in the accounts.

Among the great offices of the household which appear from the Pipe Roll to have been saleable are those of dapifer, marshal, and chancellor. The last-mentioned officer in A.D. 1130 owes £3006 13s. 4d. for the great seal; the office of treasurer was bought by Bishop Nigel for his son for £400. Inferior places in the legal staff are also sold. In Norfolk, Benjamin pays £4 5s. to be allowed to keep the pleas of the crown; in Northumberland, Uhtred son of Waltheof makes a payment for the grant of sac and soc, and a similar transaction is recorded in Suffolk; John the Marshal pays forty marks for a mastership in king's court, Humfrey Bohun four hundred marks to be dapifer regis; Richard Fitz-Alured pays fifteen marks that he may sit with Ralph Basset on the king's pleas in Buckinghamshire. At the same time the officers of the ancient courts are found purchasing relief from their responsibilities; the *judices* and *juratores* of Yorkshire pay £100 that they may be judges and jurors no longer, anxious no doubt to avoid the heavy fines exacted from them either for non-attendance or for other neglect of duty.

The sum accounted for in the single Pipe Roll of the reign of Henry I, including all the debts and other gross receipts, is not less than £66,000 for the year. The exhaustive and orderly character of the roll is in marked contrast with the very scanty details of the similar accounts at the beginning of Henry II's reign, when the whole sum accounted for is not more than £22,000: and this fully confirms the statements of the historians and of the writer of the Dialogus de Scaccario, as to the ruinous state into which the machinery of government had fallen under Stephen.

But it is not only in the department of finance that this most important record illustrates constitutional history, and we must refer to it again in examining the framework of the Norman judicature. Before doing this it will be necessary to recur to the Domesday Survey, which was not only the general record of the royal revenue, but the rate-book of valuation of all the land in the kingdom. The formation of this record afforded a precedent for a rating system which was of no small importance in its bearing on later history: and it is not a little singular that a measure taken by the Conqueror, in order to fix and make available to the utmost his hold upon the country, should be the first step in a continuous process by which the nation arrived ultimately at the power of taxing itself, and thus controlling the whole framework of the constitution and the whole policy of government.

The Domesday Survey was ordered by William in a great council held at Christmas 1085 at Gloucester, when a Danish invasion was supposed to be imminent. It was carried into execution during the following year by officers appointed by the king, who visited the several counties, and called before them all those persons of whom in ordinary times the county court was composed. Tradition recorded that, when the Conqueror wished to confirm the national laws, in order to obtain a true report of those laws he summoned to his court twelve elected representatives of each shire to declare upon oath the ancient lawful customs. A similar plan was now adopted. The king's barons exacted an oath from the sheriff and all the barons and Norman landholders of the shire; every hundred appeared also by sworn representatives, and from each township the priest, the reeve, and six villeins or ceorls. On the deposition or verdict of these jurors was drawn up the report of the name of each manor or township, and its present and late holder: its extent in hides, the number of ploughs for which it furnished work; the number of homagers, ceorls or villeins, cotters, and serfs; how many freemen, how many sokemen; the extent of wood, meadow, and pasture; the number of mills and fisheries; the increase and decrease since King Edward's time; the several and collective values of every holding. By this report an exhaustive register of the land and its capabilities was formed, which was never entirely superseded; for although the feudal taxation was, within a century after, based on the knight's fee instead of the hide, much of the general taxation continued to be assessed on the hide, and, the number of hides which the knight's fee contained being known, the number of knights' fees in any particular holding could be easily discovered. Ranulf Flambard, as Ordericus Vitalis informs us, attempted to reduce the number of acres contained in the hide from the English to the Norman computation, and if he had succeeded the measure would have compelled a new assessment; but, as Domesday continued to be the ultimate authority for the rating of the country, the attempt, if it were ever made, must be understood to have failed. But the changes in the ownership of land, the formation of new forests, and the bringing of old wastes into cultivation, must have made it difficult to secure a fair apportionment of taxation; and this compelled on the part of the exchequer proceedings which we find in close connexion with the provincial administration of justice. It is unnecessary here to anticipate in detail what must be repeated under the head of judicature: it is enough to remark that, as early as the reign of William Rufus, questions of assessment were referred by the crown to the report of the county court, and that in the reign of Henry I the assessment and levying of taxation seems to have formed one portion of the duty of the justices, who, with the functions if not with the name of itinerant judges, transacted the local business of the Exchequer in each shire.

So intimate is the connexion of judicature with finance under the Norman kings, that we scarcely need the comments of the historians to guide us to the conclusion, that it was mainly for the sake of the profits that justice was administered at all. Such no doubt was the principle upon which Ranulf Flambard and his master acted. A deeper and more statesmanlike view probably influenced Henry I and his great minister—the belief that a nation in which justice is done is safer and more contented, and presents therefore an easier and richer body to be taxed. But there is no reason to suppose that Henry acted on any higher motive; the value of justice depended in his eyes very much on the amount of treasure with which it supplied him; and accordingly there is not a single fiscal or judicial measure of his reign by which light is not thrown both on the Curia Regis and on the Exchequer.

THE CURIA REGIS

The Curia Regis, the supreme tribunal of judicature, of which the Exchequer was the financial department or session, was, as has been stated already, the court of the king sitting to administer justice with the advice of his counsellors; those counsellors being, in the widest acceptation, the whole body of tenants-in-chief, but, in the more limited usage, the great officers of the household and specially appointed judges. The great gatherings of the national council may be regarded as full sessions of the Curia Regis or the Curia

Regis, as a perpetual committee of the national council, but there is no evidence to prove that the supreme judicature originated in the idea of such a devolution of authority. In the more general meetings, as at the three annual placita, the king wore his crown, and consulted, or made a show of consulting, his vassals on all matters of state. The courts in the king's absence were presided over by the chief or great justiciar, acting 'ex praecepto regis' or 'vice sua,' 'in meo loco,' as the Conqueror expressed it. The other persons who bear the title of justiciar, the ordinary members, as they may be called, of the court, were the same as those of the Exchequer; the same persons who acted as barons in the latter acted as justices in the former; the fines paid or remitted in the Curia were recorded in the Exchequer, and the writ that was issued in the one chamber was treated by the other as being, what it was truly, its own act. The great officers of the household seem to have acted in the business of the Curia Regis simply however as justices; we have no record that apportions to them the definite seats or functions which they held in the Exchequer; accordingly when we find the chancellor or chamberlain sitting in judgment, we are not to suppose that the cause on which he decides is one belonging specially to the chancery or the chamber; he is simply a member of the king's judicial court.

The number of persons who filled the office of justice or baron of the Exchequer during the Norman reigns was not very large, nor are the relations of the members of the court to one another very well defined; it is even possible that a close examination of existing records would show that all the officers who discharged judicial functions were members, under some other title, of the king's household. Roger of Salisbury bore the name of 'justitiarius' from the year 1107 to his death; but there are several other justices, mentioned both in records and by the historians, whose position seems to be scarcely inferior to his. Ralph Basset appears early in the reign of Henry I as a very influential judge; his son Richard is called by Ordericus Vitalis and Henry of Huntingdon 'capitalis justitiarius' even during the life of Bishop Roger; and Geoffrey de

Clinton, who was the king's chamberlain or treasurer, held pleas in A.D. 1130 over all England. The Pipe Roll of that year furnishes us with the names of other justices: pleas were held not only by the two Bassets and Geoffrey de Clinton, but by William of Albini the Butler, Eustace Fitz-John and Walter Espec, Miles of Gloucester the Constable, Pain Fitz-John, Robert Arundel, and Walkelin Visdeloup. Other names may perhaps be found in the charters of Henry I and Stephen. The *capitalis justitia* however seems to be the only one of the body to whom, in formal documents, a determinate position as the king's representative is assigned.

The Curia Regis, in this aspect, was the machinery through which the judicial power of the crown was exercised in that wide sphere of legal business on which, in its now complicated relations, it was brought to bear. That business consisted largely of causes in which the king's interest was concerned, or which were brought up by way of appeal when the suitors were sufficiently powerful to obtain such a favour, or when the powers of the popular courts had been exhausted or had failed to do justice. In these particulars it succeeded to the royal jurisdiction of the Anglo-Saxon kings. It was also a tribunal of primary resort in cases of disputes between the tenants-in-chief of the crown, a feudal court in which were arranged the quarrels of the Norman lords, who were too strong to submit to the simple justice of the shire and hundred. It was however more than this: the ancient customary process of the local courts, with that strict maintenance of formalities and that incapacity for regarding equitable considerations which seems inseparable from the idea of compurgation and ordeal, was now becoming antiquated. As a special favour, suits were brought up from the view of the provincial courts to be decided by such new methods as the wisdom of the king and his counsellors might invent; and from the Curia Regis issued the writs which directed inquiry and recognition of rights as to land, the obligations of tenure, the legitimacy of heirs, and the enforcement of local justice. These writs, although not absolutely unknown in England before the Conquest, were derived no doubt in their Norman form from the process of the Karolingian lawyers; they were the expedients by which the 'jus honorarium' of the king, as fountain of justice, was enabled to remedy the defects of the 'jus civile' or 'commune,' the customary proceedings of the local moots.

The Curia Regis had criminal jurisdiction also, as Ralph Basset proved when he hanged forty-four thieves at Hundehoge. It was in fact a supreme court of justice, both of appeal and, where leave was obtained, of primary recourse.

But it was also a ministry of justice, before which the whole judicial action of the country passed in review. This was done partly by the Court of Exchequer, in which, as we have seen, the sheriffs annually rendered their accounts; but partly also by direct inspection. The provincial judicature was brought into immediate connexion with the central judicature by journeys of the king's judges. We have seen traces of this arrangement as early as the time of Alfred, who may have been acquainted with the system in use under the Frank emperors. Edgar and Canute had themselves made judicial circuits; the Conqueror's choice of the three great cities of the south of England for his annual placita brought the sense of royal justice home to the country at large. But Henry I went a step further. He sent the officers of the Exchequer through the country to assess the revenue; in one great fiscal iter of the reign the ferms of the counties were fixed; and during his reign the whole kingdom was visited by justices, officers of the Curia Regis, not perhaps with the systematic regularity enforced by his grandson, but with sufficient order to prove that he saw and satisfied the want of such an expedient. In A.D. 1130 Geoffrey de Clinton, the chamberlain, had lately visited seventeen out of the thirty-four counties of which the accounts are preserved; Ralph Basset had visited seven; Richard Basset five; Eustace Fitz-John and Walter Espec had held pleas in the northern counties; Miles of Gloucester and Pain Fitz-John in the west-midland and the Welsh March; William of Albini, Robert Arundel and others, in the forests and in the south-western counties. It is probable that this was by no means an exceptional measure: in A.D. 1124 we find Ralph Basset, as has been frequently mentioned, holding a court in Leicestershire; Ordericus Vitalis gives an account of a trial held before him in the county court of Huntingdonshire in A.D. 1115 or 1116. A measure dictated still more distinctly by this policy may be traced in the list of sheriffs for A.D. 1130. Richard Basset and Aubrey de Vere, a judge and a royal chamberlain, act as joint sheriffs in no less than eleven counties: Geoffrey de Clinton, Miles of Gloucester, William of Pont l'Arche the Treasurer, are also sheriffs as well as justices of the king's court. That such a system was open to much abuse is self-evident; these officers sitting as judges and barons in the Exchequer actually audited the accounts which they presented as sheriffs; but they were under the strong control of the king and Bishop Roger; and although there were scandals no doubt, such as that for which Geoffrey de Clinton was tried in this very year, the important fact remains that by these means the king and the justiciar kept in their hands the reins of the entire judicial administration. The justices whilst employed in provincial work sat in the shire-moot; and this usage of Henry I, with the series of similiar measures initiated by Henry II, forms the link between the old and new organisations of the country, by which that concentration of local machinery was produced, out of which the representative system arose. The parliament of the thirteenth century was the concentration of local representation in and with the national council. It was no small step in that direction when the action of the Curia Regis was brought into direct connexion with that of the shire-moot. The Norman curia met the Anglo-Saxon gemot in the visitations of the itinerant justices.

THE SHIRE COURT

We thus come to the constitution of the shire-moot. In a former chapter the history of this institution has been traced up to and past the date of the Conquest; and it has already been shown how in the inquest which preceded the Domesday Survey, as well as in the production of the record of Edward's laws, the means of gaining information which it afforded were utilised. The existence of the shire-moot through the reigns of the Conqueror and William Rufus is proved by the existence of writs addressed, as in the preceding reigns, to the sheriffs and other leading members. There is in existence a writ directed by William Rufus to the sheriff of Northamptonshire ordering him to call together his shire to examine into the rights of the monks of Ramsey. It appears from the very charter by which Henry I orders the restoration of the ancient courts that they had been used under his brother for the purposes of extortion, and the same may be inferred from the description of Ranulf Flambard 'as driving all the gemots' throughout all England. From the year 1108 onwards these courts, as well as those of the hundred, were held 'as in king Edward's days and not otherwise.' The lords of land and their stewards attended, and from each township the reeve and four men, and the parish priest. The full court met twice a year under the sheriff or his deputy, and was still competent to declare folk-right in every suit; the pleas of the crown were recorded in it for the view of the Curia Regis, whether reported by the sheriff to the Exchequer or examined by the justices in a provincial visit. It had a criminal as well as a civil jurisdiction as before, although the management of the pleas of the crown on the one side, and the interference by royal writ on the other, must have materially affected its independence. It retained however all its authority in matters of voluntary jurisdiction, witnessing transfers of land, and sanctioning by its testimony private charters and documents of all sorts. The ancient forms were also in use; witness, compurgation, and ordeal; and the old theory that in these popular courts the suitors were the judges.

The new light thrown on the shire-moot, by the increased number of records, makes it a little difficult to know what particulars of custom, now for the first time discoverable, are new or old. The composition of the court and its times of session are however clearly ancient. The custom of interference of the crown by writ, although not unprecedented, is, as a custom, new. The references to trial by battle, which now become common, show that the

Normans had introduced that custom in its legal completeness. But the most important novelty is the inquest by oath, which has been already referred to, and which forms an important link in the history of the jury. William the Conqueror directs the justiciars on one occasion to assemble the shire-moots which had taken part in a suit touching the rights of Ely; that being done, there were to be chosen a number of the English who knew the state of the disputed lands in the reign of Edward; these were to swear to the truth of their depositions; and action was to be taken accordingly. A similar writ of William Rufus to the sheriff of Northamptonshire, already mentioned, directs a like proceeding in the affairs of Ramsey; whilst two writs of William the Etheling to the sheriff of Kent order, and direct action to be taken upon, the verdict or recognition of the good men of that county in reference to the rights of S. Augustine's.

The employment of a number of sworn thegns to report on the character of accused persons, which has been traced to the laws of Ethelred, may probably have continued to be usual; and thus the growth of the jury in criminal matters may have kept pace with its development in civil affairs. But of this we have slight evidence, unless the session of Hundehoge, where the thegns of Leicestershire acted with the king's justiciar, may be again appealed to. But however this may be, it is certain that the administration of justice in the shire-moot was now vested in persons who were bound by oath to the fulfilment of their duties and to speak the truth. The Pipe Roll of Henry I proves the existence of large bodies of judices and juratores. Whether the terms are equivalent; whether they merely mean the qualified members of the courts who were summoned *nominatim* and from whose body witnesses and compurgators must be chosen; whether the judices were a permanent body of local proprietors, and the juratores a selection of freemen sworn to declare the truth in the particular case; whether the judices may not have been the presenters of the criminals, and the juratores the witnesses in the civil suits, it would be dangerous even to guess. They appear however to be distinguished, probably by special summons, from the 'minuti homines,' 'smale-manni' or mean men, who were likewise bound to attend the shire-moot and hundred-moot, either in person or by the reeve, and who probably did not possess so much land as was necessary to qualify a man for acting as judge in a suit in which land was in question. That these persons were very numerous is certain from the very large fines imposed on them for neglect of duty. In Yorkshire the sheriff accounts for thirty-one marks drawn from nine 'judicatores comitatus;' and for 336 marks five shillings and sixpence 'de minutis judicibus et juratoribus comitatus.' It is no wonder that we find almost immediately after that the unfortunate payers have undertaken to compound for their attendance: 'The judges and jurors of Yorkshire owe a hundred pounds that they may no more be judges or jurors.' The sheriff of Kent accounts for £17 3s. 4d. from the jurors of Kent, and another sum from Sussex; in Essex, £5 6s. 8d. is raised from the 'minuti homines'; in Lincolnshire, seventy-four marks and a-half; in Bedfordshire, forty shillings from the 'juratores et minuti homines;' and four judges of the isle of Axholm render account for eight marks due for the pleas of William of Albini. It can scarcely be doubted that all these fines were incurred for non-attendance, and that they prove either the dislike of the free-holders to attend the court of the justice itinerant, or a serious decline in the ancient constitution of the county courts. But this does not affect the main question, which is the continuance of the custom of employing jurors to transact the judicial work.

The use made of the shire-moot for the purpose of raising money may account for the reluctance of the suitors to attend. That this was the practice is clearly shown by Henry's writ for the restoration of the ancient custom: 'I will cause those courts to be summoned when I will for my own proper necessities, at my pleasure;' an important engagement intended to deprive the sheriffs of their opportunities of wanton exaction, but to secure to the king the right of asking for or taking money when he should deem it necessary. Unfortunately this is the only evidence that we have of the method of raising money from the shire-moot; but it seems almost certain that when the occasion arose, the counties would be consulted by the barons of the Exchequer and not by the sheriffs. The same writ directs that suits between the barons of the king's demesne for the division of land are to be decided in the Curia Regis; similar suits between vassals, 'vavassores,' in the county court and by trial by battle.   [CHE, I: 398–430]

The Norman Contribution to
Government in England

✑§ How far was the machinery [of Anglo-Norman administration] the national system of the Normans in their earlier seats? how far was it a mere translation of English institutions into Norman forms? how far was it the result of a combination which forced both elements into new developments? What was purely Norman, what was purely English, what was new? The opinions of lawyers and historians have widely differed on this point; and the differences seem in many cases traceable rather to the mental constitution than to the political or national prepossessions of the writers. One authority insists on the immemorial antiquity of every institution the origin of which cannot be fixed by date; another refuses to recognise the possible existence of a custom before it appears definitely in contemporary records: this writer regards the common features of the two systems as positive proofs that the one is derived from the other; that refuses to receive any amount of analogy as proof of historical connexion. The result has been on the one hand to treat the Norman system of government as an entire novelty, and on the other to reduce its influences to the merest and most superficial shades of change. The view that has been taken in the earlier chapters of this book has recognised to the fullest extent the permanence of the Anglo-Saxon institutions, and under each head of the present chapter have been noted the features of the Norman reigns which appeared really strange to the older rule. In the policy of the Conqueror we have traced the existence of an idea of combination, of dovetailing or welding together the administrative framework of the two races. In taxation the Danegeld is distinctly English, the feudal aid is distinctly Norman: William maintained both. In legal procedure the hundred-moot and the shire-moot are English, the custom of trial by battle is Norman; in military organisation the fyrd is Anglo-Saxon, the knight-service is Norman: in each case the Conqueror introduced the one without abolishing the other. This principle was dictated in the first instance by the necessity of providing institutions for two distinct nationalities, and was perpetuated as the nationalities coalesced, because it furnished the king with a power of holding the balance of the kingdom with a firm purpose of strong government. Just as the nationalities combined to produce one nation strengthened in character and polity by the union, so the combination of the institutions produced a new growth in which, whilst much that is old can be detected, there is much else that could not have existed but for the combination. The increase of official records in the reigns of Henry II and his sons enables us to trace this influence more accurately as we advance. But there are some points which demand notice at our present stage of inquiry.

We have considered the leading principle of the system of the Conquest to be the combination of the strongest part of the Norman system with the strongest part of the early English system; the maintenance of the local and provincial machinery of the latter with the central and sovereign authority characteristic of the former. The most important parts of the centralising system of the Norman kings are the Curia Regis and Exchequer; and here the most opposite opinions have been put forth for many years with the utmost confidence. The Curia Regis has been regarded as the simple reproduction in conquered England of the Curia Ducis of Normandy, which again was a reproduction of the court of the Karoling kings of the West Franks as it existed under Charles the

Simple when he bestowed Normandy on Rollo. From another point of view it is represented merely as the English court of Edward the Confessor, the small witenagemot of the Anglo-Saxon kings, which has under the influence of feudal ideas sustained a change rather nominal than constitutional, and which gradually tends to devolve upon the king and his more immediate household the central administration of justice in cases calling for such administration. From another point the whole central administration is viewed as the operation of the personal omnipotence of the king as conqueror and supreme administrator. Each of these theories contains a great truth: the Norman kings were despotic in fact; their highest attempts at organised government advance in the direction of law no further than that stage which has been more than once described as the stage of routine. The system of routine by which they worked was primarily the system on which they had governed Normandy; the court of the duke was reproduced in principle, as it was in the persons who constituted it, in the court of the king. The English administrative system was also so far advanced under Edward the Confessor that the transformation of the ancient witenagemot into the great court and council was—after the great change of actors caused by the substitution of Norman for native lords and prelates—possible without any still more violent innovation. But there are other facts to be considered besides theories conceived à priori. We possess a large stock of Anglo-Saxon records; laws and charters which shed a great deal of broken light on every department of the life of our forefathers. The constitutional history of Normandy, and the legal history of the whole of that kingdom of which Normandy was a nominal province, is, during the century and a half that intervenes between the extinction of the Karolingian power and the reign of Lewis VI, illustrated only in a very slight degree by fragments of legislation and scattered charters. The most ancient text-books of Norman law are later than the reign of Henry II, both in composition and in materials. No one at the present day would contend that the legal reforms of Henry II were drawn from the Grand Coûtumier of Normandy, any more than that they were the result of the lessons of his great-uncle King David of Scotland. Yet it would be almost as rash to maintain that the similarities of Norman and later English law are to be ascribed solely to the fact that both were developed under the force of Henry I and under the genius of Henry II. If, again, we ascribe to Norman sources all that is Karolingian in the measures of the Norman and Angevin kings, we are underrating the probable and almost demonstrable influence which the association of the West-Saxon dynasty with the Karoling, Saxon, and Franconian courts must have produced on native custom. Under the circumstances it might seem almost the safest plan to abstain from attempting a conclusion. But this is scarcely possible.

The regular action of the central power of the kingdom becomes known to us, as we have seen, first in the proceedings of the Exchequer. The English Exchequer appears first early in the reign of Henry I: the Norman Exchequer appears first under Henry II. There is nothing in the name to determine whether it was originally given to the court in England or in Normandy. The method of accounting in the English Exchequer is based on the English coinage, that of the Norman on the French: both England and Normandy must have had fiscal audits long before the Conquest; the systems of account, almost all the processes of the two courts, are different. Yet the results have necessarily a resemblance; the officers of the one were occasionally trained in the work of the other, and when reforms were needed in the one, a change of administrators was easy; the Treasury of Caen could lend an abbot to the Exchequer of Westminster, or the Exchequer of Westminster could lend a baron to revise the accounts of Caen. The same exigencies, so long as the rulers of England and Normandy were the same, would be met by much the same measures. There is no evidence but that of tradition for deriving the English Exchequer from Normandy: there is far more antecedent probability that whatever the Norman Exchequer has in common with the English was derived from the latter. Yet the English Exchequer was organised by Norman ministers: the Domesday Survey was carried out by Normans: Ranulf Flambard and Roger of Salisbury were both natives of the neighbourhood of Caen. If there is no Norman roll of the reign of Henry I, there is but one English roll: in the latter case all but one have perished, so that no one can safely maintain that in the former case none ever existed. Yet at the time at which the English fiscal system was developed, during the reign of William Rufus and in the early years of Henry I, the two countries were not under the same ruler.

The conclusion seems to depend on a balance of probabilities: it is most probable that in both countries there was a fiscal court or audit, that the two were developed and more fully organised under the same superintendence, and each may have borrowed from the other: but there is no historical proof, and no historical necessity to assume, that the one was an offshoot of a transplantation of the other. The importance of the name is only secondary; it matters little whether the chequered cloth were first used at Westminster or at Caen. It appears only in those countries which are connected with Normandy after the Conquest and with the Norman kings of England, so that from this point of view the English origin seems most probable.

The history of the Curia Regis, in its judicial aspect, is, as we have seen, even more complicated. The Anglo-Saxon kings heard causes in person: the judgment of the king was the last resort of the litigant who had failed to obtain justice in the hundred and the shire. He had also a court in which the disputes of his immediate dependents were settled, the 'theningmannagemot,' the existence of which is proved, but no more than its existence. The Norman duke had his feudal court of vassals like every other feudal lord, and a tribunal of supreme judicature which may or may not have been personally identical with the court of vassals. The royal judicature in England was in the reigns of the Conqueror and William Rufus exercised either by the king or justiciar in person on the great festivals, or by special commission in the shire-moot. The question then is this, Was the Curia Regis as developed under Henry I the Curia Ducis of Normandy? or was it the king himself acting as judge with the council of his witan or a portion of them?

or was it not rather a tribunal in a stage of growth, springing from a combination of the two older systems, and tending to become something very different from either?

The report of the court held on Bishop William of S. Carileph, after the rebellion of 1088, supplies us with convincing proof that the last is the true account of the matter. The bishop had joined in the conspiracy of the earls during Lent 1088; and the king's officers had on the 12th of March seized his estates; he demanded restitution; the king insisted that he should purge himself of his treason. The bishop pleaded his right to be tried as a bishop, but offered to defend himself from the charge of having broken his oath of fealty. The parties met on the 2nd of November at Salisbury, where all the bishops, earls, barons, and royal officers assembled. Lanfranc refused to listen to the bishop's plea, and he was appealed of treason by Hugh de Beaumont on the king's part. After much deliberation, every stage of which is recorded, the bishop still insisting on his right Lanfranc declares that he must first answer the king's demand: 'We are not judging you in the matter of your bishopric but of your fee, and so we judged the bishop of Bayeux before the king's father concerning his fee; nor did the king in that plea call him bishop, but brother and earl.' The bishop struggles against this and appeals to Rome. The court then deliberates on the sentence, which is finally pronounced by Hugh de Beaumont, in the name of the king's court and the barons: as the bishop will not answer the charge brought against him, he forfeits his fee. Ultimately he spends three years in exile. The record is drawn up by a friend of the bishop, and is very long; but these details are sufficient to prove that the court in which the trial was held was the witenagemot acting as a feudal court of peers.

The Curia Regis of Henry I was a regulated and modified form of that of William Rufus, as that of Henry II was an organised development of that of Henry I. The trial of Henry of Essex early in the reign of Henry II, and that of Robert of Belesme in the reign of Henry I, are links in a series which proves the fundamental identity of the earliest and latest forms.

But although we may assert an English element in the Curia Regis, and confidently deny its exclusively Norman origin, it must be granted that very much of the new forms of process was foreign. Whether Lanfranc brought it from Pavia, or William inherited it from the Norman dukes, we can scarcely on existing evidence decide. [CHE, I: 471–477]

◆§ The royal policy [in administration] is a policy of combination, whereby the strongest and safest elements in two nations were so united as to support one sovereign and irresponsible lord; the alliance between the king and the English is reflected in the measures taken to strengthen the Curia Regis and to protect the popular courts. It is the first stage in the process of amalgamation; a process which Henry I probably never contemplated as possible, but which Stephen's reign with all its troubles helped to begin, and which that of Henry II made practically safe. The age of routine dependent on the will of a despot passes by almost perceptible stages into the age of law secured by the organisation of a people which has begun at least to realise its unity and identity.

[CHE, I: 480–481]

The Shaping of the English Church

◆§ The ecclesiastical policy of the Conqueror presents marks of coincidence, and also of contrast, with his secular administration. There is the same change of administrators, but not the same fusion or modification of offices. The change of administrators is gradual in the church as in the state, and nearly as complete: the English church was drawn into the general tide of ecclesiastical politics and lost much of its insular character: it gained in symmetry and definiteness of action, and was started on a new career. But the immediate motives of William's measures are somewhat complex. His attack on England was planned and carried out with the approval of Pope Alexander II, and the hard measure dealt out to the English bishops personally was due quite as much to the desire of satisfying the pope, who had his own jealousies and grudges, as to William's belief that the influence of the great ecclesiastics was secretly working against him, or that the support of a strong Norman hierarchy was absolutely necessary for his safety. But William had no intention of following the papal guidance further than was convenient to himself; and in the great adviser whom he chose on his own responsibility he found a very able and conscientious helper. Lanfranc was a statesman as well as a theologian, a lawyer as well as a scholar, and in feeling quite as much an Englishman as a Norman: he was an Italian too, and therefore, perhaps, not a papalist. Hence whilst attempting the reformation of abuses, which either the national easiness and self-complacency, or the evil influence of the Norman clergy had originated, he adopted no violent or rigorous scheme of discipline, provoked no national antipathies, sacrificed neither the state to the church nor the church to the state. His policy was uniformly in agreement with the king's, and his personal influence kept in harmonious working two systems, which contained elements that after his death were to produce a long and bitter quarrel.

William's own ideas of managing the church were probably developed in England itself. The Norman prelates, with whom as duke he had to do, were either sons of the ruling families or personally insignificant. They had not the position of the English prelates with reference either to the people or to the duke. They were but a small element in his council, and in no close relation with the native population, whilst in England they were the most numerous and coherent body in the witenagemot; and, although many of Edward's bishops were foreigners, they had inherited the loyalty and traditional support of the districts over which they presided. The ready submission of the witan in A.D. 1066 saved the bishops for the moment: the Conqueror had no wish to make enemies, and they had no champion to take the place of Harold. But when in A.D. 1070 he had found that the influence of the episcopate was so strong that it must be put into safer hands, and when the legates of Alexander II demanded the humiliation of the ignorant supporters of the antipope Benedict, the deposition of the bishops consecrated by Stigand, and the enforcement of canonical order, he proceeded to displace most of the native bishops. Then Stigand, who occupied two sees, one of which he had taken in the lifetime of a Norman predecessor, and who had received the pall from a schismatic pope, was deposed and imprisoned. With him fell his brother, the bishop of Elmham, and the faultless bishop of Selsey whom he had consecrated, and who might be regarded as sharing his schismatic attitude. The brother bishops of Durham, Ethelwin and Ethelric, had incurred the penalties of treason. York and Lichfield were vacant by death. Dorchester had been filled up by the Norman Remigius since the battle of Hastings; he too had been consecrated by Stigand, but the offence was not so fatal in a Norman as in an Englishman; he declares in his profession of obedience to Lanfranc that he was ignorant of Stigand's uncanonical status. Hereford, Wells, Ramsbury, Exeter, and London were already in the hands of foreigners. It was by no act of extraordinary severity that the change was made; but at the end of A.D. 1070 only two sees retained native bishops, Worcester and Rochester. The way was open for Lanfranc, and his appointment satisfied both king and pope. Henceforth the bishops and most of the abbots were Norman; but they, like the king, realised their new position as Englishmen by adoption; entering immediately on all the claims of their predecessors and declaring that, so far as their power went, the churches they espoused should suffer no detriment. The Conqueror's bishops were generally good and able men, though not of the English type of character. They were not mere Norman barons, as was the case later on, but scholars and divines chosen under Lanfranc's influence. The abbots were less wisely selected, and had perhaps a more difficult part to play, for the monasteries were still full of English monks, and preserved, and probably concentrated, most of the national aspirations after deliverance which all came to naught.

The most important ecclesiastical measure of the reign, ordering the separation of the church jurisdiction from the secular busi-

ness of the courts of law, is unfortunately, like all other charters of
the time, undated. Its contents however show the influence of the
ideas which under the genius of Hildebrand were forming the
character of the continental churches. From henceforth the bishops and archdeacons are no longer to hold ecclesiastical pleas in the
hundred-court, but to have courts of their own; to try causes by
canonical not by customary law, and to allow no spiritual questions to come before laymen as judges. In case of contumacy the
offender may be excommunicated and the king and sheriff will enforce the punishment. In the same way laymen are forbidden to
interfere in spiritual causes. The reform is one which might very
naturally recommend itself to a man like Lanfranc. The practice
which it superseded was full of anomalies and disadvantages to
both justice and religion. But the change involved far more than
appeared at first. The growth of the canon law, in the succeeding
century, from a quantity of detached local or occasional rules to a
great body of universal authoritative jurisprudence, arranged and
digested by scholars who were beginning to reap the advantages of
a revived study of the Roman civil law, gave to the clergy generally a far more distinctive and definite civil status than they had
ever possessed before, and drew into church courts a mass of business with which the church had previously had only an indirect
connexion. The question of investitures, the marriage of the
clergy, and the crying prevalence of simony, within a very few
years of the conqueror's death, forced on the minds of statesmen
everywhere the necessity of some uniform system of law. The
need of a system of law once felt, the recognition of the supremacy of the papal court as a tribunal of appeal followed of course:
and with it the great extension of the legatine administration. The
clergy thus found themselves in a position external, if they chose
to regard it so, to the common law of the land; able to claim exemption from the temporal tribunals, and by appeals to Rome to
paralyse the regular jurisdiction of the diocesans. Disorder followed disorder, and the anarchy of Stephen's reign, in which every
secular abuse was paralleled or reflected in an ecclesiastical one,

prepared the way for the Constitutions of Clarendon, and the struggle that followed with all its results down to the Reformation itself. The same facility of employing the newly developed jurisprudence of the canonists drew into the ecclesiastical courts the matrimonial and testamentary jurisdiction, and strengthened that most mischievous, because most abused, system of enforcing moral discipline by spiritual penalties, at the instance of men whose first object was the accumulation of money.

The reformation of the spiritual courts, and the exemption of their proceedings from the common usages of Anglo-Saxon law, had a bearing on the relations of the church to the state in these ways; but it must not be supposed that it was in itself a sign of any disposition in either William or Lanfranc to admit extreme claims on the part of the popes. The results that have been mentioned flowed from a state of things which was now in process of development, and which attained full growth far more rapidly than they could have expected, through circumstances which they could not foresee. Anything like a direct claim on the part of the papacy William repudiated at once. Not only did he distinctly refuse the demand of fealty made by the legate Hubert on behalf of Gregory VII, but he seems to have established an understanding with the English church which had the force of a concordat for future times. The arrangement is described by the faithful historian Eadmer as a novelty, but it was a novelty necessitated by the newness of the circumstances in which the king found himself. 'He would not suffer that any one in all his dominions should receive the pontiff of the city of Rome as apostolic pope, except at his command, or should on any condition receive his letters if they had not been first shown to himself.' This principle, which was abused by William Rufus, and which could only work well when the chiefs in church and state were in thorough concert, expresses rather than overcomes the difficulty. But it is a difficulty which has never yet been overcome; and it is probable that the Conqueror's rule went as near to the solution as any state theory has ever done. A second rule was this, 'He did not suffer the primate of his king-

dom, the archbishop of Canterbury, if he had called together under his presidency an assembly of bishops, to enact or prohibit
anything but what was agreeable to his will and had been first
ordained by him.' This was a most necessary limitation of the
powers recognized as belonging to the spiritual courts, nor did it,
in an age in which there was no discord of religious opinion, create
any of the scandals which might arise under more modern conditions. The two rules together express the principle of the maxim so
well known in later times, 'cujus regio, ejus religio' in that early
form in which it recommended itself to the great Charles. A third
rule was this; 'he did not allow any of his bishops publicly to im-
plead, excommunicate, or constrain by penalty of ecclesiastical
rigour, any of his barons or servants, who was informed against
either for adultery or for any capital crime, except by his own
command.' Of this also it may be said that it might work well
when regulated by himself and Lanfranc, but that otherwise it created rather than solved a difficulty. A further usage, which was
claimed by Henry I as a precedent, was the prohibition of the exercise of legatine power in England, or even of the legate's landing
on the soil of the kingdom without royal licence.

Such precautions as these show little more than an incipient
misgiving as to the relations of church and state: a misgiving
which might well suggest itself either to the king or to the
thoughtful mind of the adviser, who saw himself at the head of a
church which had been long at uneasy anchorage apart from those
ecclesiastical tumults into the midst of which it was soon to be
hurried. There is something Karolingian in their simplicity, and
possibly they may have been suggested by the germinating
Gallicanism of the day. They are, however, of great prospective
importance and form the basis of that ancient customary law on
which throughout the middle ages the English church relied in her
struggles with the papacy.   [CHE, I: 304–311]

⊸§ The church was not Normanised by the Norman kings;
they forced bishops and abbots of their own into the rich places,
and some of these were oppressors, but they were in many cases

non-resident, and the conduct of the priests and monasteries was much as it had been before: they were plundered and perhaps persecuted, but that only made what light they had burn clearer; in some measure the shield of their oppressors was a defence to them as well—when as much as possible was extorted, the rulers took care that none else should try it. Now these priests and monks were Englishmen, and relations generally of the English families who lived near the monasteries; they had sympathy of race and blood to keep up the charity that they were bound by their vows to show to those that needed. Hence they were centres of security and civilisation, and the only centres of civilisation during the Norman reigns. Their liberties were looked on by the people as their own; their sympathies were always on the side of liberty, and their freedom was won with the freedom of the people.   [LEEH, 34]

IV

THE ANGEVIN ERA:
FROM DESPOTISM TO
CONSTITUTIONALISM
(1154–1216)

The Achievement of National Unity

❧ The sixty years that followed the death of Stephen comprise a period of English history which has a special importance. It is a period of constant growth, although the growth is far from being regular or uniform. The chain of events that connects the peace of Wallingford and the charter of Runnymede is traceable link by link. The nation which at the beginning of the period is scarcely conscious of its unity, is able, at the end of it, to state its claims to civil liberty and self-government as a coherent organised society. Norman and Englishman are now one, with a far more real identity than was produced by joint ownership of the land or joint subjection to one sovereign. England has been enabled, by the fortunate incapacity of John, to cut herself free from Normandy; and the division of interest between the two races has ceased. The royal power has curbed the feudal spirit and reduced the system to its proper insignificance. The royal power, having reached its climax, has forced on the people trained under it the knowledge that it in its turn must be curbed, and that they have the strength to curb it. The church, the baronage, and the people have found by different ways their true and common interest. This has not been done without struggles that have seemed at certain times to be internecine. The people, the baronage, and the church have been severally crushed, reformed, revived, and reorganised. More than once the balance of forces has been readjusted. The crown has humbled the baronage with the help of the people, and the church with the help of the baronage. Each in turn has been made to strengthen the royal power, and has been taught in the process to know its own strength. By law the people have been raised from the dust, the baronage forced to obedience, the clergy deprived of the immunities that were destroying their national character and counteracting their spiritual work. The three estates, trained in and by royal law, have learned how law can be applied to the very power that forced the lesson upon them. What the king has reformed and reorganised in order to gain a firm and real basis for his own power, has discovered its own strength and the strength of law, and has determined to give its service and sacrifices no longer without conditions. . . .

Henry II is the first of the three great kings who have left on the constitution indelible marks of their own individuality. What he reorganised Edward I defined and completed. The Tudor policy, which is impersonated in Henry VIII, tested to the utmost the soundness of the fabric: the constitution stood the shock, and the Stewarts paid the cost of the experiment. Each of the three sovereigns had a strong idiosyncrasy, and in each case the state of things on which he acted was such as to make the impression of personal character distinct and permanent.

Henry II at his accession found the kingdom in a state of dissolution: his only advantage was the absolute exhaustion of all the forces which had produced that dissolution. The task before him was one which might have appalled an experienced legislator, and Henry was little more than twenty-one years old. He did not succeed to the inheritance of a band of veteran counsellors; the men with whom he had to work were the survivors of the race that had caused the anarchy. He was a young man of keen bright intellect, patient, laborious, methodical; ambitious within certain well-defined limits, tenacious of power, ingenious even to minuteness in expedients, prompt and energetic in execution; at once unscrupulous and cautious. These characteristics mark also the later stages of his career, even when, disappointed of his dearest hopes and mortified in his tenderest affections, he gave way to violent passion and degrading licence; for his private vices made no mark on his public career, and he continued to the last a most industrious, active, and business-like king. There was nothing in him of the hero, and of the patriot scarcely more than an almost instinctive knowledge of the needs of his people, a knowledge which can hardly ever be said to be the result of sympathy. Thus much all the historians who have described him join in allowing; although they form very different estimates of his merit as a ruler, and of the objects of his policy. These objects seem to have been mainly the consolidation of his power: in England the strengthening and equalising of the royal administration; on the Continent the retention and thorough union of the numerous and variously constituted provinces which by marriage or inheritance had come into his hands. The English nation may gratefully recognise his merit as a ruler in the vastness of the benefits that resulted from the labours even of a selfish life. [CHE, I: 482–484]

◄§ Henry II, who was hailed as the restorer of the native line of kings, began by breaking the power of the great vassals: he ordered the destruction of the castles, and sent justices round to the counties to hold assizes. In these measures we trace the English hand of his chancellor, the great Thomas of London, Thomas Becket, to whom, whether or not [we] esteem him as a saint and martyr, English liberty as asserted against the king and the barons owes an eternal debt of gratitude. As chancellor for the first eight years of Henry's reign he was prime minister, and organised the ameliorating measures by which that king gained his popularity. When he became archbishop of Canterbury he went at once into opposition in defence of what he esteemed to be the necessary liberties of the church, and continued in that attitude until he was murdered. Even if, as many . . . will think, he was wrong in his estimate of church liberties, and still more wrong in the temper in which he supported them, he was the first Englishman who broke through the hard deadening crust of misery which had burst from the flaming volcano of Norman tyranny, and for that deserves to be counted a hero.   [LEEH, 34]

❧§ The great characteristic of the English constitutional system . . . —the principle of its growth, the secret of its construction,—is the continuous development of representative institutions from the first elementary stage, in which they are employed for local purposes and in the simplest form, to that in which the national parliament appears as the concentration of all local and provincial machinery, the depository of the collective powers of the three estates of the realm. We have traced in the Anglo-Saxon history the origin and growth of the local institutions, and in the history of the Norman reigns the creation of a strong administrative system. Not that the Anglo-Saxon rule had no administrative mechanism, or that the Norman polity was wanting in its local and provincial organism, but that the strength of the former was in the lower, and that of the latter in the upper ranges of the social system, and that the stronger parts of each were permanent. In the reigns of the three kings [of the Angevin line, the so-called early Plantagenets—Henry II, Richard I, and John], we trace a most important step in advance, the interpenetration, the growing together, of the local machinery and the administrative organisation. . . . Now we begin to trace the process by which the administrative order is worked into the common law of the people, and the common institutions of the people are admitted to a share in the administration of the state; the beginning of the process which is completed in national self-government.

The period is one of amalgamation, of consolidation, of continuous growing together and new development, which distinguishes the process of organic life from that of mere mechanic contrivance, internal law from external order.

The nation becomes one and realises its oneness; this realisation is necessary before the growth can begin. It is completed under Henry II and his sons. It finds its first distinct expression in Magna Carta. It is a result, not perhaps of the design and purpose of the

great king, but of the converging lines of the policy by which he
tried to raise the people at large, and to weaken the feudatories and
the principle of feudalism in them. Henry is scarcely an English
king, but he is still less a French feudatory. In his own eyes he is
the creator of an empire. He rules England by Englishmen and for
English purposes, Normandy by Normans and for Norman purposes; the end of all his policy being the strengthening of his own
power. He recognises the true way of strengthening his power, by
strengthening the basis on which it rests, the soundness, the
security, the sense of a common interest in the maintenance of
peace and order.

The national unity is completed in two ways. The English have
united; the English and the Norman have united also. The threefold division of the districts, the Dane law, the West-Saxon and the
Mercian law, which subsisted so long, disappears after the reign of
Stephen. The terms are become archaisms which occur in the
pages of the historians in a way that proves them to have become
obsolete; the writers themselves are uncertain which shires fall into
the several divisions. Traces of slight differences of custom may be
discovered in the varying rules of the country courts, which as
Glanvill tells us, are so numerous that it is impossible to put them
on record; but they are now mere local by-laws, no real evidence
of permanent divisions of nationality. In the same way Norman
and Englishmen are one. Frequent intermarriages have so united
them, that without a careful investigation of pedigree it cannot be
ascertained,—so at least the author of the Dialogus de Scaccario
affirms,—who is English and who Norman. If this be considered a
loose statement, for scarcely two generations have passed away
since the Norman blood was first introduced, it is conclusive evidence as to the common consciousness of union. The earls, the
greater barons, the courtiers, might be of pure Norman blood, but
they were few in number: the royal race was as much English as it
was Norman. The numbers of Norman settlers in England are
easily exaggerated; it is not probable that except in the baronial and
knightly ranks the infusion was very great, and it is very probable

indeed that, where there was such infusion, it gained ground by peaceable settlement and marriage. It is true that Norman lineage was vulgarly regarded as the more honourable, but the very fact that it was vulgarly so regarded would lead to its being claimed far more widely than facts would warrant: the bestowal of Norman baptismal names would thus supplant, and did supplant, the old English ones, and the Norman Christian name would then be alleged as proof of Norman descent. But it is far from improbable, though it may not have been actually proved, that the vast majority of surnames derived from English places are evidence of pure English descent, whilst only those which are derived from Norman places afford even a presumptive evidence of Norman descent. The subject of surnames scarcely rises into prominence before the fourteenth century; but an examination of the indices to the Rolls of the Exchequer and Curia Regis shows a continuous increase in number and importance of persons bearing English names: as early as the reign of Henry I we find among the barons Hugh of Bochland, Rainer of Bath, and Alfred of Lincoln, with many other names which show either that Englishmen had taken Norman names in baptism, or that Normans were willing to sink their local surnames in the mass of the national nomenclature.

The union of blood would be naturally expressed in unity of language, a point which is capable of being more strictly tested. Although French is for a long period the language of the palace, there is no break in the continuity of the English as a literary language. It was the tongue, not only of the people of the towns and villages, but of a large proportion of those who could read and could enjoy the pursuit of knowledge. The growth of the vernacular literature was perhaps retarded by the influx of Norman lords and clerks, and its character was no doubt modified by foreign influences under Henry II and his sons, as it was in a far greater degree affected by the infusion of French under Henry III and Edward I: but it was never stopped. It was at its period of slowest growth as rapid in its development as were most of the other literatures of Europe. Latin was still the language of learning, of law, and of ritual. English had to struggle with French as well as with Latin for its hold on the sermon and the popular poem: when it had forced its way to light, the books in which it was used had their own perils to undergo from the contempt of the learned and the profane familiarity of the ignorant. But the fact that it survived, and at last prevailed, is sufficient to prove its strength. The last memoranda of the Peterborough Chronicle belong to the year 1154: the last extant English charter can scarcely be earlier than 1155. There are English sermons of the same century, and early in the next we reach the date of Layamon's Brute and the Ormulum. These are fragments of the literature of a language which is passing through rapid stages of growth, and which has not attained a classical standard. Only fragments are left, for the successive stages pass so quickly that the monuments of one generation are only half intelligible to the next. The growth of the language and that of the literature proceed in an inverse ratio. If we were to argue from these fragments, we should infer, that whilst in the department of law the use of the native tongue was necessarily continuous, it had to rise through the stages of the song and the sermon to that point of development at which those who required history and deeper poetry demanded them in their own language. Such a sequence may imply the increase of education in the English, but it more probably implies the disuse of French in the classes that had a taste for learning: and it is still more probable that the two literatures advanced by equal steps until the crisis came which banished French from popular conversation. There are traces that seem to show that English was becoming the familiar conversational language of the higher classes. The story of Helewisia de Morville, preserved by William of Canterbury in his life of Becket, exhibits the wife or mother of one of the murderers as using English. 'Huwe of Morvill, war, war, Liulf haveth his sword ydrawen,' was her cry when she invoked the aid of her husband to punish the stubborn virtue of her English favourite. Giraldus Cambrensis, a man of high Norman descent, could not only read but criticise the language of the Chronicles and of Alfred, and compare the dialects of northern and southern England. Hugh of Nunant, a Norman of the Normans, mentions it as a strange thing that William Longchamp the chancellor was ignorant of the language of the people, and regards it in special connexion with his hatred and contempt of the English. Latin was the ordinary language of the monks of Durham, yet they conversed in English with S. Godric, who spoke French only by miracle. The hymn which the Blessed Virgin taught the same saint was in English and in English it is recorded for the reading of bishop Hugh de Puiset. At Canterbury, in the miraculous history of Dunstan, written by Eadmer, it is the devil that speaks French and corrects the indifferent idiom of an English monk. S. Hugh of Lincoln, who was a Burgundian by birth, did not understand the dialects of Kent and Huntingdonshire, but he was addressed by the natives as if it were naturally to be expected that he would comprehend what they said. Little can be safely inferred from such scattered notices, but that it was not uncommon for educated people to speak both languages. Of any commixture of French and English at this period there is no trace: the language of Chaucer owes its French elements to a later infusion: the structure of our language is affected by the foreign influence as yet in a way which may be called mechanical rather than chemical: it loses its inflexions, but it does not readily accept new grammatical forms, nor does it adopt, to any great extent, a new vocabulary.

The uniformity of legal system in its application to Norman and Englishman alike, would of necessity follow from a state of society in which Norman was undistinguishable from Englishman: but, except in one or two points of transient interest, it is not likely that any great distinctions of legal procedure had ever separated the two races. The Norman character of the Curia Regis and the English character of the shiremoot stand in contrast not so much because the former was Norman and the latter English, as because of the different social principles from which they spring. The Englishman where he is a tenant-in-chief has his claims decided in the Curia Regis; the Norman vavassor and the English ceorl alike are treated in the shiremoot. The trial by battle and the inquest by jury in its several forms are, after the first pressure of the Conquest is over, dealt with by both alike. The last vestige of difference, the presentment of Englishry, loses what significance it ever had. The tenures are the same for all; the Englishman is not disqualified from being a tenant-in-chief: the Norman may hold land in villenage: the free and common socage of the new system is really the free possession of the old, and the man who holds his acres by suit and service at the county court is as free as if he continued to call his land *ethel* or *bocland,* over which none but the king had soken. The one class which is an exception to all these generalisations, that of the *rustici* or *nativi,* is, it would appear, exclusively English: but even these, where they have recognised claims to justice, claim it according to its fullest and newest improvements. The system of recognition is as applicable to the proof or disproof of villein extraction as to the assize of mort d'ancestor or novel disseisin: nor does the disqualification under which the rustic lies, for ordination or for the judicial work of the jury and assize, arise from his nationality, but from his status. The claims of his lord forbid him to seek emancipation by tonsure; the precarious nature of his tenure forbids him to testify in matters touching the freer and fuller tenure of other men's property.

Still great promotion in Church and State does not yet commonly fall to the lot of the simple Englishman. Wulfstan of Worcester, the last of the Anglo-Saxon bishops, dies in 1095; Robert, the scholar of Melun, the first English bishop of any note after the Conquest, belongs to the reign of Henry II. The Scot, the Welshman, and the Breton reach episcopal thrones before the Englishman. Archbishop Baldwin, who was promoted to Canterbury by Henry II, seems to have been an Englishman of humble birth; Stephen Langton also was an Englishman, but by this time the term includes men of either descent, and henceforth the prelates of foreign extraction form the exceptions rather than the rule. In the service of the State however it is, as we have seen already, by no means improbable that English sheriffs and judges were employed by Henry I: and English scholars and lawyers were rising into distinction in Sicily and even in France.

The union of the races resembles not merely the mechanical union of two bodies bound together by force, or even by mutual attraction, in which, however tight the connexion, each retains its individual mass and consistency: it is more like a chemical commixture in which, although skilled analysis may distinguish the ingredients, they are so united both in bulk and in qualities, that the result of the commixture is something altogether distinct from the elements of which it is composed. The infusion of a little that is Norman affects the whole system of the English, and the mass which results is something different from either the one or the other. True the great proportion of the bulk must be English, but for all that it is not, and nothing will ever make it, as if that foreign element had never been there.

The commixture of institutions is somewhat similar: the new machinery which owes its existence to the new conception of royal power, the Curia Regis and Exchequer, does not remain side by side and unconnected with the shiremoot and the kindred institutions; it becomes just as much a part of the common law as the other: the ancient system of the shire rises to the highest functions of government; the authority of royal justice permeates the lowest regions of the popular organisation. The new consolidating process is one of organism, not of mere mechanism: the child's puzzle, the perfect chronometer, the living creature, symbolise three kinds or stages of creative skill, order, organisation, law; the point that our history reaches at the date of Magna Carta may be fixed as the transition from the second to the third stage.   [CHE, 1: 584–591]

Magna Carta

◄§ The king granted these privileges [in Magna Carta] on the understanding that he was to retain the allegiance of the nation. It is the collective people who really form the other high contracting party in the great capitulation,—the three estates of the realm, not it is true arranged in order according to their profession or rank, but not the less certainly combined in one national purpose, and securing by one bond the interests and rights of each other severally and of all together. The Charter contains a clause similar to that by which Henry I tried to secure the rights of his subjects as against the mesne lords; but now the provision is adopted by the lords themselves for the security of fair and equal justice: 'All the aforesaid customs and liberties that we have granted to be held in our kingdom, so far as pertains to us, with reference to our vassals, all men of our kingdom, as well clerk as lay, shall observe, so far as pertains to them, with reference to their men.' The barons maintain and secure the right of the whole people as against themselves as well as against their master. Clause by clause the rights of the commons are provided for as well as the rights of the nobles; the interest of the freeholder is everywhere coupled with that of the barons and knights; the stock of the merchant and the wainage of the villein are preserved from undue severity of amercement as well as the settled estate of the earldom or barony. The knight is protected against the compulsory exaction of his services, and the horse and cart of the freeman against the irregular requisition even of the sheriff. In every case in which the privilege of the simple freeman is not secured by the provision that primarily affects the knight or baron, a supplementary clause is added to define and protect his right; and the whole advantage is obtained for him by the comprehensive article which closes the essential part of the charter.

This proves, if any proof were wanted, that the demands of the barons were no selfish exaction of privilege for themselves; it proves with scarcely less certainty that the people for whom they acted were on their side. The nation in general, the people of the towns and villages, the commons of later days, the Englishmen who had fought the battles of the Norman kings against the feudatories, had now thrown themselves on the side of the barons: John's tyranny had overthrown that balance of the powers of the

State which his predecessors had striven with so much earnestness and so much policy to adjust. We do not indeed find, in the list of those who forced the king to yield, any names that prove the commons to have been influential in the drawing up of the articles: the conspicuous names are those of the northern barons, of the men of the great ministerial houses, and of that remnant of the Conqueror's baronage that had cut themselves loose from Normandy and Norman principles and reconciled themselves to the nobler position of leaders of their brother Englishmen. It was probably by the bishops, Langton in particular, and the legal members of the confederacy, that the rights of the freeholder were so carefully fenced round with provisions. These men and their successors led the commons and acted for them until the Reformation, with little discord and still less jealousy of their rising influence; and it was the extinction of the class which furnished their natural leaders that threw the Church and the nation under the tyranny that followed the Wars of the Roses.

The Great Charter is the first great public act of the nation, after it has realised its own identity: the consummation of the work for which unconsciously kings, prelates, and lawyers have been labouring for a century. There is not a word in it that recalls the distinctions of race and blood, or that maintains the differences of English and Norman law. It is in one view the summing up of a period of national life, in another the starting-point of a new period, not less eventful than that which it closes.

Magna Carta in its completed form attests the account given by the historians of its origin and growth. It is based on the charter of Henry I; it follows the arrangement of that famous document, and it amplifies and expands it, so as to bring under the principles, which were for the first time laid down in A.D. 1100, all the particular rights, claims, and duties which had come into existence during the developments of the intervening century. As the whole of the constitutional history of England is little more than a commentary on Magna Carta, a brief summary of the articles, regarded as the outgrowth of the previous history, is all that is necessary or possible at this stage of our work.

The king declares himself moved to issue the charter, as his great-grandfather had done, by his pious regard for God and his desire for the benefit of his people: the counsellors by whose advice he acts, and whose names he enumerates, are the bishops and barons who had not taken an overt part against him, or who only at the last moment had joined the confederation which compelled him to yield.

The first clause, again, as in the charter of Henry I, secures the rights of the Church; repeats and confirms the charter, twice issued already, for the free election to bishoprics, and the great principle so often appealed to both earlier and later, 'quod Anglicana Ecclesia libera sit.'

This is followed by a series of clauses protecting the tenants-in-chief of the Crown from the abuses of feudal right; a fixed sum is determined for the relief, as 'the ancient relief,' the very statement betraying the nature of the grievances; the relief is altogether abolished where the right of wardship is exercised; the latter right is carefully limited; the disparagement of heirs by unequal marriages is forbidden; and the widow is secured against spoliation as well as against compulsion to take another husband. The latter concession John had already declared himself willing to grant in that scheme of abortive reforms which he propounded, before his submission to the pope, in A.D. 1212. This portion of the charter closes with three articles in which the king renounces the oppressive means which had been used to secure the payment of debts to the Crown and to the Jews, in whose debts the Crown had an ulterior and contingent interest. These clauses show that the king's servants had departed from the rules which had prevailed in the Exchequer under Henry II, and which had been carefully drawn up so as to secure the rights of the Crown with the greatest regard to the safety of the debtor.

The twelfth and three following articles are those to which the greatest constitutional interest belongs; for they admit the right of the nation to ordain taxation, and they define the way in which the consent of the nation is to be given. No scutage or aid, other than the three regular feudal aids, is henceforth to be imposed but by the common counsel of the nation, and the common counsel of the nation is to be taken in an assembly duly summoned; the archbishops, bishops, abbots, earls, and greater barons are to be called up by royal writ directed to each severally; and all who hold of the king in chief, below the rank of the greater barons, are to be summoned by a general writ addressed to the sheriff of their shire; the summons is to express the cause for which the assembly is called together; forty days' notice is to be given; and when the day has arrived the action of those members who obey the summons is to be taken to represent the action of the whole. This most important provision may be regarded as a summing-up of the history of parliament so far as it can be said yet to exist. It probably contains nothing which had not been for a long time in theory a part of the constitution: the kings had long consulted their council on taxation; that council consisted of the elements that are here specified, and had been summoned in a way analogous to if not identical with that here defined. But the right had never yet been stated in so clear a form, and the statement thus made seems to have startled even the barons; they had not ventured to claim it, and when they had the reins of power in their own hands they seem in the subsequent editions of the charter to have shrunk from repeating the clauses which contained it. It was for the attainment of this right that the struggles of the reign of Henry III were carried on; and the realisation of the claim was deferred until the reign of his successor. In these clauses however the nation had now obtained a clear, or comparatively clear, definition of the right on which their future political power was to be based.

The limitation of royal exaction is supplemented by a corresponding limitation of the power of the mesne lords; the king is not to empower them to take aids except for the three recognised purposes, and then only such sums as are reasonable: nor is any one to be distrained to perform more than the proper service of his tenure.

The next series of clauses concern judicial proceedings: the suitors who are involved in Common Pleas are no longer to be compelled to follow the Curia Regis: the trials are to be heard in some fixed place. The recognitions of novel disseisin, mort d'ances-ter, and darrein presentment are henceforth to be taken in the county courts, before two justices who will visit each shire every quarter, and four knights chosen by the county court for the pur-pose. The freeman is not to be amerced in a way that will ruin him, the penalty is to be fixed by a jury of his neighbourhood; earls and barons are to be amerced by their peers, and clerks only in proportion to their non-ecclesiastical property. Such a clause proves that the careful provisions of the Exchequer on this point had been transgressed by the king who had, as we learn from the historians, imposed amercements of scandalous amount and with wanton tyranny, just as he compounded by fines for imaginary offences. The sheriffs, constables, coroners, and bailiffs of the king are forbidden to hold pleas of the Crown; a further limitation on the power of the local magistrates, which had been already cur-tailed by the direction issued in Richard's reign that no sheriff should be justice in his own county. Such a provision shows some mistrust of the sheriffs on the part of both king and barons; but it was probably disregarded in practice. This is the first of a series of articles by which the abuse of the sheriff's authority is restrained; the ferms of the counties and other jurisdictions are not to be in-creased; the debts due to the Crown which are collected by the sheriff are to be collected under the view of the lawful men of the neighbourhood; the goods of intestates are to go to their natural heirs; the royal officers are to pay for all the provisions which they take by requisition; they are not to take money in lieu of service from those who are willing to perform the service in person; they are not to seize the horses and carts of the freeman to do royal work, nor his wood without his consent; the lands of convicted felons are to be held by the Crown for a year and a day, and then to revert to the lords; and the weirs in the Thames, the Medway, and the other rivers in England are to be removed.

The remaining articles of general application are of a miscellaneous character; some laying down great principles, and others defining points of minute and occasional import. The use of the writ of Praecipe is limited so as not to defeat the judicial rights of the lords: the uniformity of weights and measures is directed in the words of Richard's assize; the writ of inquest in cases where life and limb are concerned is to be granted freely: the king will not claim the sole wardship of the minor who has other lords, except where he is the king's tenant by knight service: no bailiff is to force a man to compurgation or ordeal without witnesses. Merchants may go out and come in without paying exorbitant customs; and all lawful men may leave the kingdom and return except in time of war, or when the traveller belongs to a nation at war with the king. The vassals of an escheated honour are not to be treated by the king as tenants-in-chief of the Crown, but only to pay such reliefs and aids as they would owe to the mesne lord if there were one. The forest courts are not to compel the attendance of any man who is not directly concerned in the forest jurisdiction: this clause relieves the people of the shires in which the forests lie from the compulsory attendance directed by the Assize of Woodstock. It is followed by a still greater concession; all the forests made in the present reign are disforested, and all rivers placed in fence are thrown open; a thorough investigation of all the forest usages is to be made by an inquest of twelve sworn knights, and all the bad customs are to be abolished forthwith. By these clauses, which form the only forest charter issued by John, a great yet reluctant concession is made to a demand which had been increasing in intensity and listened to with stubborn disregard for a century and a half.

Other clauses are of a more general character. The thirty-ninth and fortieth are famous and precious enunciations of principles. 'No free man shall be taken, or imprisoned, or disseized, or outlawed, or exiled, or any wise destroyed; nor will we go upon him, nor send upon him, but by the lawful judgment of his peers or by the law of the land. To none will we sell, to none will we deny or delay, right or justice.' The judicium parium was indeed no novelty; it lay at the foundation of all German law; and the very formula here used is probably adopted from the laws of the Franconian and Saxon Caesars; but it was no small gain to obtain the declaration in such terms from a king who by giving the promise made a confession of past misgovernment.

Another significant article pledges the king to confer the sheriffdoms and other judicial offices of the local courts only on men skilled in the law. Another secures to the founders of religious houses their rights of custody during vacancy; and another forbids that any one should be taken or imprisoned on the appeal of a woman, except for the death of her husband.

Such, with the provision for the application of the rules thus enunciated to the whole nation, are what may be called the general articles of the Charter. The remainder is composed of clauses of special and transient interest: the king undertakes to surrender all charters and hostages placed in his hands as securities, and to dismiss the detested group of foreign servants whom he had gathered round him either as leaders of mercenaries or as ministers of small tyrannies. As soon as the pacification is completed he will dismiss all his mercenaries, forgive and recall all whom he has disseized or exiled; he will then reform, on the principles already adopted, the forests made by his father and brother, and do justice in other ways, for many of the promises made in the earlier part of the Charter had no retrospective validity. The rights of the Welsh who have been oppressed are at the same future period to be determined and recognised; the Welsh princes and the king of Scots are to have justice done; and a general amnesty for all political offences arising out of the present quarrel is to be given.

The enforcement of the Charter is committed to twenty-five barons, to be chosen by the whole baronage. These are empowered to levy war against the king himself, if he refuse to do justice on any claim laid before him by four of their number; and in con-

junction with the communa—the community of the whole realm
—to distrain him, saving his royal person and queen and children.

The last clause contains the enacting words, 'We will and
firmly enjoin,' and the oath to be taken on the part of the king and
on the part of the barons, that all these articles shall be observed in
good faith and without evasion of their plain construction.

In this mere abstract of the Great Charter we have the summing up of the rights and duties that have been growing into
recognition whilst the nation was growing into consciousness. The
Communa totius terrae, which is to join with the twenty-five
barons in the execution of the Charter, has at last entered upon its
career of constitutional life.

So great a boon as Magna Carta might almost excuse the men
by whose agency it was won from a trial at the bar of history. But
so much of the earlier fortunes of the constitution turns upon personal history, on the local, official, and family connexions of the
great men, that we cannot dismiss the subject without the inquiry,
Who were the men, and what was their training? Who were the
barons that now impose limits on royal tyranny, and place themselves in the vanguard of liberty? How have they come to sit in
the seats and wield the swords of those whom so lately we saw
arrayed in feudal might against king and people?

The barons who took part in the transactions out of which
Magna Carta emerges—and the whole baronage was in one way or
another directly concerned in it—fall into four classes: those who
began the quarrel in A.D. 1213 by refusing to follow the king to
France; those who joined them after the councils held at S. Alban's
and in S. Paul's; those who left the king in the spring of A.D. 1215
after the adhesion of the Londoners; and those who continued
with him to the last. Each of these divisions contained men who
acted on the ground of public right, and others who were mainly
influenced by private friendship and gratitude, or by the desire of
avenging private wrongs.

The first class was chiefly composed of the north country
barons, the Northumbrani, Norenses, Aquilonares of the chroni-

clers. No list of them is given, but they can easily be distinguished in the roll of chiefs enumerated by Matthew Paris in connexion with the assembly at Stamford: they are Eustace de Vesci, Richard de Perci, Robert de Ros, Peter de Bruis, Nicolas de Stuteville, William de Mowbray, Simon de Kyme, Gilbert de la Val, Oliver de Vaux, John de Lacy the constable of Chester, and Thomas of Multon. All these are well-known names in the north; many of them appear in Domesday; but, with the exception of Mowbray and Lacy, not among the greater tenants-in-chief at the time of the Survey. They had sprung into the foremost rank after the fall of the elder house of Mowbray, and had many of them done service under Richard de Lucy and Ranulf Glanvill in the defence of the north. Eustace de Vesci, however, was closely connected by marriage with the king of Scots, and is said to have had, like Robert Fitz-Walter and William of Salisbury, cruel wrongs to avenge upon the king.

The second division, containing the rest of the confederates who met at Stamford, embraced the remnant of the Conquest baronage, and the representatives of the families which had earned lands and dignities under Henry I and Henry II. Amongst these the most prominent is Robert Fitz-Walter, a grandson of Richard de Lucy and a descendant in the male line from the Norman house of Brionne. With him are Saer de Quenci earl of Winchester, the possessor of half the inheritance of the great house of Leicester; Henry Bohun earl of Hereford, and Roger Bigod earl of Norfolk, who appear side by side as their descendants did when they defied Edward I; Richard of Clare earl of Hertford, the brother-in-law, and Geoffrey de Mandeville earl of Essex, the husband, of the king's divorced wife; William Marshall the younger, the son of the great earl whose adhesion was the main support of John; Roger de Creissi, William Malduit, William de Lanvalei, and others, whose names recall the justices of Henry II's Curia; and with them Robert de Vere, Fulk Fitz-Warin, William Mallet, William de Beauchamp, two of the house of Fitz-Alan, and two of the house of Gant. Many of these have names the glories of which belong to later history: such of them as are of earlier importance may be referred to the two sources already indicated; the great baronial families that had been wise enough to cast away the feudal aspirations of their forefathers, and the rising houses which had sprung from the ministerial nobility.

The third class, which clung to John as long as he seemed to have any hope in resistance, was headed by those earls who were closely connected by blood or by marriage with the royal house: Earl William of Salisbury, the king's natural brother; William of Warenne, the son of Earl Hamelin and cousin of John, and Henry earl of Cornwall, grandson of Henry I. With them were William de Forz, titular count of Aumâle and lord of Holderness, a feudal adventurer of the worst stamp, whose father had been one of the captains of Richard's crusading fleet; Ranulf earl of Chester, and William Marshall earl of Pembroke, two men of long and varied experience as well as great social importance, who seem up to the last moment to have hoped that their own influence with the king might make it unnecessary for them to go into open opposition. In the second rank come Geoffrey de Lucy, Geoffrey de Furnival, Thomas Basset, Henry de Cornhell, Hugh de Neville, and William Briwere, the men who were at present in power in the Curia Regis and Exchequer; who were bound in honour to adhere to their master or to resign their dignities and who had in many cases been too willing ministers of the iniquities that provoked the struggle.

The few who adhered to John to the last were chiefly those who had everything to fear and nothing to hope from the victory of the confederates; Richard de Marisco, the chancellor, Peter de Mauley, Falkes de Breauté, Philip son of Mark, Gerard de Atie, Engelard de Cygonies, Robert de Gaugi, and others whose names testify to their foreign extraction, and some of whom were expressly excluded by the Great Charter from ever holding office in England.

Of the bishops, Peter des Roches the justiciar was probably the only one who heartily supported John: he was a foreign favourite and an unpopular man. Pandulf the papal envoy was also on the

king's side; and some of the bishops who had been lately consecrated, such as Walter Gray of Worcester, who had been chancellor for some years, and Benedict of Rochester, probably avoided
taking up any decided position. Even archbishop Langton himself,
although he sympathised with, and partly inspired and advised the
confederates, remained in attendance on the king.

It is worth while to compare with these lists the names of those
counsellors by whose advice John declares that he issues the charter, as well as those of the twenty-five barons to whom the execution was committed. The former body is composed of the bishops,
with Stephen Langton and Pandulf at their head, and those earls
and barons who only left John after the adhesion of the Londoners: it contains none of the northern barons, none of the second list
of confederates; and the selection was perhaps made in the hope of
binding the persons whom it includes to the continued support of
the hard-won liberties. The twenty-five executors are selected
from the two latter classes; they are as follows: of the north country lords, Eustace de Vesci, William de Mowbray, Robert de Ros,
John de Lacy, Richard de Perci; of the Stamford confederates, the
earls of Hertford, Gloucester, Winchester, Hereford, Norfolk,
and Oxford; Robert Fitz-Walter, William Marshall the younger,
Gilbert de Clare, Hugh Bigod, William Mallet, John Fitz-Robert,
Roger de Mumbezon, Richard de Muntfitchet, William de Hunt-
ingfield. Two of the third list, William of Aumâle and William of
Albini, represent a body less hostile to John. Geoffrey de Say, who
is found shortly after in arms against John, and the mayor of London, complete the number.

In a further stage of our inquiry we shall be able to trace the
subsequent divisions of party and policy that sprang out of these
several combinations, in that altered state of affairs which followed
the French invasion, and through the difficulties which beset the
minority of Henry III. The analysis of the lists confirms the evidence of the historians, and proves that the first cry for freedom
came from the North, that it was taken up and maintained by the
strength of the baronial party, which had learned the benefit of

law, peace, and good government, and that the demands of the confederates took a definite and defensible form under the hand of the archbishop, and on the model of Henry I's charter: that this basis of agreement was accepted by the people at large, and especially by the Londoners, who to some extent represent the town population of the kingdom; and was finally adhered to by the most important members of the government, with William Marshall at their head. John remained contumacious till all but his foreign creatures had forsaken him, and, when he yielded, he yielded with a full intention of eluding by papal connivance all his promises. The Great Charter is then the act of the united nation, the church, the barons, and the commons, for the first time thoroughly at one. It is in form only the act of the king: in substance and in historical position it is the first effort of a corporate life that has reached full consciousness, resolved to act for itself and able to carry out the resolution. [CHE, 1: 570–583]

The Growth of Representative Institutions

ANGEVIN KINGSHIP

⚜ The very idea of kingship had developed since the age of the Conqueror. This had been one result of the struggle with the Church. The divine origin of royalty had been insisted on as an argument to force on the kings the sense of responsibility. This lesson had been familiar to the ancient English rulers, and its application had been summarily brought home. Edwy, like Rehoboam, had spurned the counsels of the fathers, and the men of the north had left him, and taken Edgar to be king. But the truth was less familiar, and the application less impressive to the Norman. The Conqueror had won England by the sword; and, though he tried to rule it as a national king, it was not as one who would be brought to account: William Rufus had defied God and man: Henry I had compelled Anselm to give him a most forcible reminder of the source from which both king and prelate derived their power: Stephen had sinned against God and the people, and the hand of supreme power was traced in his humiliation. The events that were taking place on the Continent conveyed further lessons. In the old struggles between pope and emperor the zeal of righteousness was on the side of the latter: since the reign of Henry IV the balance of moral influence was with the popes; and the importance of that balance had been exemplified both in Germany and in France. The power of the pen was in the hands of the clergy: Hugh of Fleury had elaborately explained to Henry I the duties and rights which his position owed to its being ordained of God. John of Salisbury, following Plutarch and setting up Trajan as the model of princes, had urged the contrast between the tyrant and the king such as he hoped to find in Henry II. Yet these influences were thwarted by another set of ideas, not indeed running counter to them, but directed to a different aim. The clergy had exalted royalty in order to enforce its responsibilities on the conscience of the king; the lawyers exalted it in order to strengthen its authority as the source of law and justice; making the law honourable by magnifying the attributes of the lawgiver. And, as the lawyers grew more powerful as a class, the theory of royalty approached more closely to absolutism: their language has a tone, a force, and a consistent logic that is wanting to the exhortations of the churchmen. Yet even to the lawyer this ideal king was not the man who sat on the throne, but the power that would enforce the law. Glanvill cites and applies to Henry II the maxim of the Institutes, 'quod principi placuit, legis habet vigorem,'—a principle which, as Fortescue points out, is absolutely foreign to the ideas of English law; and the author of the Dialogus de Scaccario, who, although himself an ecclesiastic, represented both in life and in doctrine the ministerial lawyer, lays down that the deeds of kings are not to be discussed or condemned by inferior men, their hearts are in the hands of God, and it is by divine not by human judgment that their cause must stand or fall. Happily a theory of absolutism is compatible with very strong and strict limitations in practice: yet it was probably under the idea that the king is the sovereign lord of his people that Richard I and John forsook the time-honoured practice of issuing a charter of liberties at the coronation. John's idea of his own position was definitely that of an absolute prince: when he heard the demands of the barons he inquired why they had not asked for the kingdom also, and swore that he would never grant them such liberties as would make himself a slave: yet the liberties they asked were those which his forefathers had been glad to offer to their people. Curiously enough it is in John that the territorial idea of royalty reaches its typical enunciation: all the kings before him had called themselves on their great seals kings of the English: John is the first whose title appears on that solemn and sovereign emblem as *Rex Angliae*.

The growth of real power in the king's hands had advanced in proportion to the theory. Every measure of internal policy by which the great vassals had been repressed, or the people strengthened to keep them in check, had increased the direct influence of the crown; and the whole tendency of the ministerial system had been in the same direction. Hence it was that John was able so long to play the part of a tyrant, and that the barons had to enforce the Charter by measures which for the time were an exercise on their part of sovereign power.   [CHE, 1: 592-594]

THE NATIONAL COUNCIL

◢§ The national council under Henry II and his sons seems in one aspect to be a realisation of the principle which was introduced at the Conquest, and had been developed and grown into consistency under the Norman kings, that of a complete council of feudal tenants-in-chief. In another aspect it appears to be in a stage of transition towards that combined representation of the three estates and of the several provincial communities which especially marks our constitution, and which perhaps was the ideal imperfectly grasped and more imperfectly realised, at which the statesmen of the middle ages almost unconsciously aimed. The constituent members of this assembly are the same as under the Norman kings, but greater prominence and a more definite position are assigned to the minor tenants-in-chief; there is a growing recognition of their real constitutional importance, a gradual definition of their title to be represented and of the manner of representation, and a growing tendency to admit not only them, but the whole body of smaller landowners, of whom the minor tenants-in-chief are but an insignificant portion, to the same rights. This latter tendency may be described as directed towards the concentration of the representation of the counties in the national parliament, —the combination of the shiremoots with the witenagemot of the kingdom.

The royal council, as distinct from the mere assembly and court of the household, might consist of either the magnates, the greater barons, the 'proceres' of the Conqueror's reign; or of the whole body of tenants-in-chief, as was the accepted usage under Henry II; or of the whole body of landowners, whoever their feudal lords might be, which was the case in the great councils of 1086 and 1116, and which, when the representative principle was fully recognised, became the theory of the medieval constitution. These three bodies were divided by certain lines, although those lines were not very definite. The greater barons held a much greater extent of land than the minor tenants-in-chief: they made a separate agreement with the Crown for their reliefs, and probably for their other payments in aid: they had, as we learn from Magna Carta, their several summonses to the great councils, and they led their vassals to the host under their own banners. The entire body of tenants-in-chief included besides these the minor barons, the knightly body, and the socage tenants of the crown, who paid their reliefs to the sheriff, were summoned to court or council through his writ, and appeared under his banner in the military levy of the county. The general body of freeholders comprised, besides these two bodies, all the feudal tenants of the barons and the freemen of the towns and villages, who had a right or duty of appearing in the county court, who were armed in the fyrd or under the assize of arms, who were bound to the Crown simply by the oath of allegiance taken in the shiremoot, and were qualified to determine by their sworn evidence the rights of their neighbours, the assessment of their goods, and the report of their neighbourhood as to criminals.

These three possible assemblies may be regarded again as the assembly in its ordinary, extraordinary, and theoretical form: the national council usually contained only the magnates; on great occasions it contained the whole body of the tenants-in-chief; in idea it was the representation of the nation; and on one or two very rare occasions that idea was partially realised. But there were departments of national action in which the uncertainty and indefiniteness of such a theory were inadmissible. For the payment of taxes all men must be brought under contribution; for the efficiency of the national host all men must be brought together in arms. For the first of these purposes they might be visited in detail, for the second they must be assembled in person. Accordingly we find that the military levies in which Henry II brought together the whole kingdom in arms, as for the siege of Bridgnorth in 1155 or for the expedition to Normandy in 1177, may have really been steps towards the assembling of the nation for other purposes; and when, as in the latter case, we find the king acting by the counsel of the assembled host, we recur in thought to that ancient time when the only general assembly was that of the nation in arms. But the nation in arms was merely the meeting of the shires in arms: the men who in council or in judgment made up the county court, in arms composed the 'exercitus scirae:' on occasion of taxation or local consultation they were the wise men, the legales homines of the shiremoot. The king's general council is then one day to comprise the collective wisdom of the shires, as his army comprises their collective strength. But it is very rarely as yet that the principle of national concentration, which has been applied to the host, is applied to the council.

The point at which the growth of this principle had arrived during the period before us is marked by the fourteenth article of the Great Charter: 'To have the common council of the kingdom' for the assessment of extraordinary aids and scutages, 'we will cause to be summoned the archbishops, bishops, abbots, earls, and greater barons singly by our letters; and besides we will cause to be summoned in general by our sheriffs and bailiffs all those who hold of us in chief; to a certain day, that is to say, at a term of forty days at least; and to a certain place; and in all the letters of such summons we will express the cause of the summons; and the summons having been so made, the business shall on the day assigned proceed according to the counsel of those who shall be present, although not all who have been summoned shall have come.' The council is thus no longer limited to the magnates: but it is not extended so as to include the whole nation, it halts at the tenants-in-chief: nor are its functions of advising on all matters recognised, it is simply to be assembled for the imposing of taxation. The provision, that the determination of the members present shall be regarded as the proceeding of the whole body summoned, enunciates in words the principle which had long been acted upon, that absence, like silence, on such occasion implies consent.

The use of a written summons to call together the council must have been very ancient, but we have no evidence of the date at which it became the rule. The great courts held on the festivals of the Church might not indeed require such a summons, but every special assembly of the sort—and very many such occur from the earliest days of the Norman reigns—must have been convoked by a distinct writ. Such writs were of two kinds: there was first a special summons declaring the cause of meeting, addressed to every man whose presence was absolutely requisite; thus for the sessions of the Exchequer each of the king's debtors was summoned by a writ declaring the sum for which he was called upon to account: and secondly there was a general summons such as those addressed to the several counties through their sheriffs to bring together the shiremoot to meet the justices or the officers of the forest. The former was delivered directly to the person to whom it was addressed; the latter was proclaimed by the servants of the sheriff in the villages and market towns, and obeyed by those who were generally described in the writ itself, as their business, inclination, or fear of the penalty for non-attendance, might dispose them. On this analogy the writs of summons to the national council were probably of two sorts: those barons who in their military, fiscal, and legal transactions dealt directly with the king were summoned by special writ: those tenants-in-chief who transacted their business with the sheriff were convened, not by a writ in which they were severally named, but by a general summons. Of the greater barons the first person summoned was the archbishop of Canterbury, and it is from the mention by the historians of the offence offered to Becket by neglecting this customary respect that we learn the existence of the double system of summons in the early years of Henry II. There is still earlier evidence of the special summons: Gilbert Foliot, in reference to the homage and oaths taken to the empress, describes the greater magnates as those who were accustomed to be summoned to council in their own proper names; evidently as distinguished from those who were cited by a collective summons. The Pipe Rolls contain very frequent mention of payments made to the summoners, and that in direct connexion with meetings of the council. In 1175 Henry went so far as to forbid those who had been lately in arms against him to appear at his court at all without summons. It is a strange thing that so very few of these early writs are now in existence: the most ancient that we have is one addressed to the bishop of Salisbury in 1205, ten years before the granting of the charter. This document fixes the date of the assembly, which is to be held at London on the Sunday before Ascension Day, and the cause of the meeting, which is to discuss the message brought by the envoys from Philip of France; and it also contains a clause of general summons, directing the bishop to warn the abbots and priors of his diocese to be present on the occasion. Of the general forms of summons addressed to the sheriffs, we have no specimens earlier than the date at which representative institutions had been to a great extent adopted: but, if we may judge of their tenour from the like writs issued for military and fiscal purposes, they must have enumerated the classes of persons summoned in much the same way as they were enumerated in the writs ordering the assembly of the county court. Of this however it is impossible to be quite certain. That the county court had a special form of summons for the purpose of taxation we learn from a writ of Henry I, which has been already quoted. It is probable that the fourteenth clause of Magna Carta represents no more than the recognised theory of the system of summons; a system which was already passing away; for, besides that council at S. Alban's in 1213, in which the several townships of royal demesne were represented as in the county court by the reeve and four best men, a council was called at Oxford in the same year, in which each county was represented by four discreet men, who were to attend on the king 'to talk with him on the business of the kingdom.' In the writ by which this council is summoned, and which is dated on the 7th of November at Witney, we have the first extant evidence of the representation of the counties in the council; they were already accustomed to elect small numbers of knights for legal and fiscal purposes, and the practice of making such elections to expedite the proceeding of the itinerant justices is confirmed by the Great Charter itself. It is then just possible that the 14th clause may have been intended to cover the practice of county representation which had been used two years before. The further development of the system belongs to a later stage of our inquiries.

The character of the persons summoned requires no comment: the archbishops and bishops were the same in number as before, but the abbots and priors were a rapidly increasing body. The number of earls increased very slowly: it may be questioned whether Henry II founded any new earldoms, or whether the two or three ascribed to him were not merely those which, having been created by his mother or Stephen, he vouchsafed to confirm. None were created by Richard; and by John only the earldom of Winchester, which was founded in favour of one of the coheirs of the earldom of Leicester, the latter title being taken by the other coheir. The number of great baronies however was probably on the increase, although we have not sufficient data, either as to the possessors or as to the exact character of such baronies, to warrant a very positive statement. The number of minor tenants-in-chief who attended cannot even be conjectured: but, as the clergy of inferior dignity formed an appreciable part of the council, it is probable that the knights who, without yet possessing a representative character, came up from the shires in consequence of the general summons, were a considerable body: and sometimes they were very numerous. The presence of a large number of deans and archdeacons is mentioned on some special occasions, which seem to indicate a plan of assembling the three estates in something like completeness: but we have no reason to suppose that they were ever summoned as a matter of right or as tenants-in-chief.

The times of assembly were very irregular. In many cases, especially in the early years of Henry II, they coincided with the great festivals, or with the terminal days which were already beginning to be observed by the lawyers. But so great a number of occasional councils were called by Henry, and so few by his sons, that obviously no settled rule can have been observed. And the same remark is true as regards the place of meeting. The festival courts were still frequently kept at Winchester and Westminster; but for the great national gatherings for homage, for proclamation of Crusade, or the like, some central position, such as Northampton or its neighbourhood, was often preferred. Yet some of Henry II's most important acts were done in councils held in the forest palaces, such as Clarendon and Woodstock. Richard's two councils were held in middle England, one at Pipewell in Northamptonshire, the other at Nottingham; both places in which the weariness of state business might be lightened by the royal amusement of the chase.

The name given to these sessions of council was often expressed by the Latin *colloquium:* and it is by no means unlikely that the name of parliament, which is used as early as 1175 by Jordan Fantosme, may have been in common use. But of this we have no distinct instance in the Latin Chroniclers for some years further, although when the term comes into use it is applied retrospectively; and in a record of the twenty-eighth year of Henry III the assembly in which the Great Charter was granted is mentioned as the 'Parliamentum Runimedæ.'

The subjects on which the kings asked the advice of the body thus constituted were very numerous: it might almost seem that Henry II consulted his court and council on every matter of importance that arose during his reign; all the business that Richard personally transacted was done in his great councils; and even John, who acted far more in the manner and spirit of a despot than did his father or brother, did little in the first half of his reign without a formal show of respect towards his constitutional advisers. Nor is there any reason to suppose that such a proceeding was, in the great proportion of instances, merely a matter of form: a sovereign who is practically absolute asks counsel whenever he wants it; and such a sovereign, if he is a man of good sense, with reason for self-confidence, is not trammeled by the jealousies or by the need of self-assertion which are inseparable from the position of a monarch whose prerogatives are constitutionally limited. Hence it was perhaps that these kings, besides constantly laying before their barons all questions touching the state of the kingdom,—matters of public policy such as the destruction of the illegal castles and the maintenance of the royal hold on the fortresses, matters relating to legislation, to the administration of justice, to taxation, and to military organisation,—also took their opinion on peace and war, alliances, royal marriages, and even in questions of arbitration between foreign powers which had been specially referred to the king for decision. Of such deliberations abundant instances have been given in the last chapter. It is very rarely that any record is preserved of opposition to or even remonstrance against the royal will. In 1175 Richard de Lucy ventured to remind Henry II, when he was enforcing the law against the destroyers of the forests, that the waste of vert and venison had been authorised by his own writ; but his mediation was summarily set aside: the remonstrances likewise of the one or two counsellors, who during the Becket quarrel interposed on behalf of the archbishop, were either tacitly disregarded or resented as an advocacy of the king's enemy. Still less are we to look for any power of initiating measures of either public policy or particular reform in any hands but those of the king. Yet the assize of measures in 1197 was made not only with the advice but by the *petition* of the magnates. The justiciar however probably advised the king on all these matters, and perhaps suggested the administrative changes which he had to work out in their details; in this respect acting as the spokesman of the barons, as the archbishop acted as the spokesman of the Church, and exercising over the king a less overt but more effectual influence than could have been asserted by the barons except at the risk of rebellion. John certainly chafed under the advice of the justiciar, without venturing to dismiss him. In all these matters the regard, even if merely formal, shown by the king to the advice and consent of his barons has a constitutional value, as affording a precedent and suggesting a method for securing the exercise of the right of advising and consenting when the balance of power was changed, and advice and consent meant more than mere helpless acquiescence. The part taken by the national council in legislation, taxation, and judicature may be noticed as we proceed with the examination of those departments of public work.

The ecclesiastical councils of the period did their work with very little interference from the secular power, and with very little variation from the earlier model. Their privilege of legislating with the royal acquiescence was not disputed, and their right to a voice in the bestowal of their contributions towards the wants of the state came into gradual recognition in the reign of John: but although his expedients for the raising of money may now and then have served as precedents upon which the claim to give or refuse might be raised on behalf of the several orders in Church and State, no complete system of separate action by the clergy on secular matters was as yet devised, nor was their position as a portion of the common council of the realm defined by the Great Charter apart from that of the other tenants-in-chief. The theory

of the Three Estates had yet to be worked into practice; although
there were signs of its growing importance.

HENRY II'S LEGISLATION

Great as was the legal reputation of Henry II, and greatly as
the legal system of England advanced under him and his sons, the
documentary remains of the legislation of the period are very
scanty. The work of Glanvill is not a book of statutes, but a man-
ual of practice; and, although it incorporates no doubt the words
of ordinances which had the force of laws, it nowhere gives the
literal text of such enactments. The formal edicts known under the
name of Assizes, the Assizes of Clarendon and Northampton, the
Assize of Arms, the Assize of the Forest, and the Assizes of Measures, are the only relics of the legislative work of the period. These
edicts are chiefly composed of new regulations for the enforcement of royal justice. They are not direct re-enactments or
amendments of the ancient customary law, and are not drawn up
in the form of perpetual statutes: but they rather enunciate and
declare new methods of judicial procedure, which would either
work into or supersede the procedure of the common law,
whether practised in the popular or in the feudal courts. In this respect they strongly resemble the Capitularies of the Frank kings,
or, to go farther back, the edicts of the Roman Praetors: they
might indeed, as to both form and matter, be called Capitularies.
The term Assize, which comes into use in this meaning about the
middle of the twelfth century, both on the Continent and in England, appears to be the proper Norman name for such edicts; but it
is uncertain whether it received this particular application from
the mere fact that it was a settlement like the Anglo-Saxon *asetniss*
or the French *établissement*, or from a verbal connexion with the
session of the court in which it was passed, or from the fact that it
furnished a plan on which sessions of the courts reformed by it
should be held. The assize thus differs widely from the charter of
liberties, the form which the legislation of Henry I and Stephen

had taken, and is peculiar in English history to the period before us, as the form of Provisions marks the legislative period of Henry III, and that of Statute and Ordinance belongs to that of Edward I and his successors. The special sanctity of the term *law*, as used in Holy Scripture and in the Roman jurisprudence, may perhaps account for the variety of expressions, such as those quoted above, by means of which men avoided giving the title of law to their occasional enactments. The Assizes of England, Jerusalem, Antioch, Sicily, and Romania, the Establishments of S. Lewis, the Recesses of the German diets, and many other like expressions, illustrate this reluctance.

The Assize possesses moreover the characteristic of tentative or temporary enactment, rather than the universal and perpetual character which a law, however superficially, seems to claim: its duration is specified in the form; it is to be in force so long as the king pleases; it may have a retrospective efficacy, to be applied to the determination of suits which have arisen since the king's accession, or since his last visit to England; it is liable to be set aside by the judges where they find it impossible to administer it fairly. But, on the other hand, it is to the assize that the most important legal changes of the period owe their origin: the institution of jury and the whole procedure of the Curia Regis can have come into existence in no other way.

In the drawing up of the assize, the king acted by the advice and consent of his national council. This is distinctly stated in the preamble or title of the Assizes of Clarendon and Woodstock: the former is made 'de assensu archiepiscoporum, episcoporum, abbatum, comitum, baronum, totius Angliae;' the latter 'per consilium et assensum archiepiscoporum, episcoporum et baronum, comitum et nobilium Angliae.' The Assize of Northampton was the work, we are told, of the king, made by the counsel of King Henry his son and by the counsel of his earls, barons, knights, and vassals (homines) in a great council, consisting of bishops, earls, barons, and the rest, held 'de statutis regni.' The ordinance by which trial by the Great Assize was instituted was, according to Glanvill, an act of royal beneficence, bestowed on the nation by the clemency of the prince according to the counsel of the magnates. The Assize of Measures was issued in the name of Richard I by the justiciar in 1197, as made by the lord Richard king of England at Westminster, although the king was at the time in France, by the petition and advice of his bishops and all his barons. In this act of legislation the justiciar represented the king. The instructions given to the itinerant justices had likewise the force of laws, and might with justice be termed Assizes. They too were issued by the justiciar in the king's absence, and contained old as well as new regulations for the courts. The Assize of Arms issued in 1181 is not distinctly said to be framed under the advice of the council, and it may possibly have been regarded by the barons with some jealousy as putting arms into the hands of the people; but, when John in 1205 summoned the nation to arms in conformity with the principle embodied in his father's assize, he declares that it is so provided with the assent of the 'archbishops, bishops, earls, barons, and all our faithful of England.' These instances are sufficient to prove the share taken by the national council in legislation. The duty of proclaiming the law in the country fell upon the sheriffs and the itinerant justices, whose credentials contained perhaps the first general promulgation. The Great Charter was read, by the king's order, publicly in every county, no doubt in the shiremoot and hundred court; duplicates of it were deposited in the cathedral churches.

In all this there was nothing new: it was simply the maintenance of ancient forms, which prove their strength by retaining their vitality under the strongest of our kings. The advice and consent of the council may have been, no doubt in many cases was, a mere formality: the enacting power was regarded as belonging to the king, who could put in respite or dispense with the very measures that he had ordained. Yet in this an advantage may be incidentally traced. If the barons under Henry II had possessed greater legislative power, they might have kept it to themselves, as they did to a certain extent keep to themselves the judicial power of the later parliament; but, as it was, legislation was one of the nominal rights that belonged to the whole council as the representative of the nation, and the real exercise of which was not attained until the barons had made common cause with the people, and incorporated their representatives in their own assembly. The period of national as distinct from royal legislation begins when the council has reached its constitutional development as the national parliament. The legislation of the Great Charter was to a certain extent an anticipation, a type, a precedent, and a firm step in advance towards that consummation.

TAXATION

The subject of taxation may be arranged under three heads, —the authority by which the impost is legalised, the description of persons and property on which it is levied, and the determination of the amount for which the individual is liable; in other words, the grant, the incidence, and the assessment.

The reticence of historians during the reigns of the Norman kings leaves us in doubt whether the imposts which they levied were or were not exacted simply by their own sovereign will. Two records have been mentioned, however, of the reign of Henry I, in one of which the king describes a particular tax as 'the aid which my barons gave me,' whilst in another he speaks of the summoning of the county courts in cases in which his own royal necessities require it. From the two passages it may be inferred that some form was observed, by which the king signified, both to his assembled vassals and to the country at large through the sheriffs, the sums which he wanted, and the plea on which he demanded them. The same method was observed by Henry II and Richard I; and it is only towards the end of the reign of Richard that we can trace anything like a formal grant or discussion of a grant in the national council. It was commonly said that the king took a scutage, an aid, or a carucage; and, where the barons are said to have given it, the expression may be interpreted of the mere payment of the money. Of any debate or discussion on such exactions in the national council we have rare evidence: the opposition of S. Thomas to the king's manipulation of the Danegeld, and the refusal by S. Hugh of Lincoln to furnish money for Richard's war in France, are however sufficient to prove that the taxation was a subject of deliberation, although not sufficient to prove that the result of such discussion would be the authoritative imposition of the tax. For the shadow of the feudal fiction, that the tax-payer made a voluntary offering to relieve the wants of his ruler, seems to have subsisted throughout the period: and the theory that the promise of the tax bound only the individual who made it, helped to increase the financial complications of the reign of John. Archbishop Theobald had denounced the scutage of 1156, and it is doubtful whether it was raised on his lands. S. Thomas had declared at Woodstock that the lands of his church should not pay a penny to the Danegeld; the opposition of S. Hugh was based not on his right as a member of the national council, but on the immunities of his church; and, when Archbishop Geoffrey in 1201 and 1207 forbade the royal officers to collect the carucage on his estates, it was on the ground that he himself had not promised the payment. The pressing necessity of raising the ransom of Richard probably marks an epoch in this as in some other points of financial interest. The gentle terms *donum* or *auxilium* had signified under his father's strong hand as much as Danegeld or tallage; but now not only was the king absent and the kingdom in a critical condition, but the legal reforms in the matter of assessment had raised up in the minds of the people at large a growing sense of their rights. The taxes raised for the ransom were imposed by the justiciar, probably but not certainly, with the advice of the barons, and were no doubt collected without any general resistance; but both the amount and the incidence were carefully criticised, and in some cases payment was absolutely refused. The clergy of York, when the king's necessities were laid before them by the archbishop in their chapter, declared that he was infringing their liberties, and closed their church as in the time of interdict.

This idea, which is indeed the rudimentary form of the principle that representation should accompany taxation, gained ground after the practice arose of bringing personal property and income under contribution. It was the demand of a quarter of their revenues, not a direct tax upon their land, that provoked the opposition of the canons of York; and although Archbishop Geoffrey is found more than once in trouble for forbidding the collection of a carucage, the next great case in which resistance was offered to the demands of the Crown occurred in reference to the exaction of a thirteenth of moveable property in 1207. On this occasion it was not an isolated chapter, but a whole estate of the realm that protested. The king in a great council held on January 8 at London proposed to the bishops and abbots that they should permit the parsons and beneficed clerks to give him a certain portion of their revenues. The prelates refused to do so. The matter was debated in an adjourned council at Oxford on February 9, and there the bishops repeated their refusal in still stronger terms. The king therefore gave up that particular mode of procedure, and obtained from the national council a grant of an aid of a thirteenth of all chattels from the laity. That done, having on the 26th of May forbidden the clergy to hold a council at S. Alban's, he issued, the same day, a writ to the archdeacons and the rest of the clergy, informing them of the grant of aid, and bidding them follow the good example. Archbishop Geoffrey, who acted as the spokesman of the clergy, now gave up the struggle and went into exile; other circumstances were leading to a crisis: the thirteenth was no doubt generally collected; but early in the following year the interdict was imposed and constitutional law was in abeyance during the remainder of the reign. The twelfth article of the charter, in which the king promises that no scutage or aid, save the three regular aids, should henceforth be imposed without the advice and consent of the national council, does not explicitly mention the imposition of a tax on moveables, nor does it provide for the representation in the council of the great majority of those from whom such a tax would be raised. But in this, as in other points, the progress of events was outstripping and superseding the exact legal definitions of right. The fourteenth article does not provide for the representation of the shires, or for the participation of the clergy as an estate of the realm, distinct from their character as feudal freeholders, yet in both respects the succeeding history shows that the right was becoming practically established. So neither is the principle as yet formally laid down that a vote of the supreme council is to bind all the subjects of the realm in matter of taxation without a further consent of the individual. The prevalence of the idea that such consent was necessary brings the subject of the grant into close connexion with that of the assessment.

.   .   .   .   .

The taxable property may be divided into land and moveables, and again, according to the character of their owners, into lay and clerical; these may be subdivided in the former case according as the layman is a tenant-in-chief, a knight, a freeholder, a burgher, or a villein, in the latter according as the possessor is a prelate, a beneficed clerk, a chapter, or a religious house. Each division of property was brought under contribution at a different period, and for each there was a distinct name and method of taxation.

All the imposts of the Anglo-Saxon and Norman reigns were, so far as we know, raised on the land, and according to computation by the hide: the exceptions to the rule would be only in the cases of those churches which claimed entire immunity, and those boroughs which paid a composition for their taxes in a settled sum, as they paid the composition for the ferm in the shape of an annual rent. This generalisation covers both the national taxes like the Danegeld, and the feudal exactions by way of aid; both were levied on the hide. Henry I had exempted from such payments the lands held in demesne by his knights and barons, in consideration of the expenses of their equipments; but this clause of his charter can have been only partially observed. Henry II, from the very beginning of his reign, seems to have determined on attempting important changes. He brought at once under contribution the lands held by the churches, which had often claimed but had never perhaps secured immunity.

In the Assize of Arms in 1181 he took a long step towards taxing rent and chattels, obliging the owner of such property to equip himself with arms according to the amount which he possessed. In the ordinance of the Saladin Tithe personal property is rendered liable to pay its tenth. Under Richard I the rule is extended: for the king's ransom every man pays a fourth part of his moveables: in 1204 John exacted a seventh of the same from the barons, and in 1207 a thirteenth from the whole of the laity. This change in the character of taxation serves to illustrate the great development of material wealth in the country which followed the reforms of Henry II. The burdens would not have been transferred from the land to the chattels if the latter had not been found much more productive of revenue than the former.

But this was not the only change. Henry II adopted the knight's fee instead of the hide as the basis of rating for the knights and barons: and on this basis established a somewhat minute system of distinctions. As early as his second year we find him collecting a scutage, at twenty shillings on the 'scutum' or knight's fee, from the knights who held land under the churches. In 1159, for the war of Toulouse, he raised a much larger sum under the same name, from the tenants by knight service; as a commutation for personal service he accepted two marks from each, and with the proceeds paid an army of mercenaries. The word scutage, from its use on this occasion, acquired the additional sense of a payment in commutation of personal service, in which it is most frequently used. In 1163, as has been already mentioned, the ancient Danegeld disappears from the Rolls; but it is succeeded by a tax which, under the name of donum or auxilium, and probably levied on a new computation of hidage, must have been a reproduction of the old usage. Such a change must indeed have been necessary, the Danegeld having become in the long lapse of years a mere composition paid by the sheriff to the Exchequer, while the balance of the whole sums exacted on that account went to swell his own income. Under Richard the same tax appears under the name of carucage: the normal tax being laid on the carucate instead of the hide, and each carucate containing a fixed extent of one hundred acres.

Each of these names represents the taxation of a particular class: the scutage affects the tenants in chivalry; the donum, hidage or carucage, affects all holders of land; the tenth, seventh, and thirteenth, all people in the realm. Each has its customary amount; the scutage of 1156 was twenty shillings on the fee; those of 1159 and 1161 were two marks; the scutage of Ireland in 1171 was twenty shillings, and that of Galloway in 1186 at the same rate. The scutages of Richard's reign,—one for Wales in the first year and two for Normandy in the sixth and eighth,—were, in the first case ten, in the other cases twenty shillings. John in his first year raised a scutage of two marks; on nine other occasions he demanded the same sum, besides the enormous fines which he extorted from his barons on similar pretexts. Other aids to which the name is not commonly given were raised in the same way and at similar rates. Such were especially the aid pur fille marier, collected by Henry in 1168 at twenty shillings on the fee, and that for the ransom of Richard I at the same amount.

The carucage of Richard was probably intended, as the Danegeld had been, to be fixed at two shillings on the carucate. In 1198 however it was raised to five, and John in the first year of his reign fixed it at three shillings.

Under the general head of donum, auxilium, and the like, come a long series of imposts, which were theoretically gifts of the nation to the king, and the amount of which was determined by the itinerant justices after separate negotiation with the payers. The most important of these, that which fell upon the towns and demesne lands of the Crown, is known as the tallage. This must have affected other property besides land, but the particular method in which it was to be collected was determined by the community on which it fell, or by special arrangement with the justices.

It was only on rare occasions that all these methods of raising money were resorted to at once. Such an occasion might be the aid to marry the king's daughter, or to ransom his person; but not the ordinary contributions towards the regular expenses of the Crown. On these great occasions, the knights paid aid or scutage, the freeholders carucage, the towns tallage: the whole and each part bore the name of auxilium. More frequently only one tax was raised at once; a year marked by a scutage was not marked by a donum or a carucage. It was the accumulation and increased rate of these exactions that created the discontent felt under Hubert Walter's administration in the later years of Richard and the early years of John. In this division of burdens, and distinction of class interests, may be traced another step towards the system of three estates: the clergy and laity were divided by profession and peculiar rights and immunities; scutage and carucage drew a line between the tenant in chivalry and the freeholder, which at a later time helped to divide the lords from the commons. The clergy had in their spiritual assemblies a vantage-ground, which they used during the thirteenth century, to vindicate great liberties; and their action led the way to general representative assembling, and made easier for the commons the assertion of their own definite position.

The method of assessment varied according to the incidence of the tax. So long as all the taxation fell on the land, Domesday book continued to be the rate-book of the kingdom; all assessments that could not be arranged directly by it, such as the contributions of the boroughs, were specially adjusted by the sheriffs, or by the officers of the Exchequer in their occasional visitations, or were permanently fixed in a definite proportion and at round sums. This system must have proved sufficient so long as the changes of occupation, which had occurred since the Domesday Survey, could be kept in living memory. As soon however as Henry II began to rate the land by the knight's fee, a new expedient was requisite. Hence, when he was preparing to levy the aid pur fille marier, the king issued a writ to all the tenants-in-chief of the Crown, lay and clerical, directing each of them to send in a cartel or report of the number of knights' fees which had been enfeoffed and the amount of their service. This was done, and the reports so made are still preserved in the Black Book of the Exchequer, to which reference has been more than once made in former chapters. The scutages continued to be exacted on the same assessment, compared from year to year with the Pipe Rolls, until the reign of John, who on several occasions took advantage of the reluctance which his barons showed for foreign war to make arbitrary exactions. A clause of the Great Charter issued by Henry III in 1217 directs that the scutages shall be taken as they were in his grandfather's time. A few years after this Alexander of Swerford, who compiled the Red Book of the Exchequer, reduced the computation of knights' fees to something like order by a careful examination of the Pipe Rolls; but, so long as scutages were collected at all, the assessment of the individual depended very much on his own report, which the Exchequer had little means of checking.

The donum, auxilium, or tallage, which Henry imposed in lieu of the ancient Danegeld, was assessed by the officers of the Exchequer. In 1168 the whole of England was visited by a small commission of judges and clerks, who rated the sums by which the freeholders and the towns were to supplement the contributions of the knights. In 1173 a tallage on the royal demesne was assessed by six detachments of Exchequer officers, and throughout the remainder of the reign the fiscal circuits correspond with those of the justices, or the fiscal business is done by the justices in their judicial circuits. This method of assessment, like that of scutage, failed to secure either party against the other; either the justices had to accept the return of the tax-payer, or the tax-payer had to pay as the judges directed him. Little help could be expected from the sheriff, who indeed was generally an officer of the Exchequer. The assessment of the justices sometimes varied considerably from that of the payer, and in one recorded instance we find the tender of the former accepted in preference to the valuation of the latter. In 1168 the men of Horncastle pay £29 13s. 4d. for an aid, 'quod ipsi assederunt inter se concessu justitiarum ailter quam justitiae.' It is obvious that an exaction, the amount of which was settled as in these two cases by the statement of the payer, was removed by only one step from the character of a voluntary contribution. That step might be a very wide one, and the liberty which it implied might be very limited, but the right of grant and the right of assessment were brought into immediate juxtaposition.

When however, as was the case under the Assize of Arms and the Saladin Tithe, personal property was to be rated, it became clear that no safe assessment could be based either on the taxpayer's statement of his own liability, or on the uninformed opinion of the sheriff and justices. To remedy this, Henry had recourse to his favourite expedient of the jury. He directed that the quantity and character of armour which each man was to provide should be determined by the report of a number of sworn knights and other lawful men of each neighbourhood, who were to draw up a list of the men within their district, with a distinct statement of their liability. In the collection of the Saladin Tithe, in which the king himself took an active part, the same plan was adopted: where suspicion arose that any man was contributing less than his share, four or six lawful men of the parish were chosen to declare on oath what he ought to give. The great precedent for this proceeding was found of course in the plan by which the Domesday Survey had been made, and the occasional recognitions of fiscal liability which had been taken under special writs. The plan was so successful that in 1198 it was applied to the assessment of the carucage, an account of which has been given already. The assessment of the thirteenth in A.D. 1207 was however not made by juries, but by the oath of the individual payer taken before the justices; the contributions of the clergy being a matter of special arrangement made by the archdeacons. The carucage of 1198 is then the land-mark of the progress which the representative principle expressed by the jury had as yet attained in the matter of taxation.

The further question, which arose chiefly in the towns, how the sums agreed to between the special community and the Exchequer were to be adjusted so as to insure the fair treatment of individuals, also came into importance as soon as personal property was liable to assessment. We learn from the story of William Fitz-Osbert, that in London the taxes were raised by capitation or poll-tax, every citizen poor or rich contributing the same amount, the unfairness of the rule being compensated by the lightness of the burden which so many joined in bearing. William came forward as the advocate of the poor, and declared that an assessment should be made by which each man should pay in proportion to his wealth: but we are not told by what means he intended to carry the idea into execution, and his intemperate conduct produced the riot with which our knowledge of the matter terminates.

The whole subject of taxation illustrates the gradual way in which king and people were realising the idea of self-government. The application of a representative scheme to the work of assessment, and the recognition that the liability of the payer was based on his own express consent, either to the grant itself or to the amount of his own contribution, mark a state of things in which the concentration of local interests in one general council was all that was needed to secure the tax-payer from arbitrary treatment on the part of either the sovereign or his ministers. This becomes still more evident as we approach the wider but equally important sphere of judicial action, in which not only the principle, but the actual details of the representative system seem progressively to assert themselves. [CHE, 1: 604–629]

LAW AND ADMINISTRATION

◄§ The judicial measures of Henry II constitute a very important part of his general policy. . . . We have . . . seen how the original impulse was given to his reforms by the terms on which the Crown was secured to him, how those reforms were moulded by his peculiar genius or by the influence of well-chosen advisers, the tradition of the Exchequer forming an important element; how the several steps in advance were partly guided by a desire to limit the judicial power of the great feudal vassals, and to protect the people against the misuse by the local magnates of that influence in the county courts which had fallen into their hands. We have accordingly noted the chief occasions on which the sheriffs, and even the royal judges, were brought to special account, and displaced to make way, either for men who had received a better legal training, or for such as were less closely connected with the ruling families of the district, or for those who would bring the shire administration into more thorough concert with the supreme administration, if not completely under its control. We have traced, under the history of Hubert Walter and Geoffrey Fitz-Peter, a growing spirit of legal reform, a rapid invention of new machinery or adaptation of the old machinery to new ends, not indeed free from the imputation that it was chiefly stimulated by financial considerations, but still in its ultimate results conducive to the growth and conscious realisation of the idea of self-government. And we have further inferred that the attitude taken by the clergy, the barons, and the commons at the date of the Great Charter was produced by the altered circumstances in which the kingdom was placed by these changes: that whilst on the one hand they had given to the king an overwhelming power, they had on the other revealed to the Three Estates the unity of their interests, and the possibility of erecting a well-compacted fabric of liberty. We have now to trace the mechanical workings involved in this history.

Henry at his accession found the administrative system in the most attenuated state. Twenty years of misrule had seen the polity of his grandfather broken up rather than suspended, and very few of the old servants of the State survived. Such judicial machinery as existed seems to have been sustained by Richard de Lucy, but the year which had elapsed since the pacification had only given time to attempt the uprooting of the evils of misrule, not to lay the foundations or to rebuild the fabric of a sound government. Hence Henry's reforms, although, so far as he was able to get aid from his grandfather's ministers, they were based upon the older system, owe very much to the king himself, and, from the outset of the reign, exhibit marks of decided growth and difference from the former state of things. The Exchequer was restored under Bishop Nigel as it had existed under Bishop Roger, but the Curia Regis from the first presents a much more definite appearance than before. Still one with the Exchequer in its personal staff, it has much more independent action and a wider sphere; it developes a new and elaborate system of rules and customs. The king's personal tribunal continues to be a supreme and ultimate resort, but the royal judicature from time to time throws off offshoots, which before the end of the period constitute a system of courts and jurisdictions that with some developments and modifications have subsisted to our own day.

The judicature may be divided into three branches, the central and supreme court or courts, the provincial, popular, or common law tribunals, and the visitatorial jurisdiction by which the first interfered with, regulated, and remodelled the second: and these may be noticed in the order of their authority; first, the king's courts; secondly, the itinerant justices; thirdly, the local tribunals.

The Exchequer and the Curia Regis continue throughout this period to exist in that close union which proves their original identity; but whereas under Henry I the financial character of the board is the most prominent, under Henry II more importance attaches to its judicial aspect. In the former reign the Curia Regis, except when the king takes a personal share in the business, seems to be a judicial session of the Exchequer, and adaptation of Exchequer machinery to judicial purposes; under the latter the Exchequer seems to be rather a financial session of the Curia Regis. The king is ostensibly the head of the one, the justiciar the principal actor in the other; but still the fabric is the same: the judges are the same; the transactions of the Curia frequently take place in the chamber of the Exchequer, and are recorded in its Rolls; and, through all the changes by which the Curia is modelled and divided, the Exchequer forms a rallying-point, or common ground, on which all the members of the supreme judicature seem to meet, as in the more modern Court of Exchequer Chamber in modern days.

The financial system of the Exchequer, as it existed under Henry I, has been already described, and illustrated from the single Pipe Roll of the reign as well as from the Dialogus de Scaccario. The latter work describes the practice of the year 1178, in language which shows a substantial agreement with the system presented in the Roll of 1130. This organisation therefore it is unnecessary to recapitulate here. The points in which change and development are traceable are either minute matters of procedure, which scarcely come within the view of constitutional history, or matters of legal interest which belong more strictly to the history of the Curia Regis and itinerant jurisdictions. The Court of Exchequer, taking special cognisance of suits touching the revenue, possessing a different body of judges and a distinct code of customs, has not yet a separate existence; but it may be justly presumed that, where such suits were entertained, the judges before whom they were tried would be those who were most familiar with the financial work. The fines levied for legal purposes, which were originally the determinate agreements between litigants drawn up and recorded in the king's court, and were a source of constant income to the Crown, were regularly concluded 'ad scaccarium;' but the judges who witnessed the transaction were not a permanent committee of officers; they were apparently a selection for each occasion from the whole body of the Curia, all of whom were, it is probable, equally eligible and of equal authority. The records of the Exchequer grow during the period in bulk and in number: the Pipe Rolls of Henry II are supplemented under John by Oblate, Liberate, and Mise Rolls, in which the particular outgoings on the heads of royal allowances, benefactions, and other payments are circumstantially recorded. The Great Rolls of the Pipe however continue to contain the summaries and authoritative details of the national account.

The Curia Regis of Henry II attained its ultimate constitution by a long series of somewhat rapid changes. In the early years of the reign it appears to be, as it had been under Henry I, a tribunal of exceptional resort to which appeals, although increasing in number, were still comparatively rare, and the action of which is scarcely distinguishable from that of the national council. The king himself took a leading part in the business, much of which was done in his presence; and even in his absence the action of the justiciar seems to depend on the royal pleasure as indicated by special writs . . . .

In 1166 we come to the Assize of Clarendon, which marks an epoch in the administration of, at least, the criminal law. During these years—for such is the reasonable inference—the judicial work of the Curia Regis had been growing until it was more than the king and his regular ministers of state could dispatch, and was thus falling, even more completely than it had done under Henry I, into the hands of the officers of the Exchequer. The system of recognition was, as the Constitutions of Clarendon prove, in full play, and the superior chances of justices which that system afforded were drawing larger business to the court, and at the same time involved a vast 'officina brevium,' with a body of trained clerks and a regular code of practical jurisprudence. Unfortunately we are unable to discover the date at which the Great Assize was issued; if this were known, it would probably be found to coincide with one of the periods at which great changes were made in the judicial staff.

The first however of these epochs is the year 1166. The changes in the Curia Regis at this date were so great as to call for especial notice from John of Salisbury, even in the height of the Becket controversy; and the Assize of Clarendon, which belongs to the same year, denotes the character of the changes. Yet the Assize of Clarendon was directed to the improvement of provincial justice; and it was carried out, not by a new body of judges, but by two of the king's ministers, the justiciar and the earl of Essex, with the assistance of the sheriffs, who, acting under royal writ as administrators of the new law, still engrossed the title of 'justitiae errantes.' The development of the central jurisdiction is traceable by inference from that of the provincial judicature. The four Exchequer officers who assessed the aid *pur fille marier* in 1168 are found hearing placita and attesting concords shortly after; it follows that they acted not only as taxers but as judges. The six circuits of the tallagers of 1173 were no doubt suggestive of the two circuits of the justices in 1175 and the six circuits of the judges in 1176. It is then to these years, from 1166 to 1176, that we must refer the creation or development of the large staff of judges in the Curia Regis which we find acting in 1178. All the eighteen justices of 1176 were officers of the Exchequer; some of them are found in 1175 holding 'placita Curiae Regis' in bodies of three or four judges, and not in the same combinations in which they took their judicial journeys. We can scarcely help the conclusion that the new jurisprudence was being administered by committees of the general body of justices, who were equally qualified to sit in the Curia and Exchequer and to undertake the fiscal and judicial work of the eyre.

The year 1178 furnishes another epoch. Henry finding that the eighteen judges of the Curia were too many, that they caused entanglements in the business of the court, and expense and distress to the suitors, reduced them at once to five. Some were dismissed perhaps for misconduct; but very many of the existing judges reappear again in functions scarcely distinguishable from those which they had discharged before. Yet the statement of the diminution of their number, which is made by a historian singularly well informed as to the affairs of the court, has considerable significance. From this date we may fix the existence of the sittings of the Curia Regis 'in Banco.' Their proceedings are still nominally transacted 'coram rege,' but nominally only. 'The five are to hear all the complaints of the kingdom and to do right, and not to depart from the Curia Regis.' Questions which are too hard for them are to be referred to the king in person, who will decide them with the advice of the wise men of the kingdom.

The year 1179 witnessed another change, possibly however of persons rather than of system. The great justiciar had resigned, and

Henry had put the office as it were into commission, employing the bishops of Norwich, Ely, and Winchester as heads of three bodies of itinerant judges, each containing two clerks and three knights. A fourth body, to which the northern counties were assigned, contained Ranulf Glanvill, who was to succeed, the next year, to the justiciarship, with five other judges. This fourth committee, according to the chronicler, entered into the place assigned in 1178 to the five judges retained in the Curia; 'these six are the justices constituted in the Curia Regis to hear the complaints of the people:' why the circuit most remote from the capital was assigned to them we are not told, but as the whole business of the eyre was concluded between April 1 and August 27, there could have been no insuperable difficulty.

This is the last notice of the constitution of the Curia Regis which the historians of Henry's reign have preserved to us: and the modifications which are traceable in records from this point to the date of Magna Carta are of personal rather than legal importance. The work of Glanvill furnishes us with the rules of procedure; the Rotuli Curiae Regis which begin in 1194 afford a record of the actual business done, and the names of the judges employed are discoverable from these and other records.

So far then as concerns the framework of the supreme judicature, our conclusion for the present is this: from the year 1179 the sessions of 'justitiarii in Banco' are regularly held in the Curia Regis, nominally but not actually 'coram rege.' These justices are a selection from a much larger staff, before whom Exchequer business is done, and who undertake the work of the circuits: and it would appear probable that the selection was altered from time to time, possibly from year to year. Their work was to hear all suits that were brought before the king, not only criminal but civil, cases in which the revenue or rights of the king were touched, and cases of private litigation with which the king, except as supreme judge, had no concern: all the business in fact which came at a later period before the courts of King's Bench, Exchequer, and Common Pleas. Although their deliberations were not held in the king's presence, they followed his person, or the justiciar in the king's absence; a rule which must have been most burdensome to ordinary suitors, and which accordingly, so far as touches private civil suits or 'communia placita,' was abolished by Magna Carta. The fixing of the Common Pleas at Westminster broke up the unity of the Curia; but it was not until the end of the reign of Henry III that the general staff was divided into three distinct and permanent bodies of judges, each under its own chief.

But the court or courts thus organised must no longer be regarded as the last resource of suitors. The reservation of knotty cases to be decided by the king with the council of his wise men, cases which, as we learn from the Dialogus de Scaccario, included questions of revenue as well as of law in general, continues the ancient personal jurisdiction of the sovereign. The very act that seems to give stability and consistency to the ordinary jurisdiction of the Curia, reduces it to a lower rank. The judicial supremacy of the king is not limited or fettered by the new rule; it has thrown off an offshoot, or, as the astronomical theorists would say, a nebulous envelope, which has rolled up into a compact body, but the old nucleus of light remains unimpaired. The royal justice, diffused through the close personal council, or tempered and adapted by royal grace and equity under the pen of the chancellor, or exercised in the national assembly as in the ancient witenagemot, or concentrated in the hands of an irresponsible executive in the Star Chamber, has for many generations and in many various forms to assert its vitality, unimpaired by its successive emanations.

In tracing the history of the central judicature we have had to anticipate the leading points of interest in the development of the visitatorial jurisdiction. The whole may be briefly summed up. The circuits of the royal officers for fiscal and judicial purposes, which we have traced in the reign of Henry I, continue to have the same character under Henry II, the judicial forms following rather than preceding the fiscal. In 1166 the itinerant court receives new and full instructions from the Assize of Clarendon, but it is still the Curia Regis in progress, a great part of the work being done by the sheriffs. In 1176 six circuits are formed, eighteen judges are specially told off in six detachments, as had been done in the fiscal iter of 1173: in 1178, 1179, and 1180 there seem to be four circuits, and the arrangements in the later years vary between two and six. Under Richard we have still further modifications, and the same in the early years of John, none of them however involving a new principle of construction, but all perhaps implying a restriction of the local jurisdictions of the sheriff and the shiremoot. At last, in the eighteenth clause of Magna Carta, the king undertakes to send two justices four times a year to take the Assizes of Mort d'ancester, Novel disseisin, and Darrein present- ment. This arrangement proved no doubt far too burdensome to be continued, but the changes indicated in the re-issues of the Charter and carried into effect in periodical iters of the judges lie beyond our present inquiry. The justices of the year 1176 are the first to whom the name *Justitiarii Itinerantes* is given in the Pipe Rolls: the commissioners of 1170 are called *Barones errantes:* 'perlustrantes judices' is the term used by the author of Dialogus; the sheriffs were the 'errantes justitiae' known to John of Salisbury in 1159. The various applications of the terms may mark the growth and consolidation of a system by which the sheriffs were deprived of the most important of their functions.

The visits of the itinerant justices form the link between the Curia Regis and the Shire-moot, between royal and popular justice, between the old system and the new. The courts in which they preside are the ancient county courts, under new conditions, but substantially identical with those of the Anglo-Saxon times. The full shire-moot consists, as before, of all the lords of land and their stewards, and the representatives of the townships, the parish priest, the reeve and four men from each; but the times of meet- ing, the sphere of business, and the nature of procedure during the period before us have undergone great and significant changes, some of which can be minutely traced, whilst others can be ac- counted for only by conjecture.

The Anglo-Saxon shire-moot was held twice a year: the county court of Henry I was held as it had been in King Edward's days, that is, according to the 'Leges Henrici I,' twice a year still. Yet in the confirmation of the Great Charter, issued by Henry III in 1217, it is ordered that the county court shall meet not more than once a month, or less frequently where such has been the custom; the sheriff is to hold his tourn twice a year in the hundreds. An edict issued in 1234 further provides that the hundred courts, which under Henry II had been held fortnightly, should be held from three weeks to three weeks, but not under general summons. It is not easy to determine the date or the causes of so great a multiplication of sessions of the shire-moot, unless, as it would be rash to argue, we suppose the sessions of the hundred court to be included in the term *comitatus*. Possibly the sheriffs had abused their power of summoning special meetings and of fining absentees; a custom which comes into prominence in the reign of Henry III, and which shows that it was the direct interest of the sheriffs to multiply the occasions of summons. Possibly it may have arisen from the increase of business under the new system of writs and assizes, which involved the frequent adjournment of the court for short terms: possibly from an earlier usage by which the practice of the county court was assimilated to that of the hundred with the special object of determining suits between litigants from different hundreds or liberties. Or it may have been caused by the gradual withdrawal of the more important suits from the shire-moot, the natural result of which would be the increase of the number of less important meetings for the convenience of petty suitors.

The power of the sheriff, again, had been very much limited, not only by the course of political events noticed in the last chapter, but by the process of centering the administration of justice in the hands of the itinerant justices and the Curia Regis,—a process the stages of which may be more easily traced. At the beginning of the period the sheriffs were the 'errantes justitiae,' only occasionally superseded and superintended by the itinerant justices. As sheriffs, probably, they presided in the court of the county in which the suitors were the judges, and were answerable for the maintenance of the peace: as royal justices they acted under special writ, managed the pleas of the Crown, and conducted the tourn and leet, or the courts which were afterwards so called. In 1166 they were still in the same position; the itinerant justices by themselves, and the sheriffs by themselves, received and acted on the presentment of the grand juries. But from 1170, after the great inquest into their exactions, their authority is more and more limited. In the Assize of Northampton they are rather servants than colleagues of the itinerant justices; in 1194 it is provided that they shall no more be justices in their own counties, and the elective office of coroner is instituted to relieve them from the duty of keeping the pleas of the Crown. In 1195 the duty of receiving the oath of the peace is laid, not on the sheriffs, but on knights assigned in each county, the duty of the sheriffs being only to receive and keep the criminals taken by these knights until the coming of the justices. In 1215 the barons propose that the sheriffs shall no longer meddle with the pleas of the Crown, without the coroners; whilst the Great Charter, in the clause founded on that proposal, forbids either sheriff or coroner to hold such pleas at all. We may question whether these regulations were strictly observed, especially as before the year 1258 the sheriffs seem to be as powerful as ever, but they show a distinct policy of substituting the action of the justices for that of the sheriffs, a policy which might have led to judicial absolutism were it not that the growing institution of trial by jury vested in the freemen of the county far more legal power than it took away from the sheriffs. These officers too had long ceased even remotely to represent the local feeling or interest.

The shire-moot which assembled to meet the itinerant judges was, however, a much more complete representation of the county than the ordinary county court which assembled from month to month. The great franchises, liberties, and manors which by their tenure were exempted from shire-moot and hundred were, before these visitors, on equal terms with the freeholders of the geldable, as the portion of the county was called, which had not fallen into the franchises. Not even the tenants of a great escheat in the royal hands escaped the obligation to attend their visitation. The representation was thoroughly organized: side by side with the reeve and four men of the rural townships appeared the twelve legal men of each of the chartered boroughs which owed no suit to the ordinary county court. In the formation of the jury of presentment the same principle is as clear; each hundred supplies twelve legal men, and each township four, to make report to the justices under the Assize of Clarendon, and in 1194 twelve knights or legal men from each hundred answer for their hundred under all the articles of the eyre, whether criminal, civil, or fiscal. The court thus strengthened and consolidated is adopted by the royal officers as an instrument to be used for other purposes. All who are bound to attend before the itinerant justices are, in the forest counties, compelled to attend the forest courts; and they probably form the 'plenus comitatus' which elects, according to Magna Carta, the knights who are to take the assizes, and the twelve knights who are to inquire into the abuses which Magna Carta was designed to reform.

THE COMMON LAW BACKGROUND
TO REPRESENTATION

It is in the new system of recognition, assizes, and presentments by jury that we find the most distinct traces of the growth of the principle of representation; and this in three ways. In the first place, the institution of the jury was itself based on a representative idea: the jurors, to whatever fact or in whatever capacity they swore, declared the report of the community as to the fact in question. In the second place, the method of inquest was in England brought into close connexion with the procedure of the shire-moot, and thus the inquisitorial process, whether its object was the recognition of a right or the presentment of a criminal, was from the moment of its introduction carried on in association with the previously existing representative institutions, such as were the reeve and four best men, the twelve senior thegns, and the later developments of the same practice which have been just enumerated in our account of the formation of the county court and the usage of legal assessment. In the third place, the particular expedients adopted for the regulation of the inquests paved the way in a remarkable manner for the system of county representation in the parliament as we saw it exemplified on the first occasion of its appearance in the reign of John. The use of election and representation in the courts of law furnished a precedent for the representation of the county by two sworn knights in the national council. On each of these heads some detail is necessary which may throw light incidentally on some kindred points of interest.

The history of the Jury has been treated by various writers from every possible point of view: its natural origin, its historical development, the moral ideas on which it is founded, and the rational analysis of its legal force, have all been discussed many times over with all the apparatus of learning and the acute penetration of philosophical research. Some of these aspects are foreign to our present inquiry. Yet the institution is of so great interest both in itself and in its relations that some notice of it is indispensable.

We have sketched, in an earlier stage of this work, the formation of the primitive German courts: they were tribunals of fully qualified members of the community, a selection it might be from a body of equally competent companions, able to declare the law or custom of the country, and to decide what, according to that custom, should be done in the particular case brought before them. They were not set to decide what was the truth of facts, but to determine what action was to be taken upon proof given. The proof was itself furnished by three means, the oaths of the parties to the suit and their compurgators, the production of witnesses, and the use of the ordeal: the practice of trial by battle being a sort of ultimate expedient to obtain a practical decision, an expedient partly akin to the ordeal as a judgment of God, and partly based on the idea that where legal measures had failed recourse must be had to the primitive law of force,—the feud or right of private war,—only regulated as far as possible by law and regard for the saving of life. For each of these methods of proof there were minute rules and formalities, the infringement or neglect of which put the offender out of court. The complainant addressed his charge to the defendant in solemn traditional form; the defendant replied to the complainant by an equally solemn verbal and logical contradiction. The compurgators swore, with joined hands and in one voice, to the purity and honesty of the oath of their principal. Where the oath was inconclusive, the parties brought their witnesses to declare such knowledge as their position as neighbours had given them; the court determined the point to which the witnesses must swear, and they swore to that particular fact. They were not examined or made to testify all they knew; but swore to the fact on which the judges determined that evidence should be taken. If the witnesses also failed, the ordeal was used. And where the defeated party ventured to impugn the sentence thus obtained, he might challenge the determination of the court by appealing the members of it to trial by combat; or as was the later practice, by applying to the king for a definitive sentence. Trial by combat, however common among some branches of the German stock, was by no means universal, and, as has been pointed out, was not practised among the native English.

In these most primitive proceedings are found circumstances, which on a superficial view seem analogous to later trial by jury: but on a closer inspection they warrant no distinct impression of the kind. The ancient judges who declare the law and give the sentence—the rachinburgii, or the scabini—are not in any respect the jurors of the modern system, who ascertain the fact by hearing and balancing evidence, leaving the law and sentence to the presiding magistrate; nor are the ancient witnesses, who depose to the precise point in dispute, more nearly akin to the jurors who have to inquire the truth and declare the result of the inquiry, than to the modern witnesses who swear to speak not only the truth and nothing but the truth, but the whole truth. The compurgators again swear to confirm the oath of their principal, and have nothing in common with the jury but the fact that they swear. Yet although this is distinctly the case, the procedure in question is a step in the history of the jury: the first form in which the jury appears is that of witness, and the principle that gives force to that witness is the idea that it is the testimony of the community: even the idea of the compurgatory oath is not without the same element; the compurgators must be possessed of qualities and legal qualifications which shall secure their credibility.

Beyond this stage, modified it is true here as elsewhere by different circumstances and local usages, the Anglo-Saxon system did not proceed. The compurgation, the sworn witness, and the ordeal, supplied the proof; and the sheriff with his fellows, the bishop, the shire-thegns, the judices and juratores, the suitors of the court, declared the law. Only in the law of Ethelred, by which the twelve senior thegns in each wapentake are sworn not to accuse any falsely, do we find the germ of a more advanced system, in which the community seems to undertake the duty of prosecution: but the interpretation of the passage is disputed, and its bearing contested, although it seems to imply no more than that the English were not far in arrear of the Frank jurisprudence.

The whole system of recognition by sworn inquest, with the single exception, if it be an exception, which has just been mentioned, was introduced into England by the Normans: the laws of Edward, the Domesday Survey, the fiscal recognitions of the reigns of William Rufus and Henry I, are distinctly a novelty, a part of the procedure of the newly-developed system of government. Various theories have been invented for their origin. Many writers of authority have maintained that the entire jury system is indigenous in England, some deriving it from Celtic tradition based on the principles of Roman law and adopted by the Anglo-Saxons and Normans from the people they had conquered. Others have regarded it as a product of that legal genius of the Anglo-Saxons of which Alfred is the mythic impersonation; or as derived by that nation from the customs of primitive Germany or from their intercourse with the Danes. Nor, even when it is admitted that the system of recognition was introduced from Normandy, have legal writers agreed as to the source from which the Normans themselves derived it. One scholar maintains that it was brought by the Norsemen from Scandinavia; another that it was derived from the processes of the canon law; another that it was developed on Gallic soil from Roman principles; another that it came from Asia through the Crusades, a theory which has little more to recommend it than the still wilder supposition that it is of Slavonic origin, and borrowed by the Angles and Saxons from their neighbours in Northern Europe. But all these theories on examination show that their inventors have either been misled by superficial coincidences, or argue on hypothesis only. The only principle which the systems on which the theories are built have in common is the use of the oath as an instrument of judicial procedure, and this use is universal. The truth seems to be that the inquest by sworn recognitors is directly derived from the Frank Capitularies, into which it may be adopted from the fiscal regulations of the Theodosian Code, and thus own some distant relationship with the Roman jurisprudence. The Karolingian kings issued instructions to their Missi very much as Henry II issued instructions to his itinerant justices, and they gave special commissions of inquiry into fiscal and judicial matters to be answered by the oath of sworn witnesses in the district court. These answers then embodied the belief or knowledge of the local court as representing the community, every qualified member of the community being a member also of the court. The persistence of the inquisitorial system is proved not only by Norman charters and customs, but by the existence of the kindred principle, undeveloped indeed and early forgotten, in the jurisprudence of the rest of France. The order to hold such inquest was a royal, or in Normandy a ducal privilege, although it was executed by the ordinary local officers; primarily it was employed to ascertain the rights and interests of the Crown; by special favour permission was obtained to use it in the concerns of the churches and of private individuals. Even under this system the sworn recognitors were rather witnesses than judges; they swore to facts within their own knowledge; the magistrate to whom the inquiry was entrusted was the inquirer, and he inquired through the oath of men sworn to speak the truth and selected in consequence of their character and local knowledge.

Such was the instrument which, introduced in its rough simplicity at the Conquest, was developed by the lawyers of the Plantagenet period into the modern trial by jury. Henry II expanded and consolidated the system so much that he was not unnaturally regarded as the founder of it in its English character. From being an exceptional favour, it became under his hand a part of the settled law of the land, a resource which was open to every suitor. The recognitions are mentioned by Ralph Niger as one of his expedients of tyranny; by Ranulf Glanvill as a boon conferred by royal benevolence on the people, and with the counsel and consent of the nobles. John, in a charter granted to the church of Beverley, forbids that the rights of that church should be damaged by assizes or recognitions, and adds that the pleas shall be held in the court of the provost as they were in the reign of Henry I, before recognitions or assizes had been ordained in the kingdom. So early had Henry II acquired the fame of having instituted the system, which he had indeed remodelled and made a part of the common right of his subjects, but which had certainly existed under his four predecessors.

The application of the principle to legal matters—for we have already noticed its fiscal use—may be placed under two heads: the inquest in civil matters exemplified in the Great Assize and in the Assizes of Novel disseisin, Mort d'ancestor, Darrein presentment, and others; and the inquest of presentment in criminal matters, which appears in the Assizes of Clarendon and Northampton. The Great Assize is, according to Glanvill, a royal boon by which wholesome provision is made for the lives of men and the integrity of the State, so that in maintaining their right to the possession of their freeholds the suitors may not be exposed to the doubtful issue of trial by battle. This institution proceeds from the highest equity, for the right, which after much and long delay can scarcely be said to be proved by battle, is by the beneficial use of this constitution more rapidly and more conveniently demon-

strated. It is in fact the most distinct mark of the original equity
with which the royal jurisdiction, as civilisation and legal knowledge advanced, was applied to remedy the evils inherent in the
rough and indiscriminating formality of the popular tribunals:
such the inquest had been under the Karolings, such was the
recognition or assize under the Plantagenets. The trial by battle
was in England an innovation; it was one from which the English
recoiled as an instrument associated with tyranny, if not devised
for the purposes of tyrants; and the charters of the boroughs frequently contain a provision, dearly bought no doubt but greatly
valued, that the burghers shall not be liable to its use. In the place
of this barbarous foreign custom, the following machinery is applied; the possessor of the freehold in dispute applies to the Curia
Regis to stop all proceedings in the local courts until a recognition
has taken place as to the right of the claimant: and thereupon a
writ is issued to the sheriff to that effect. The party in possession is
thus said to have placed himself on the assize; and the next step is
taken by the claimant, who demands a writ by which four lawful
knights of the county or neighbourhood shall be empowered to
choose twelve lawful knights of the same neighbourhood, who
shall declare on oath which of the two litigants has the greater
right to the land in question. The writ accordingly is issued, addressed to the sheriff, directing him to summon four knights to
appear at Westminster to choose the twelve. They appear in due
course, and under oath nominate the twelve recognitors, who are
then summoned to appear before the king or his justices prepared
to make their declaration. On the day fixed they present themselves, and the suit proceeds; if the twelve are acquainted with the
circumstances in dispute and are unanimous, the transaction is
complete; they are sworn 'that they will not speak falsehood nor
conceal truth' according to knowledge gained by eye-witness or
'by the words of their fathers and by such words as they are
bound to have such confidence in as if they were their own.' The
declaration made, the sentence is issued. If however the twelve
knights or any of them are ignorant, or if they disagree, others are

to be called in who have the requisite information; and, when the complete number of twelve unanimous witnesses will depose to the fact, their verdict is of the same account. The proceedings in the other assizes are of the same kind, save that the twelve recognitors are nominated by the sheriff himself without the intervention of the four knights electors.

The date of the original enactment of the Great Assize is unknown; but the use of recognition by twelve sworn witnesses is prescribed in the Constitutions of Clarendon for cases of dispute as to lay or clerical tenure. It there appears as a part of the work of the 'capitalis justitia.' From Glanvill it is clear that such litigation might be transacted before the itinerant justices; and the Assize of Northampton of 1176 places among the agenda of the eyre recognitions of the seisin of heirs, and of 'disseisin upon the assize,' under which descriptions we may detect the cases of Mort d'ancester and Novel disseisin. In 1194 the grand jury of the hundred are empowered to act on all the business of the session, in which are included all recognitions and assizes ordered by the king's writ, and even recognitions under the Great Assize where the property in dispute is worth five pounds a year or less. In 1198 the sum is raised to ten pounds, and the elections under the Great Assize are to be made before the itinerant justices. The great charter of John likewise retains the three recognitions of Novel disseisin, Mort d'ancester, and Darrein presentment, to be heard in the quarterly county courts by the justices and four chosen knights: and the charter of 1217 orders the same rule to be observed once a year, except in cases of Darrein presentment, which are reserved for the justices of the bench. The recognitions have become a permanent and regular part of the county business.

The development of the jury of presentment is, after its reconstitution or creation by Henry II, marked by corresponding stages of progress. But its origin is less clear. By some jurists it is brought into close connexion with the system of compurgation, the jurors who present the list of criminals representing the compurgators of the accuser, and the jury which at a later period was impanelled to traverse the presentment representing the compurgators of the accused. Others again connect it with the supposed institution of the collective frankpledge, the corporate responsibility of the tithing, the hundred, and the shire for the production of offenders, which has played so large a part in constitutional theories, but which rests on very slight foundation of fact. The *frithborh* was neither a body of compurgators nor a jury of presentment. As a matter of history it seems lawful to regard the presentment as a part of the duty of the local courts for which an immemorial antiquity may be claimed with at least a strong probability. The leet juries of the small local courts do not draw their origin from any legal enactment, and bear every mark of the utmost antiquity. By them amercements are still made and presentments offered under oath, although their action is restricted and superseded by newer expedients. But their procedure affords some warrant for believing that the twelve senior thegns, who swore in the county court to accuse none falsely, were a jury of presentment. The *juratores synodi*, in the ecclesiastical courts of the ninth century, might furnish a precedent or parallel. If so, the mention of the juratores of the shire and hundred which occurs in the Pipe Roll of Henry I is accounted for, and with it the mention of a criminal jury in the Constitutions of Clarendon. The obscurity of this side of the subject may be regarded as parallel with the scantiness of evidence which we have already noticed as to the recognition. From the year 1166 however the history of the criminal jury is clear. By the Assize of Clarendon inquest is to be made through each county and through each hundred, by twelve lawful men of the hundred and by four lawful men of each township, 'by their oath that they will speak the truth.' By these all persons of evil fame are to be presented to the justices, and then to proceed to the ordeal: if they fail in the ordeal they undergo the legal punishment; if they sustain the ordeal, yet, as the presentment against them is based on the evidence of the neighbourhood on the score of bad character, they are to abjure the kingdom. The jury of presentment is reduced to a still more definite form, and receives a more distinct representative character, in the Assize of Northampton, and in the Articles of Visitation in 1194: in the latter capitulary the plan used for nominating the recognitors of the Great Assize is applied to the Grand Jury, for so the body now constituted may be termed:—'In the first place, four knights are to be chosen from the whole county, who by their oath shall choose two lawful knights of each hundred or wapentake, and those two shall choose upon oath ten knights of each hundred or wapentake, or, if knights be wanting, legal and free men, so that these twelve may answer under all heads concerning their whole hundred or wapentake.' The heads on which they answer include not only the assizes which have been already referred to in connexion with the jury, but all the pleas of the Crown, the trial of malefactors and their receivers as well as a vast amount of fiscal business. The later development of these juries does not fall under our present inquiry, but it may be generally stated thus: at an early period, even before the abolition of ordeal by the Lateran Council of 1215, a petty jury was allowed to disprove the truth of the presentment, and after the abolition of ordeal that expedient came into general use. The further change in the character of the jurors, by which they became judges of fact instead of witnesses, is common to the civil and criminal jury alike. As it became difficult to find juries personally well informed as to the point at issue, the jurors summoned were allowed first to add to their number persons who possessed the requisite knowledge, under the title of afforcement. After this proceeding had been some time in use, the afforcing jurors were separated from the uninformed jurors and relieved them altogether from their character of witnesses. The verdict of the jury no longer represented their previous knowledge of the case, but the result of the evidence afforded by the witnesses of the fact; and they become accordingly judges of the fact, the law being declared by the presiding officer acting in the king's name.

In all these points we see distinctly the growth of a principle of representation, especially applied to the work of the county courts or growing up in them. The 'judicium parium' however, which is mentioned in Magna Carta, has a wider application than this. It covers all cases of amercement in the county, the hundred, and the manorial courts, and exhibits a principle which, rooted in primitive antiquity, is capable of infinite development and beneficial application; and this we have seen exemplified in the assessment processes described above.

It remains then briefly to point out the direct connexion between the jury system and county representation. In the earliest existing records of recognitions, the way in which the jurors are to be selected is not clearly laid down. The recognitions of the Norman reigns are regarded as acts of the county court, and the possibility of election by the suitors is not excluded: it is however more probable that the recognitors were selected by the sheriff, possibly by rotation from a general list, possibly according to their nearness to the spot or acquaintance with the business in hand. On the institution of the assizes of Novel disseisin, Mort d'ancester, and Darrein presentment, the sheriff summoned the requisite number of jurors at his discretion, and the plea was held at a place named in the writ of summons in such a way as to imply that it was to be heard not in the regular county court, but in a special session. The Great Assize was differently constituted: there the sheriff nominated four electors to choose the twelve recognitors, and the trial took place before the justices itinerant in the county, or before the court at Westminster. The articles of 1194 place the election of the recognitors, with all the other business of the eyre, in the hands of the grand jury; those of 1198 direct that it shall take place before the justices in the full county court; Magna Carta completed the process, enacting that the assizes shall be taken quarterly in the county court before two justices sent by the king, and four knights of the county, chosen by the county. The constitution of the grand jury of inquest is similarly developed. The twelve legal knights of the shire, the twelve lawful men of the hundred, and the four men of the township mentioned in the Assize of Clarendon, may have appeared in rotation, or may have been selected by the sheriff or the hundredman or the reeve: but in 1194 they are nominated, through a process of co-optation, by four elected knights. These elected knights may still have been nominated by the sheriff, but it is more probable that they were chosen by the suitors, first because the appointment of coroners, which is directed in the same document, was made by election of the freeholders, and intended as a check on the power of the sheriff; and, secondly, because the term 'eligendi' may be reasonably interpreted by the clause of Magna Carta just referred to. The mode of nominating the grand jury was modified in later practice, and the element of popular election was altogether eliminated; in the period before us, however, it furnishes an important illustration of the usage of election which was so soon to be applied to parliamentary representation. In both the systems of judicial jury we have thus the same result, a body of four knights representing the county court for this special purpose, in one case certainly, and in the other probably, chosen by the county court itself. In the fiscal business we have another analogy; the carucage of 1198 is assessed before a knight and a clerk of the Exchequer acting on behalf of the Crown, and the sheriff and lawful knights 'electi ad hoc' acting on behalf of the shire: it was collected by two knights of the hundred, who paid it to the sheriff, and he accounted for it at the Exchequer.

We are thus prepared for the great executory measure of 1215, under which the articles of the charter were to be carried out by an inquest of twelve sworn knights in each county, chosen in the county court and of the county itself: and we understand the summons to the council at Oxford of 1213, in which the sheriff of each county is ordered to send four discreet men of his county to speak with the king on the business of the realm. In the four discreet men of the shire we detect the old representative idea of the four good men of the township, who appeared in the shire-moot: now they are summoned to a national assembly which is itself a concentration of the county courts. It is not however yet certain whether the four discreet men, the predecessors of the two discreet knights of later times, were on this occasion elected by the shire. On the analogy of the other elections it might be presumed that they were; but the fact that only a week's notice was given to the sheriffs seems to preclude the possibility of a general election. Nor is it necessary to antedate the growth of an institution, when the later steps of its development are distinctly traceable. Whether or no the fourteenth article of the Great Charter intended to provide for a representation of the minor tenants-in-chief by a body of knights elected in the county court, we see now the three principles involved in such representation already in full working, although not as yet distinctly combined for this purpose. We have a system of representation, we have the practice of election, and we have a concentration of the shires in the great council. The struggle of eighty years which followed the act of Runnymede not only had to vindicate the substantial liberties involved in that act, but to sharpen and perfect and bring into effective and combined working every weapon which, forged at different times and for different purposes, could be made useful for the maintenance of self-government. The humble processes by which men had made their by-laws in the manorial courts and amerced the offenders; by which they had assessed the estates or presented the report of their neighbours; by which they had learned to work with the judges of the king's court for the determination of questions of custom, right, justice, and equity, were the training for the higher functions, in which they were to work out the right of taxation, legislation, and political determination on national action.

URBAN GOVERNMENT

The history of the towns presents some points of marked contrast with that of the shires; and these shed light on the later separation of interest between the two classes of communities. The whole period was one of great development in this respect; Henry II and the ministers of his sons encouraged the growth of the mercantile spirit, and reaped the benefit of it in a very great increase of revenue. The privileges of self-government and self-assessment, exemption from the interference of the sheriffs and their arbitrary exactions, the confirmation of guilds, the securing of corporate property, the free election of magistrates, and the maintenance of ancient customs, in many cases to the exclusion of the general reforms, are all of them matters of grant liberally bestowed or sold without reservation. The charters of Richard and John are very numerous; those of Henry II are fewer in number, and do not furnish us with a clue to any progressive policy on the king's part, such as might have been inferred from his general practice in other matters. In those few to which an approximate date can be assigned, the privileges granted are not much greater than was the case in the reign of Henry I: but the Pipe Rolls contain great numbers of instances in which the purchase of additional favours is recorded. In some of these, perhaps, the favour is obtained merely for the single occasion, and in such cases no charter need have been drawn up. In others, where a permanent privilege was bought, the charter in which it was contained must have been lost or destroyed when its importance had been diminished by a new grant of still greater favours. The charters of Richard belong chiefly to his early years, especially to the first year, when he was anxiously raising money for the Crusade. Those of John, however, extend throughout the reign, and, being enrolled among the royal records, have survived in great measure the dangers in which the earlier grants perished. They exhibit the town constitution in almost every stage of development, and in every part of the kingdom. Helston and Hartlepool are alike striving for municipal organisation: one town is rich enough to purchase a constitution like that of Oxford or Winchester, another is too poor or too humble to ask for more than the merchant guild, or the *firma burgi,* or the condition of a free borough. Amongst the more privileged communities great varieties of custom prevail, and provincial laws of considerable antiquity probably underlie the customs of the larger towns. London, Winchester, Oxford, Norwich, and others, appear as typical constitutions on the model of which privileges are granted to the more humble aspirants; and to their practice the newly-enfranchised boroughs are referred, in case of a dispute as to the interpretation of the charter. Thus, beside the common instinct which would lead the mercantile communities to act together in cases in which there was no ground for rivalry, and beside the common privilege which exempted them from the jurisdictions to which their country neighbours were amenable, they possessed in common a quantity of peculiar customs, which kept the *burgenses* of the kingdom as a class by themselves, although they never, as was the case in Scotland and in Germany, adopted a confederate bond of union or organised themselves in leagues. [CHE, 1: 638–669]

&§ Free election of magistrates, independent exercise of jurisdiction in their own courts and by their own customs, and the direct negotiation of their taxation with the officers of the Exchequer, were no unimportant steps in the attainment of municipal independence. Nor was any such step retraced; every new charter confirmed, and many of them rehearsed in detail, the customs allowed by the earlier grants which they superseded.

The city of London still furnishes the type of the most advanced privilege, and the greatest amount of illustrative detail. Yet even the history of London is obscure. We can trace changes in the constitution of the sheriffdom, we have the date of the foundation of the *communa* and the mayoralty; we come upon occasional marks of royal jealousy, and exaggerations of civic independence; we can see two parties at work, the one moved by the court, the other by the municipal instinct; we can discern the points at issue between the rich and the poor. Still these features scarcely blend into a distinct picture, or furnish a consecutive story.

London was represented at the Exchequer, during the first fifteen years of Henry II, by two sheriffs, instead of the four who appeared in 1130, and who reappear in the sixteenth year. In 1174 the smaller number recurs: from 1182 to 1189 only one sheriff acts. At the coronation of Richard I the two sheriffs are Richard Fitz-Reiner and Henry of Cornhell, the latter of whom was Master of the Mint and sheriff of Kent; the former was the head of a great civic family; his father Reiner had been sheriff from 1155 to 1170, and Berengar his grandfather may not improbably have served before him. In the struggle between John and Longchamp in 1191 these two magnates are found on different sides: Richard Fitz-Reiner is the host and supporter of John, Henry, as his duty to the court compelled him, takes the part of the chancellor. When accordingly in the midst of the struggle John took the oath to the communa of London and was followed by the whole body of barons who adhered to him, it is probable that he acted at the suggestion of Richard Fitz-Reiner, and gave completeness to a municipal constitution which had long been struggling for recognition. Immediately after this confirmation of the communa we find Henry the son of Alwyn mayor of London: the sheriffs cease to be the ruling officers, and become merely the financial representatives of the citizens, who are themselves properly the 'fermers' or sheriffs of London and Middlesex. It is a saying among the citizens, that 'come what may, the Londoners should have no king but their mayor.' Henry Fitz-Alwyn is mayor for life; two years after his death, when John, a month before the Great Charter was extorted from him, was buying help on every side, he granted to the 'barones' of the city of London the right of annually electing the mayor. The privilege was ineffectual so far as it was intended to win the support of the Londoners, for a fortnight after it was granted they received the barons with open arms. The duty of sustaining their privileges fell accordingly on the barons: their customs were guaranteed by the thirteenth article of the Charter, and a clause was added preserving like rights to all the cities, boroughs, towns, and seaports of the realm. Lastly, as one of the twenty-five barons chosen to execute the Charter, appears the Mayor of London.

The establishment of the corporate character of the city under a mayor marks the victory of the communal principle over the more ancient shire organisation which seems to have displaced early in the century the complicated system of guild and franchise. It also marks the triumph of the mercantile over the aristocratic element. Henry Fitz-Alwyn may have been an hereditary baron of

London, but his successors, Serlo le Mercer, Ralph Eswy the gold-smith, and others, were clearly tradesmen. It would, doubtless, be unsafe to argue that mercantile pursuits were at this time regarded with anything like contempt in England. The feeling is one of the results of the growth of fictitious and superficial chivalry in the fourteenth century. The men of London had made their pilgrim-ages to Palestine, and fought their sea-fights on the way, in com-pany or in emulation with the noblest of the Norman lords. The story of Gilbert Becket may be fabulous, but Andrew of London and his fellow-citizens in 1147 had done good work for Christen-dom at the capture of Lisbon, the only real success of the second Crusade; and in 1190 William Fitz-Osbert and Geoffrey the goldsmith of London were among the chief men of the fleet which saved the infant kingdom of Portugal from Moorish conquest. The struggle, so far as we can trace it, was not between nobility and trade, but between the territorial franchise and the mercantile guild. Nor was the victory of the communa to any appreciable de-gree a victory of the Englishman over the foreigner. The popula-tion of London was less English probably than that of the other great towns such as Winchester and York. The names of the lead-ing citizens who are mentioned throughout the twelfth century are with few exceptions, such as Henry Fitz-Alwyn, of alien derivation. Richard the son of Reiner the son of Berengar was very probably a Lombard by descent: the influential family of Buc-quinte, Bucca-uncta, which took the lead on many occasions, can hardly have been other than Italian; Gilbert Becket was a Norman. The form of the communa in which the corporate life asserted its independence was itself foreign. From the beginning of its political importance London acts constantly as the purse, sometimes as the brain, never perhaps in its whole history as the heart, of England. The victory of the communa is no guarantee of freedom or fair treatment to the poorer citizens; we no sooner find it in supreme authority than the riot of William Fitz-Osbert occurs to prove that an oligarchy of the purse has as little of tender mercy as an oligarchy of the sword. The real importance of London in this region of history is rather that it affords an example of local independence and close organisation which serves as a model and standard for other towns, than that it leads the way to the attainment of general liberties or peculiarly English objects. Still its position and the action of its citizens give it no small political power, and no insignificant place in history.

CHURCH AND STATE

. . . The clergy in the great struggles of the period, . . . by their vindication of their own liberties showed the nation that other liberties might be vindicated as well, and that there are bounds to the power and violence of princes. They had fought the battle of the people in fighting their own. From them too, as subjects and not merely as churchmen, the first movements towards national action had come. They had bound up the wounds of the perishing State at the accession of Henry II; they had furnished the first if not the only champions of freedom in the royal councils, where S. Thomas, S. Hugh, and Archbishop Geoffrey had had courage to speak where the barons were silent. They had, on the other side, not, it may be fairly allowed, without neglecting their spiritual work, laboured hard to reduce the business of government to something like the order which the great ecclesiastical organisation of the West impressed on every branch of its administration. What the Church had borrowed from the Empire in this respect it repaid with tenfold interest to the rising State system of Europe. And this was especially the case in England. We have seen that the Anglo-Saxon Church made possible and opened the way to national unity: it was the common Church which combined Norman and Englishman in one service, when law and language, land tenure and political influence, would have made them two races of lords and slaves. It was the action of Lanfranc and Anselm that formed the strongest link between the witenagemot of the Confessor and the court and council of the Conqueror and his sons. It was the hard and systematic work of Roger of Salisbury that gave order to the Exchequer and the Curia. The work of Becket as Chancellor is thrown into the shade by his later history, but he certainly was Henry's right hand in the initial reforms of the reign, and the men who carried on those reforms, in a direction contrary to the policy which Becket as archbishop adopted, were men who trod in the footsteps of his earlier life. Hubert Walter, the administrator of Henry's system, who under Richard and John completed the fabric of strong government by means of law, and Stephen Langton, who deserves more than any other person the credit of undoing the mischiefs that arose from that system, maintaining the law by making the national will the basis of the strength of government, were both representative men of the English Church. No doubt there were evils in the secular employments of these great prelates: but if for a time the spiritual work of the Church was neglected, and unspiritual aims fostered within her pale, the State gained immensely by being administered by statesmen whose first ideas of order were based on conscience and law rather than on brute force. Nor was the spiritual part of the work unprovided for. Three archbishops of Canterbury, Anselm, Ralph, and William, all of them belonging to the religious rather than the secular type, had sanctioned the employment of Bishop Roger as justiciar; and without the consent of the Pope, it is said, he refused to bear the title. Innocent III, when he insisted that Hubert Walter should resign the like office, showed that the growing sense of the age forbade what so great a saint as Anselm had connived at; but that growing sense had been educated in great measure by the system which it was soon to discard.

. . . The systematic order of the growing polity was not a little indebted to the fact that there existed in the Church system a set of models of work. The Church had its ranks and degrees, codes of laws and rules of process, its councils and courts, its central and provincial jurisdictions, its peculiar forms of trial and arbitration, its system of writ and record. In a crisis in which representation and election were growing into importance, and in which all forms were manipulated by clerical administrators, the newer forms must needs be moulded in some degree on the older. The legislation of the period, the assizes and constitutions, bear, in common with the Karolingian capitularies, a strong resemblance to ecclesiastical canons, a form which was universal and vigorous when the capitulary was forgotten. The local and territorial divisions of the dioceses made indelible the civil boundaries which feudal aggression would have gladly obliterated. The archdeaconries, deaneries, and parishes preserved the local unities in which they had themselves originated; and the exempt jurisdictions of the convents were in their nature an exact parallel with the franchises of the feudal lords, and, in the case of great ecclesiastical establishments, possessed both characters. The assemblies of the clergy kept up forms that were easily transferred to the local moots: the bishop's visitation was a parallel to that of the sheriff; the metropolitical visitation to that of the Curia or Exchequer; spiritual excommunication was parallel with civil outlawry; clerical procurations with royal purveyance and the payments to the sheriff for his aid; the share of the clergy in determining their assessments suggested the like action on the part of the lay communities, or at least familiarised men with a system of the kind.

In no particular is this more apparent than in the very important question of election and representation. In the latter point we shall be able to trace, as we proceed, very close analogies: the fact that the early representative members in the national council were frequently, if not always, invested with the character of procurators or proxies, bearing letters of credence or ratification that empowered them to act on behalf of their constituents, suggests at once that the custom was borrowed from the ecclesiastical practice, of which such procuratorial representation was a familiar part, in negotiation with the Holy See, and in the formation of Church councils at home. The appearance of the proctors of the cathedral and diocesan clergy in the central assemblies of Church and State precedes by a few years the regular incorporation of the knights of the shire in parliament; and Convocation as well as the House of Commons owes its representative character to the great period of definition, the reign of Edward I. In the case of election the connexion is perhaps less close: but there can be little doubt that the struggles for ecclesiastical freedom of election kept in use forms which made the extension of elective liberty possible in other quarters. The Church recognised three modes of election: the 'via compromissi,' by which the electors deputed to a small committee of their body—an uneven number, three or five—the function of choosing the bishop or abbot; the 'via scrutinii,' in which the several votes were taken in order and the choice determined by the majority; and the 'via inspirationis Spiritus Sancti,' in which at one moment, and in one breath, the whole body uttered the name of the same person, just as in the court of justice the compurgators took their oath. The last-mentioned method in its exact form was of course inapplicable to the cases of popular election; but the acclamations of the crowd of suitors at the county court represents a similar idea; the show of hands corresponds with the 'via scrutinii;' and the 'via compromissi' has its parallel doubtless in the gradual reservation of the choice of members, both in town and shire, to a small deputed body, who in the former case finally engrossed the right of election.   [CHE, I: 672–679]

⋙ We have now, however imperfectly, traced the process of events by which the English nation had reached that point of conscious unity and identity which made it necessary for it to act as a self-governing and political body, a self-reliant and self-sustained nation,—a power in Europe, basing its claims for respect not on the accidental position or foreign acquisitions of its kings, but on its own internal strength and cohesion, its growth in good government, and its capacity for a share in the common polity of Christendom. We have also tried to trace the process by which its internal organisation has been so framed, modified, and strengthened, that when the occasion came it was able to answer to the strain: by which, when the need of representative institutions made itself felt, the mere concentration and adaptation of existing machinery supplied all that was required. The century that follows Magna Carta was an age of growth, of luxuriant, even premature, development, the end of which was to strengthen and likewise to define the several constituent parts of the organic whole. The three estates made their way, through this time of training, to a realisation of their distinct identity, and gained such a consciousness of their distinct spheres of work as enabled them to act without entanglement of machinery or waste of power. The constitution which reached its formal and definite maturity under Edward I had to learn easy and economic working under his successors. In that lesson it had also severe experiences of struggle, defect, and failure: its representative men lose the grace and simplicity of the earlier times; personal and territorial aims waste the energies of the better and wiser, and divide into permanent factions the ignorant and more selfish. Yet the continuity of life, and the continuity of national purpose, never fails: even the great struggle of all, the long labour that extends from the Reformation to the Revolution, leaves the organisation, the origin of which we have been tracing, unbroken in its conscious identity, stronger in the strength in which it has preserved, and grown mightier through trial. The further investigation of this history, in its political as well as in its mechanical aspect, must begin from Magna Carta as a new starting-point.   [CHE, I: 681–682]

V

THE SHAPING OF THE PARLIAMENTARY CONSTITUTION (1216–1307)

The Comparative History of European Representative Government

⚜ The idea of a constitution in which each class of society should, as soon as it was fitted for the trust, be admitted to a share of power and control, and in which national action should be determined by the balance maintained between the forces thus combined, never perhaps presented itself to the mind of any medieval politician. The shortness of life, and the jealousy inherent in and attendant on power, may account for this in the case of the practical statesman, although a long reign like that of Henry III might have given room for the experiment; and, whilst a strong feeling of jealousy subsisted throughout the middle ages between the king and the barons, there was no such strong feeling between the barons and the commons. But even the scholastic writers, amid their calculations of all possible combinations of principles in theology and morals, well aware of the difference between the 'rex politicus' who rules according to law and the tyrant who rules without it, and of the characteristics of monarchy, aristocracy and democracy, with their respective corruptions, contented themselves for the most part with balancing the spiritual and secular powers, and never broached the idea of a growth into political enfranchisement. Yet, in the long run, this has been the ideal towards which the healthy development of national life in Europe has constantly tended, only the steps towards it have not been taken to suit a preconceived theory. The immediate object in each case has been to draw forth the energy of the united people in some great emergency, to suit the convenience of party or the necessities of kings, to induce the newly admitted classes to give their money, to produce political contentment, or to involve all alike in the consciousness of common responsibility.

The history of the thirteenth century fully illustrates this. Notwithstanding the difference of circumstances and the variety of results, it is to this period that we must refer, in each country of Europe, the introduction, or the consolidation, for the first time since feudal principles had forced their way into the machinery of government, of national assemblies composed of properly arranged and organised Estates. The accepted dates in some instances fall outside the century. The first recorded appearance of town representatives in the Cortes of Aragon is placed in 1162; the first in Castille in 1169. The general courts of Frederick II in Sicily were framed in 1232: in Germany the cities appear by deputies in the diet of 1255, but they only begin to form a distinct part under Henry VII and Lewis of Bavaria; in France the States General are called together first in 1302. Although in each case the special occasions differ, the fact that a similar expedient was tried in all, shows that the class to which recourse was for the first time had was in each country rising in the same or in a proportional degree, or that the classes which had hitherto monopolised power were in each country feeling the need of a reinforcement. The growth of the towns in wealth and strength, and the decline of properly feudal ideas in kings, clergy and barons, tended to the momentary parallelism. The way in which the crisis was met decided in each country the current of its history. In England the parliamentary system of the middle ages emerged from the policy of Henry II, Simon de Montfort and Edward I; in France the States General were so managed as to place the whole realm under royal absolutism; in Spain the long struggle ended in the sixteenth century in making the king despotic, but the failure of the constitution arose

directly from the fault of its original structure. The Sicilian policy
of Frederick passed away with his house. In Germany the disruption of all central government was reflected in the Diet; the national paralysis showed itself in a series of abortive attempts, few
and far between, at united action, and the real life was diverted
into provincial channels and dynastic designs.

The parliamentary constitution of England comprises, as has
been remarked already, not only a concentration of local machinery but an assembly of estates. The parliament of the present
day, and still more clearly the parliament of Edward I, is a combination of these two theoretically distinct principles. The House of
Commons now most distinctly represents the former idea, which is
also conspicuous in the constitution of Convocation, and in that
system of parliamentary representation of the clergy which was an
integral part of Edward's scheme: it is to some extent seen in the
present constitution of the House of Lords, in the case of the representative peers of Ireland and Scotland, who may also appeal for
precedent to the same reign. It may be distinguished by the term
local representation as distinct from class representation; for the
two are not necessarily united, as our own history as well as that of
foreign countries abundantly testifies. In some systems the local
interest predominates over the class interest; in one the character
of delegate eclipses the character of senator; in another all local
character may disappear as soon as the threshold of the assembly is
passed; in one there may be a direct connexion between the local
representation and the rest of the local machinery; in another the
central assembly may be constituted by means altogether different
from those used for administrative purposes, and the representative
system may be used as an expedient to supersede unmanageable
local institutions; while, lastly, the members of the representative
body may in one case draw their powers solely from their delegate
or procuratorial character, and in another from that senatorial
character which belongs to them as members of a council which
possesses sovereignty or a share of it. The States General of the
Netherlands under Philip II were a mere congress of ambassadors

from the provincial estates; the States General of France under Philip the Fair were a general assembly of clergy, barons, and town communities, in no way connected with any system of provincial estates, which indeed can hardly be said to have existed at the time. In Germany the representative elements of the Diet, —the prelates, counts and cities,—had a local arrangement and system of collective as distinct from independent voting; and in the general cortes of Aragon the provincial estates of Aragon, Catalonia and Valencia, were arranged in three distinct bodies in the same chamber. Nor are these differences confined to the systems which they specially characterise. The functions of a local delegate, a class representative, and a national counsellor, appear more or less conspicuously at the different stages of parliamentary growth, and according as the representative members share more or less completely the full powers of the general body. A detailed examination of these differences however lies outside our subject, and in the constitutional history of foreign nations the materials at our command are insufficient to supply a clear answer to many of the questions they suggest.

An assembly of Estates is an organised collection, made by representation or otherwise, of the several orders, states or conditions of men, who are recognised as possessing political power. A national council of clergy and barons is not an assembly of estates, because it does not include the body of the people, 'the plebs,' the simple freemen or commons, who on all constitutional theories have a right to be consulted as to their own taxation, if on nothing else. So long as the prelates and barons, the tenants-in-chief of the crown, met to grant an aid, whilst the towns and shires were consulted by special commissions, there was no meeting of estates. A county court, on the other hand, although it never bore in England the title of provincial estates, nor possessed the powers held by the provincial estates on the continent, was a really exhaustive assembly of this character.

The arrangement of the political factors in three estates is common, with some minor variations, to all the European constitutions, and depends on a principle of almost universal acceptance. This classification differs from the system of caste, and from all divisions based on differences of blood or religion, historical or prehistorical. It is represented by the philosophic division of guardians, auxiliaries and producers, of Plato's Republic. It appears, mixed with the idea of caste, in the *edhilingi*, *frilingi*, and *lazzi* of the ancient Saxons. In Christendom it has always taken the form of a distinction between clergy and laity, the latter being subdivided according to national custom into noble and non-noble, patrician and plebeian, warriors and traders, landowners and craftsmen. The English form, clergy, lords and commons, has a history of its own which is not quite so simple, and which will be noticed by and by. The variations in this classification when it is applied to politics are numerous. The Aragonese cortes contained four brazos, or arms, the clergy, the great barons or ricos hombres, the minor barons, knights or infanzones, and the towns. The Germanic diet comprised three colleges, the electors, the princes, and the cities, the two former being arranged in distinct benches, lay and clerical. The Neapolitan parliament, unless our authorities were misled by supposed analogies with England, counted the prelates as one estate with the barons, and the minor clergy with the towns. The Castilian cortes arranged the clergy, the *ricos hombres*, and the *communidades*, in three estates. The Swedish diet was composed of clergy, barons, burghers and peasants. The Scottish parliament contained three estates, prelates, tenants-in-chief great and small, and townsmen, until James I, in 1428, in imitation of the English system, instituted commissioners of shires, to supersede the personal appearance of the minor tenants-in-chief; then the three estates became the lords, lay and clerical, the commissioners of shires, and the burgesses, these throughout their history continued to sit in one house. In France, both in the States General and in the provincial estates, the division is into 'gentz de l'eglise,' 'nobles,' and 'gentz des bonnes villes.' In England, after a transitional stage, in which the clergy, the greater and smaller barons, and the cities and boroughs, seemed likely to adopt the system used in Aragon and Scotland, and another in which the county and borough communities continued to assert an essential difference, the three estates of clergy, lords, and commons, finally emerge as the political constituents of the nation, or, in their parliamentary form, as the lords spiritual and temporal and the commons. This familiar formula in either shape bears the impress of history. The term 'commons' is not in itself an appropriate expression for the third estate; it does not signify primarily the simple freemen, the plebs, but the plebs organised and combined in corporate communities, in a particular way for particular purposes. The commons are the 'communitates' or 'universitates,' the organised bodies of freemen of the shires and towns; and the estate of the commons is the 'communitas communitatum,' the general body into which for the purposes of parliament those communities are combined. The term then, as descriptive of the class of men which is neither noble nor clerical, is drawn from the political vocabulary, and does not represent any primary distinction of class. The communities of shires and boroughs are further the collective organisations which pay their taxes in common through the sheriffs or other magistrates, and are represented in common by chosen knights or burgesses; they are thus the represented freemen as contrasted with the magnates, who live among them but who are specially summoned to parliament, and make special terms with the Exchequer; and so far forth they are the residue of the body politic, the common people, so called in a sense altogether differing from the former. It is not to be forgotten, however, that the word 'communitas,' 'communauté,' 'la commune,' has different meanings, all of which are used at one time or another in constitutional phraseology. In the coronation oath 'la communauté,' 'vulgus,' or folk, that chooses the laws, can be nothing but the community of the nation, the whole three estates: in the Provisions of Oxford 'le commun de la terre' can only be the collective nation as represented by the barons, in other words the governing body of the nation, which was not yet represented by chosen deputies; whilst in the Acts of Parliament, in which 'la commune' appears with 'Prelatz et

Seigneurs' as a third constituent of the legislative body, it can mean only the body of representatives. The inconsistency of usage is the same in the case of the boroughs, where 'communitas' means sometimes the whole body of burghers, sometimes the governing body or corporation, sometimes the rest of the freemen, as in the form 'the mayor, aldermen, and commonalty.' As ordinarily employed then the title of 'commons' may claim more than one derivation, besides that which history supplies.

The commons are the third estate: between the clergy and baronage the question of precedency would scarcely arise, but it is clear from the arrangement of the estates in the common constitutional formulae, both in England and in other countries, that a pious courtesy gave the first place to the clergy. For the term first or second estate there does not seem to be any sufficient early authority. It is scarcely necessary to add that on no medieval theory of government could the king be regarded as an estate of the realm. He was supreme in idea if not in practice; the head, not a limb, of the body politic; the impersonation of the majesty of the kingdom, not one of several co-ordinate constituents.

[CHE, II: 166–176]

The Rise of Parliament

◄§ It is obvious that, notwithstanding the great admissions and concessions of the Charter, in the hands of a strong, irresponsible, and unscrupulous king, all would be a dead letter unless supported by an authority that could limit the actions of the monarch within the bounds of law and public expedience. Nor could any council nominated by the king himself have authority strong enough even if inclined so to limit his power and compel the observance of his promises. An assembly was required which should represent the taxpayers and check public expenditure by drawing the purse strings close or relaxing them in emergency—a council, moreover, which should fairly represent the wealth and wisdom of the coun-

try as well as the land, and so should be able to advise and compel
the redress of grievances, draw up bills for the king to authorise as
laws, and see to their execution, not by minute interference, but
by securing the responsibility of the king's ministers. Now, such
an institution could not grow up all at once, nor were all the parts
of its machinery instituted with a direct view to the ends which in
process of time they were made to serve. Our constitution in parliament is not the creation of any one mind or the expedient of any
one crisis.

There was, as we have seen, a general council and assembly of
the people in Anglo-Saxon times, called the witenagemot, or meeting of the wise. It was attended by the king and the bishops and
ealdormen of the shires; perhaps by the thanes of higher rank, each
in a manner representing the freemen under his protection, but not
either an elected nor a theoretically representative assembly. The
witenagemot regulated the amount of taxation, enacted laws, heard
appeals, and acted as council to the king in all measures domestic
and foreign. With the Anglo-Saxon dynasty the witenagemot
passed away. But the early Norman kings, well aware that none of
their dependants dare lift up a finger against them, assembled a similar court every year at the great festivals, and made a show of
consulting them on measures on which the apparent concurrence
of the country seemed desirable, so that the notion of a great national council was never lost. As the power of the king was weak-
ened either by personal character or by quarrels such as Henry
II's with his family and the church, it became necessary to the
monarch to gain the real as well as the apparent support of his
council. True, the council was composed of his feudal dependants,
but these were now becoming quickly rather united with the body
of the people by sympathy and affinity than slavishly bound to a superior who always when strong enough was an oppressor. Stephen
was elected king by a parliament of this sort, and compelled to
grant a charter. Henry II made use of it to pass all his great measures: the constitutions of Clarendon, the council of Northampton,
in which Becket was tried, and the great parliament of Northamp-

ton of 1176, to which I have referred as passing the statutes by which the assize of novel disseisin was established. Richard I also held parliaments at Pipewell before his crusade, and at Winchester after his return. John was elected king by a parliament to the prejudice of his nephew Arthur; and if it had not been for his subsequent cruel conduct to him, would never have been counted as a usurper. Magna Carta was forced upon him by the great council of the king, which was becoming, and soon to be, the great council of the nation.

This council, court, or parliament was composed of very different ingredients from those which we look on as necessary to a constitutional assembly. It was, for instance, but one chamber; lords and commons were not divided; nor was the representation of the commons anything like what it was shortly to become. It seems that it was little more than the assembly of the king's feudal tenants; the barons holding their estates directly from him, the bishops and abbots not appearing by virtue of their wisdom as in the Anglo-Saxon witenagemot, but as tenants in barony of the crown. But besides the barons, that is those noble landholders who held sufficient fiefs to entitle them to the baronage, there were smaller holders also, holding directly by knight service of the king. These, by the breaking up of the original great fiefs, and by subinfeudations where the principal fief had become forfeit or escheated, had become very numerous by the time of King John, so numerous that it was desirable for their own sakes that they should not be put to the expense of attending parliament, and that it was desirable for the parliament's sake that it should not be overcrowded with unwise and inexperienced countrymen. There are records extant which tend to show that these smaller tenants, holding directly of the crown, were on some occasions represented in parliament by certain elected out of their number—knights of the shire, as they were called—even as early as the reign of John; but it does not appear that their presence was thought necessary to the constitution of parliament until the forty-ninth year of Henry III, 1265. In that year the arrangement by representation, to which I have referred, became a part of the parliament; two knights were summoned from every shire to represent the body of the county. It is a matter of doubt among lawyers by whom these county members or knights of the shire were elected. Perhaps, at first, it was only by the tenants *in capite*, the lords of manors; but later, as the distinction between these and ordinary freeholders became less and less, all the freeholders joined in the election, until, in the eighth year of Henry VI., 1430, an act was passed which, reciting that elections of knights of shires have now of late been made by very great outrageous and excessive number of people dwelling within the same shires, of the which most part were people of small substance and of no value, confines the elective franchise to freeholders of lands or tenements to the value of forty shillings. There is reason to believe that before the passing of this act the county members were elected not by the freeholders only in whom the right was vested, but by all persons whatever who came to the county court.

The representation of the towns in parliament dates from the same year, 1265. Before that time there are no trustworthy traces of any such thing; but then Simon de Montfort ordered the sheriffs to return two citizens or burgesses for every city or borough contained within their shires. . . . In 1265, fifty years after the signing of Magna Carta, the principle was admitted by the summoning of the borough members, that town and country alike ought not to be taxed without their own consent. These borough members were no doubt from the beginning elected properly by the burgage tenants; but the privilege easily fell into the hands of the managing body, the corporation, by whom in some cases it was retained even until the Reform Bill. But, you will ask, how came it about that this year 1265 was signalised by so great an event; and who was Simon de Montfort, who had the wisdom or policy to found so exceedingly important a part of the institutions of the country as the house of commons? To clear up this, we must return to the accession of Henry III. He came to the crown, as you know, very young: as people who come early into their property, he learned habits of extravagance; he had a large connection of half-brothers and sisters. So had his wife. She was extravagant too. The pope was sorely in want of money, for he was an extravagant pope; or, rather, there was a run of them, and no money to be got but out of the English nation. In vain were the Jews forced to ransom their teeth; in vain were the clergy taxed to the very utmost, and the livings of the church given away to pay the pope's debts. Money could not be got; and so the kingdom went on for no less than forty years, the king begging, borrowing, and extorting all he could get from the parliament, and spending it quicker than he got it. The barons, who then constituted the parliament, kicked very hard: sometimes they refused money altogether, but generally were persuaded or forced to give in after a remonstrance that the king ought not to undertake wars and expenses without their knowledge and advice, and expect them to pay for them. At length, however, things came to a head. King and pope together were too much for English patience. In 1255 Pope Innocent IV offered the kingdom of Sicily to Henry's second son, Edmund. Without asking the advice of his people the king accepted the offer, and borrowed money of the pope to pay the expense of the war in which it involved him. The pope had not the power to secure the kingdom of Sicily to his nominee; that nominee was brought forward merely to gratify his personal dislike to the house of Frederick II. No result followed as far as Sicily is concerned, except the spending of the 14,000 marks for which Henry had pawned the credit of the kingdom. Judge of the indignation with which, in this year 1257, the king was received by the parliament when he informed them that, without advising with them, he had pledged their honour to repay the money; that his son Edmund was made a king at their expense; and that the pope had granted him the tenths and first-fruits of all benefices in England. The nobility of the realm were indignant to think that one man's folly should thus bring them to ruin. It was not so much the amount, though that was very great, as the principle that was at stake; grant this, and another year might see them sold to the Jews. The barons insisted that a council of twenty-four persons should be nominated, half by the king and half by themselves, to reform the state of the kingdom. In consequence, a council of state was formed, with Simon de Montfort, earl of Leicester, the king's brother-in-law, at the head, which named the chancellor, justiciar, and great officers, and assumed all the functions of government. The king and the prince of Wales swore to this constitution, called the Provisions of Oxford; but the foreign favourites, who had been enriched by Henry's lavishness, refused, and seceded to France.

Matters remained in this uneasy state for about a year, when, in 1260, King Henry being on a visit to France, in which he sold Normandy to the French, the prince of Wales began to hire mercenaries; De Montfort quarrelled with the other lords, and a civil war broke out. In 1261 the king repudiated the new constitution, seized the Tower, and held it with troops against the country. From the Tower next year he went to France, and on his return swore again to the Provisions of Oxford, but brought back his foreign relations, who were particularly disagreeable to the English, and in 1263 provoked another outbreak. The barons consented to an arbitration; the king of France was to decide, and he decided that the Provisions of Oxford should be abolished, but that an amnesty should be declared, and that the people should preserve their ancient liberties. This very fair decision offended both sides, and directly after war broke out in earnest. On May 13, 1264, at the battle of Lewes the king and the prince were taken prisoners, and De Montfort became virtually the ruler in the name of Henry. The pope excommunicated the barons and all who adhered to the Provisions; and this is the triumphant moment when De Montfort assembled the parliament on its present basis—two knights from every county, two burgesses from every city and borough.

[LEEH, 346–350]

⇜§ Important as this assembly is in the history of the constitution, it was not primarily and essentially a constitutional assembly. It was not a general convention of the tenants-in-chief, or of the three estates, but a parliamentary assembly of the supporters of the existing government. This was a matter of necessity. It would have been a mere mockery to summon the men who were on the other side of the channel uttering anathemas or waiting for an opportunity of invasion. Archbishop Boniface therefore was not cited, nor the other bishops who were avowedly hostile. The archbishop of York, the bishops of Durham and Carlisle, ten abbots and nine priors of the northern province, ten bishops and four deans of the southern were summoned, and by a later writ, issued December 24 at Woodstock, fifty-five abbots, twenty-six priors, and the heads of the military orders: a sufficient proof that the clergy as a body were on the side of the earl. With the baronial body this was not the case; only five earls (Leicester, Gloucester, Norfolk, Oxford, and Derby) were summoned, and with them only eighteen barons, of whom ten had acted with Simon in the arbitration of Amiens. But the great feature of the parliament was the representation of the shires, cities, and boroughs: each sheriff had a writ ordering him to return two discreet knights from each shire; a like summons addressed to the cities and boroughs ordered two representatives to be sent from each, and the barons of the Cinque Ports had a similar mandate. The writs to the cities and boroughs are not addressed to them through the sheriff of the county, as was the rule when their representatives became an integral part of the parliament, and so far the proceedings of Simon do not connect themselves directly with the machinery of the county courts; nor is there any order for the election of the representatives, but the custom of election was so well established that it could not have been neglected on this occasion.   [CHE, II: 96–97]

§ The tide of fortune soon turned. This same year De Montfort fell at the battle of Evesham. But his great work did not perish. The system he had introduced was found too effective and too strong to be dispensed with. He himself, although a foreigner, was looked on as a popular martyr; although excommunicated, he was canonised by the national affection; and his tomb was visited by the pious country people for ages as the scene of wonderful miraculous cures. It is remarkable that the very barons, who from their dislike to De Montfort had restored Henry to the crown, forced upon him when victorious the most important of the Provisions of Oxford. The long reign of Henry is remarkable for the fact that during its convulsions Magna Carta was suffered to last untouched, nay was confirmed by several special confirmations extorted from the king in consideration of the subsidies that he could not dispense with. The principle was firmly established that money should not be had without consent of parliament; and parliament was founded on a reasonable principle, a lasting basis.

The reign of Edward I saw these principles strengthened by constant trial. This king, like his father, was an extravagant prince; unlike him, he was a faithful and honourable man.   [LEEH, 350]

◄§ Edward was by instinct a lawgiver, and he lived in a legal age, the age that had seen Frederick II legislating for Sicily, Lewis IX for France, and Alfonso the Wise for Castille . . . . Legal reforms . . . have gained for Edward the title of the English Justinian; a title which, if it be meant to denote the importance and permanence of his legislation and the dignity of his position in legal history, no Englishman will dispute.

A comparison of the legislation of Edward I with that of Henry II brings out conclusively the fact that the permanent principles of the two were the same; that the benefits of a sound administration of the law conferred by the first were adapted by his great-grandson to the changed circumstances and amplified to suit the increasing demands of a better educated people. The principle of restricting the assumptions of the clergy, which, although enunciated by the Conqueror, had in the Norman polity been neutralised by the practical independence of the church-courts and by the arbitrary action of the kings, had been made intelligible in the Constitutions of Clarendon. The institution of scutage had disarmed the feudal lords whilst it had compelled them to a full performance of their duties either in arms or in money; the assize of arms had entrusted the defence of the country to the people at large and placed arms in the hands of all. The extension of the itinerant judicature in like manner had broken down the tyranny of the feudal franchises and brought the king's justice within the reach of all. The intervening century had seen these three points contested, now extended, now restricted, sometimes enforced and sometimes obstructed; but the course of events had amply justified the principles on which they rested. Edward's statute 'de religiosis' and the statute of Carlisle prove his confidence in Henry's theory, that the church of England as a national church should join in bearing the national burdens and should not risk national liberty or law by too great dependence on Rome. What the statute 'de religiosis' was to the church the statute 'quia emptores' was to feudalism; but it was only one of a series of measures by which Edward attempted to eliminate the doctrine of tenure from political life. Henry had humbled the feudatories, Edward did his best to bring up the whole body of landowners to the same level, and to place them in the same direct relation to the crown, partly no doubt that he might, as William the Conqueror had done at Salisbury, gather the whole force and counsel of the realm under his direct control, but chiefly that he might give to all alike their direct share and interest in the common weal. Hence the policy of treating the national and the feudal force alike; the extension of compulsory knighthood from the tenants-in-chief to all landowners of sufficient means; hence the expansion of the assize of arms by the statute of Winchester. The legal reforms of the statutes of Westminster and Gloucester bear the same relation to the assizes of Clarendon and Northampton, the inquest of 1274 and the 'quo warranto' of 1279 to the inquest of sheriffs in 1170. Edward's legislation was no revolution, nor in its main principles even an innovation; the very links which connect it with that of Henry II are traceable through the reign of Henry III; the great mark of his reign, the completion of the parliamentary constitution by which an assembly of estates, a concentration of all national energies, was substituted for a court and council of feudal tenants, was the result of growth rather than of sudden resolution of change. But he contributed an element that marks every part of his policy, the definition of duties and spheres of duty, and the minute adaptation of means to ends. [CHE, II: 109–111]

⋙ How far the events of [Edward's] reign justify us in regarding him as an original worker, as founder, reviver or reformer of the Constitution,—with what moral intention he worked, for the increase of his power, for the retention of it, or for the benefit of his people,—it is scarcely within the province of the historian to determine. Personally he was a great king, although not above being tempted to ambition, vindictiveness, and impatient violence. He was great in organising: every department of administration felt his guiding and defining hand. The constitution of parliament which was developed under his hands remains, with necessary modifications and extensions, the model of representative institutions at this day. His legislation is the basis of all subsequent legislation, anticipating and almost superseding constructive legislation for two centuries. His chief political design, the design of uniting Britain under one crown, premature as it was at the moment, the events of later ages have fully justified. [CHE, II: 165]

⋙ [In 1295] Edward took the last formal step which established the representation of the commons. On the 30th of September and on the 1st of October he issued writs for a parliament to meet on the 13th of November at Westminster. The form of summons addressed to the prelates is very remarkable, and may almost be regarded as a prophetic inauguration of the representative system. It begins with that quotation from the Code of Justinian . . . which was transmuted by Edward from a mere legal maxim into a great political and constitutional principle: 'As the most righteous law, established by the provident circumspection of the sacred princes, exhorts and ordains that that which touches all shall be approved by all, it is very evident that common dangers must be met by measures concerted in common:' the whole nation, not merely Gascony, is threatened: the realm has already been invaded; the English tongue, if [the French king] Philip's power is equal to his malice, will be destroyed from the earth: your interests, like those of your fellow citizens, are at stake. The writs to the barons and sheriffs are shorter but in the same key. The assembly constituted by them is to be a perfect council of estates; the archbishops and bishops are to bring the heads of their chapters, their archdeacons, one proctor for the clergy of each cathedral, and two for the clergy of each diocese. Every sheriff is to cause two knights of each shire, two citizens of each city, and two burghers of each borough, to be elected and returned. Seven earls and forty-one barons have special summons. The purpose of the gathering and the time of notice are definitely expressed, as the great charter prescribed. The share of each estate in the forthcoming deliberation is marked out; the clergy and the baronage are summoned to treat, ordain, and execute measures of defence; and the representatives of the commons are to bring full power from their several constituencies to execute, 'ad faciendum,' what shall be ordained by common counsel. This was to be a model assembly, bearing in its constitution evidence of the principle by which the summons was dictated, and serving as a pattern for all future assemblies of the nation.   [CHE, II: 133–134]

⋙ [Edward, particularly in 1296–1297] wanted . . . to reign despotically, and the country not only would not let him, but compelled him to confirm Magna Carta, with the additional clauses that no taxes whatever should be taken without consent of the realm, save the ancient aids and prisage; tallages are abolished, and the toll upon wool, which had formerly been exacted by prerogative, was released. This great confirmation—a second and more effective Magna Carta—was granted in the 25th [year] of Edward I, 1297. It was obtained in the usual way: the king was waging war abroad, the people were oppressed with taxation at home; the barons met together and refused to serve in the war or to grant any money for it. Edward was forced to give way. The names of these great liberators are: Roger Bigod, earl of Norfolk; Humphrey Bohun, earl of Essex; and Robert Winchelsey, archbishop of Canterbury. From this moment English liberty may be considered achieved.

The weak reign of Edward II gave it time to grow; the civil war weakening the royal authority without being waged at all for purposes of liberation. Liberty profited by the quarrels of those who united might have oppressed her.

The reign of Edward III established three great principles by bringing them into actual usage: 1. That it was illegal to raise money without consent of the nation; 2. That both lords and commons should agree before an act should become law; 3. The commons established their right of inquiring into public abuses and impeaching public counsellors. All this was done quietly, without bloodshed or an appeal to popular violence.   [LEEH, 350–351]

The Foundations of
Thirteenth-Century Constitutionalism

⋙§ On a review of the circumstances of the great struggle which forms the history of England during the thirteenth century, and after realising as well as we can the constitution that emerges when the struggle is over, a question naturally arises as to the comparative desert of the actors, their responsibility for the issue, and the character of their motives. It is not easy to assign to the several combatants, or the several workers, their due share in the result. The king occupies the first place in the annals; the clergy appear best in the documentary evidence, for they could tell their own tale; the barons take the lead in action; the people are chiefly conspicuous in suffering. Yet we cannot suppose either that the well-proportioned and well-defined system which we find in existence at the death of Edward I grew up without a conscious and intelligent design on the part of its creators, or that the many plans which, under his father, had been tried and failed, failed merely because of the political weakness or accidental ill-success of their promoters. Comparing the history of the following ages with that of the past, we can scarcely doubt that Edward had a definite idea of government before his eyes, or that that idea was successful because it approved itself to the genius and grew out of the habits of the people. Edward saw, in fact, what the nation was capable of, and adapted his constitutional reforms to that capacity. But, although we may not refuse him the credit of design, it may still be questioned whether the design was altogether voluntary, whether it was not forced upon him by circumstances and developed by a series of successful experiments. And in the same way we may question whether the clerical and baronial policy was a class policy, the result of selfish personal designs, or a great, benevolent, statesmanlike plan, directed towards securing the greatness of the country and the happiness of the people.

First, then, as to the king . . . the result of the royal action upon the constitution during the thirteenth century was to some extent the work of design; to some extent an undesigned development of the material which the design attempted to mould and of the objects to which it was directed; to some extent the result of compulsion, such as forced the author of the design to carry out his own principles of design even when they told against his momentary policy and threatened to thwart his own object in the maintenance of his design. Each of these factors may be illustrated by a date; the design of a national parliament is perfected in 1295; the period of development is the period of the organic laws, from 1275 to 1290; the date of the compulsion is 1297. The complete result appears in the joint action of the parliaments of Lincoln in 1301 and of Carlisle in 1307.

The design, as interpreted by the result, was the creation of a national parliament, composed of the three estates, organised on the principle of concentrating local agency and machinery in such a manner as to produce unity of national action, and thus to strengthen the hand of the king, who personified the nation.

This design was perfected in 1295. It was not the result of compulsion, but the consummation of a growing policy. Edward did not call his parliament, as Philip the Fair called the States General, on the spur of a momentary necessity, or as a new machinery invented for the occasion and to be thrown aside when the occasion was over, but as a perfected organisation, the growth of which he had for twenty years been doing his best to guide. Granted that he had in view the strengthening of the royal power, it was the royal power in and through the united nation, not as against it, that he designed to strengthen. In the face of France, before the eyes of Christendom, for the prosecution of an occasional war with Philip, for the annexation of Wales and Scotland, or for the recovery of the Holy Sepulchre, a strong king must be the king of a united people. And a people, to be united, must possess a balanced constitution, in which no class possesses absolute and independent power, none is powerful enough to oppress without remedy. The necessary check on an aspiring priesthood and an aggressive baronage, the hope and support of a rising people, must be in a king too powerful to yield to any one class, not powerful enough to act in despite of all, and fully powerful only in the combined support of all. Up to the year 1295 Edward had these ends steadily in view; his laws were directed to the limitation of baronial pretensions, to the definition of ecclesiastical claims, to the remedy of popular wrongs and sufferings. The peculiar line of his reforms, the ever-perceptible intention of placing each member of the body politic in direct and immediate relation with the royal power, in justice, in war, and in taxation, seems to reach its fulfilment in the creation of the parliament of 1295, containing clergy and people by symmetrical representation, and a baronage limited and defined on a distinct system of summons.

But the design was not the ideal of a doctrinaire, or even of a philosopher. It was not imposed on an unwilling or unprepared people. It was the result of a growing policy exercised on a growing subject-matter. There is no reason to suppose that at the beginning of his reign Edward had conceived the design which he completed in 1295, or that in 1295 he contemplated the results that arose in 1297 and 1301. There was a development co-operating with the unfolding design. The nation, on whom and by whom he was working, had now become a consolidated people, aroused by the lessons of his father's reign to the intelligent appreciation of their own condition, and attached to their own laws and customs with a steady though not unreasoning affection, jealous of their privileges, their charters, their local customs, unwilling that the laws of England should be changed. The reign of Henry III, and the first twenty years of Edward, prove the increasing capacity for self-government, as well as the increased desire and understanding of the idea of self-government. The writs, the laws, the councils, the negotiations, of these years have been discussed in this and the preceding chapter: they prove that the nation was becoming capable and desirous of constitutional action; the capacity being proved by the success of the king's design in using it, the conscious desire by the constant aspiration for rights new or old.

The adaptability of his people to the execution of his design may well have revealed to Edward the further steps towards the perfection of his ideal. The national strength was tried against Wales, before Scotland opened a scene of new triumphs, and the submission of Scotland encouraged the nation to resist Wales, Scotland, and France at once. In the same way the successful management of the councils of 1283 and 1294 led to the completion of the parliament in 1295. In each case the development of national action had led to the increase of the royal power. Edward could not but see that he had struck the very line that must henceforth guide the national life. The symmetrical constitution, and the authoritative promulgation of its principle, mark the point at which the national development and the fullest development of Edward's policy for his people met. He was successful because he built on the habits and wishes and strength of the nation, whose habits, wishes, and strength he had learned to interpret.

But the close union of 1295 was followed by the compulsion of 1297: out of the organic completeness of the constitution sprang the power of resistance, and out of the resistance the victory of the principles, which Edward might guide, but which he failed to coerce. With the former date then the period closes during which the royal design and the national development work in parallel lines or in combination; henceforth the progress, so far as it lies within the compass of the reign, is the resultant of two forces differing in direction, forces which under Edward's successors became stronger and more distinctly divergent in aim and character. It seems almost a profanation to compare the history of Edward I with that of John; yet the circumstances of 1297 bear a strong resemblance to those of 1215: if the proceedings of 1297 had been a fair example of Edward's general dealings with his people, our judgment of his whole life must have been reversed. They were, however, as we have seen, exceptional; the coincidence of war at home and abroad, the violent aggression of Boniface VIII, and the bold attempt at feudal independence, for which the earls found their opportunity in the king's difficulties, formed together an exigency, or a complication of exigencies, that suggested a practical dictatorship: that practical dictatorship Edward attempted to grasp; failing, he yielded gracefully, and kept the terms on which he yielded.

In an attempt to ascertain how far Edward really comprehended the constitutional material on which he was working, and formed his idea according to the capacity of that material, we can scarcely avoid crediting him with measures which he may have inherited, or which may have been the work of his ministers. Little as can be said for Henry III himself, there was much vitality and even administrative genius in the system of government during his reign. Local institutions flourished, although the central government languished under him. Some of his bad ministers were among the best lawyers of the age. Stephen Segrave, the successor of Hubert de Burgh, was regarded by Bracton as a judge of consummate authority; Robert Burnell and Walter de Merton, old servants of Henry, left names scarcely less remarkable in their own line of work than those of Grosseteste and Cantilupe. No doubt these men had much to do with Edward's early reforms. We can trace the removal of Burnell's influence in the more peremptory attitude which the king assumed after his death, and the statesmanship of the latter years of the reign is coloured by the faithful but less enlightened policy of Walter Langton. But, notwithstanding all this, the marks of Edward's constitutional policy are so distinct as to be accounted for only by his own continual intelligent supervision. If his policy had been only Burnell's, it must have changed when circumstances changed after Burnell's death, as that of Henry VIII changed when Cromwell succeeded Wolsey; but the removal of the minister only sharpens the edge of the king's zeal. His policy, whatever were his advisers, is uniform and progressive. That he was both well acquainted with the machinery of administration, and possessed of constructive ability, is shown by the constitutions which he drew up for Wales and Scotland: both bear the impress of his own hand. The statute of Wales not only shows a determination closely to assimilate that country to England in its institutions, to extend with no grudging hand the benefits of good government to the conquered province, but furnishes an admirable view of the local administration to which it was intended to adapt it. The constitution devised for Scotland is an original attempt at blending the Scottish national system as it then existed with the general administration of the empire, an attempt which in some points anticipates the scheme of the union which was completed four centuries later. A similar conclusion may be drawn from Edward's legislation: it is not the mere registration of unconnected amendments forced on by the improvement of legal knowledge, nor the innovating design of a man who imagines himself to have a genius for law, but an intelligent development of well-ascertained and accepted principles, timed and formed by a policy of general government. So far, certainly, Edward seems qualified to originate a policy of design.

But was the design which he may be supposed to have originated the same as that which he finally carried out? Was the design which he actually carried out the result of an unimpeded constructive policy, or the resultant of forces which he could combine but could not thwart? Was it a policy of genius or of expediency? It may be fairly granted that the constitution, as it ultimately emerged, may not have been that which Edward would have chosen. Strong in will, self-reliant, confident of his own good-will towards his people, he would have no doubt preferred to retain in his own hands, and in those of his council, the work of legislation, and probably that of political deliberation, while his sense of justice would have left the ordinary voting of taxation to the parliament as he constructed it in 1295 out of the three estates. Such a constitution might have been more like that adopted by Philip the Fair in 1302 than like that embodied in the statement of parliament in 1322, or enunciated by Edward himself in his answer to the pope. The importance actually retained by the council in all the branches of administration proves that a simple parliamentary constitution would not have recommended itself to Edward's own mind. On the other hand, his policy was far more than one of expediency. It was diverted from its original line no doubt by unforeseen difficulties. Edward intended to be wholly and fully a king, and he struggled for power. For twenty years he acted in the spirit of a supreme lawgiver, admitting only the council and the baronage to give their advice and consent. Then political troubles arose and financial troubles. The financial exigencies suggested rather than forced a new step, and the commons were called to parliament. In calling them he not only enunciated the great principle of national solidarity, but based the new measure on the most ancient local institutions. He did not choose the occasion, but he chose the best means of meeting the occasion consonant with the habits of the people. And when he had taken the step he did not retrace it. He regarded it as a part of a new compact that faith and honour forbad him to retract. And so on in the rest of his work. He kept his word and strengthened every part of the new fabric by his own adhesion to its plan, not only from the sense of honour, but because he felt that he had done the best thing. Thus his work was crowned with the success that patience, wisdom, and faith amply deserve, and his share in the result is that of the direction of national growth and adaptation of the means and design of government to the consolidation and conscious exercise of national strength. He saw what was best for his age and people; he led the way and kept faith.

Thus he appears to great advantage even by the side of the great kings of his own century. Alfonso the Wise is a speculator and a dreamer by the side of his practical wisdom; Frederick II a powerful and enlightened self-seeker in contrast with Edward's laborious self-constraint for the good of his people. S. Lewis, who alone stands on his level as a patriot prince, falls below him in power and opportunity of greatness. Philip the Fair may be as great in constructive power, but he constructs only a fabric of absolutism. The legislation of Alfonso is the work of an innovator who, having laid hold on what seems absolute perfection of law, accepts it without examining how far it is fit for his people and finds it thrown back on his hands. Frederick legislates for the occasion; in Germany to balance opposing factions, in Italy to crush the liberty of his enemies or to raise the privileges of his friends: S. Lewis legislates for the love of his people and for the love of justice, but neither he nor his people see the way to reconcile freedom with authority. These contrasts are true if applied to the Mainzer-recht or the Constitutions of Peter de Vineis, the Establishments of S. Lewis or the Siete Partidas. Not one of these men both saw and did the best thing in the best way: and not one of them founded or consolidated a great power.

In estimating the share of the baronage in the great work there is the difficulty, at the outset, of determining the amount of action which is to be ascribed to persons and parties. In Henry III's reign we compare, without being able to weigh, the distinct policies of the Marshalls, of the earls of Chester and Gloucester, Bohun and Bigod. Even the great earl of Leicester [Simon de Montfort] appears in different aspects at different parts of his career, and the great merit of his statemanship is adaptative rather than originative: what he originates perishes, what he adapts survives. In the earlier period the younger Marshalls lead the opposition to the crown partly from personal fears and jealousies, but mainly on the principles of Runnymede; they perish however before the battle. The earl of Chester, the strongest bulwark of the royal power, is also its sharpest critic, and, when his own rights are infringed, its most independent opponent; his policy is not that of the nation but of the great feudal prince of past times. The earls of Gloucester, father and son, neither of them gifted with genius, try to play a part that genius only could make successful: like Chester, conscious of their feudal pretensions, like the Marshalls, ready to avail themselves of constitutional principles to thwart the king or to overthrow his favourites. In their eyes the constitutional struggle was a party contest: should the English baronage or the foreign courtiers direct the royal councils. There was no politic or patriotic zeal to create in the national parliament a properly-balanced counterpoise to royal power. Hence, when the favourites were banished, the Gloucesters took the king's side; when the foreigners returned, they were in opposition. They may have credit for an unenlightened but true idea that England was for the English, but on condition that the English should follow their lead. They have the credit of mediating between the English parties and taking care that neither entirely crushed the other. Further, it would seem absurd to ascribe to the Gloucesters any statesmanlike ability corresponding to their great position. The younger earl, the Gilbert of Edward I's reign, is bold and honest, but erratic and self-confident, interesting rather personally than politically. To Leicester alone of the barons can any constructive genius be ascribed; and as we have seen, owing to the difficulty of determining where his uncontrolled action begins and ends, we cannot define his share in the successive schemes which he helped to sustain. That he possessed both constructive power and a true zeal for justice cannot be denied. That with all his popularity he understood the nation, or they him, is much more questionable: and hence his greatest work, the parliament of 1265, wants that direct relation to the national system which the constitution of 1295 possesses. In the aspect of a popular champion, the favourite of the people and the clergy, Simon loses sight of the balance of the constitution; an alien, he is the foe of aliens; owing his real importance to his English earldom, he all but banishes the baronage from his councils. He is the genius, the hero of romance, saved by his good faith and righteous zeal. Bohun and Bigod, the heroes of 1297, are but degenerate sons of mighty fathers; greater in their opportunity than in their patriotism; but their action testifies to a traditional alliance between barons and people, and recalls the resistance made with better reason and in better company by their forefathers to the tyranny of John. We cannot form a just and general judgment on the baronage without making these distinctions. On the whole, however, it must be granted that, while the mainspring of their opposition to Henry and Edward must often be sought in their own class interests, they betray no jealousy of popular liberty, they do not object to share with the commons the advantages that their resistance has gained, they aspire to lead rather than to drive the nation; they see, if they do not fully realise, the unity of the national interest whenever and wherever it is threatened by the crown.

It is in the ranks of the clergy that we should naturally look, considering the great men of the time, for a moderate, constructive policy. The thirteenth century is the golden age of English churchmanship. The age that produced one Simon among the earls, produced among the bishops Stephen Langton, S. Edmund, Grosseteste, and the Cantilupes. The Charter of Runnymede was drawn under Langton's eye; Grosseteste was the friend and adviser of the constitutional opposition. Berksted, the episcopal member of the electoral triumvirate, was the pupil of S. Richard of Chichester: S. Edmund of Canterbury was the adviser who compelled the first banishment of the aliens; S. Thomas of Cantilupe, the last canonised Englishman, was the chancellor of the baronial regency.

These men are not to be judged by a standard framed on the experience of ages that were then future. It is an easy and a false generalisation that tells us that their resistance to royal tyranny and the aid that they gave to constitutional growth were alike owing to their desire to erect a spiritual sovereignty and to depress all dominion that infringed upon their own liberty of tyrannising. The student of the history of the thirteenth century will not deny that the idea of a spiritual sovereignty was an accepted principle with both clerk and laymen. The policy of the papal court had not yet reduced to an absurdity the claims put forth by Gregory VII and Innocent III. It was still regarded as an axiom that the priest-hood which guided men to eternal life was a higher thing than the royalty which guided the helm of the temporal state: that the two swords were to help each other, and the greatest privilege of the state was to help the church. Religious liberty, as they understood it, consisted largely in clerical immunity. But granting that principle,—and until the following century, when the teaching of Ockham and the Minorites, the claims of Boniface VIII and their practical refutation, the quarrel of Lewis of Bavaria and John XXII, the schism in the papacy, and the teaching of Wycliffe, had opened the eyes of Christendom, that principle was accepted,—it is impossible not to see, and ungenerous to refuse to acknowledge, the debt due to men like Grosseteste. Grosseteste, the most learned, the most acute, the most holy man of his time, the most devoted to his spiritual work, the most trusted teacher and con-fidant of princes, was at the same time a most faithful servant of the Roman Church. If he is to be judged by his letters, his leading principle was the defence of his flock. The forced intrusion of for-eign priests, who had no sympathy with his people and knew nei-ther their ways nor their language, leads him to resist king and pope alike; the depression of the priesthood, whether by the plac-ing of clergymen in secular office, or by the impoverishment of ecclesiastical estates, or by the appointment of unqualified clerks to the cure of souls, is the destruction of religion among the laity. Taxes and tallages might be paid to Rome when the pope needed it, but the destruction of the flock by foreign pastors was not to be endured. It may seem strange that the eyes of Grosseteste were not opened by the proceedings of Innocent IV to the impossibility of reconciling the Roman claims with his own dearest principles: pos-sibly the idea that Frederick II represented one of the heads of the Apocalyptic Beast, or the belief that he was an infidel plotting against Christendom, affected his mental perspicacity. Certainly as he grew older his attitude towards the pope became more hostile. But he had seen during a great part of his career the papal influence employed on the side of justice in the hands of Innocent III and Honorius III. Grosseteste's attitude towards the papacy however was not one of unintelligent submission. The words in which he expresses his idea of papal authority bear a singular resemblance to those in which Bracton maintains the idea of royal authority. The pope could do no wrong, for if wrong were done by him he was not acting as pope. So the king as a minister of God can only do right; if he do wrong, he is acting not as a king but as a minister of the devil. In each case the verbal quibble contains a virtual negation: and the writer admits without identifying a higher principle than authority. But it is not as a merely ecclesiastical politician that Grosseteste should be regarded. He was the confidential friend of Simon de Montfort, and the tutor of his children. He was more than once the spokesman of the constitutional party in parliament, and he was the patron of the friars who at the time represented learning and piety as well as the doctrines of civil independence in the Universities and country at large. Bolder and more persevering than S. Edmund, he endured the same trials, but was a less conspicuous object of attack and gained greater success.

Grosseteste represents a school of which S. Richard of Chichester and his disciple Berksted, with archbishops Kilwardby and Peckham, were representatives; a school, part of whose teaching descended through the Franciscans to Ockham and the Nominalists, and through them to Wycliffe. The baronial prelate was of another type. Walter of Cantilupe no doubt had his sympathies with the English baronage as well as with the clergy and was as hostile to the alien favourites of the court as to the alien nominees of Rome. A man like Thomas of Cantilupe united in a strong degree the leading principles of both schools; he was a saint like Edmund, a politician like his uncle, and a bishop like Grosseteste. Another class, the ministerial prelate, such as was bishop Raleigh of Winchester, was forced into opposition to the crown rather by his personal ambitions or personal experiences than by high principle: the intrusion of the foreigner into the court and council was to him not merely the introduction of foreign or lawless procedure, but the exclusion from the rewards that faithful service had merited; and his feeling, as that of Becket had been, was composed, to a large extent, of a sense of injury amounting to vindictiveness. Yet even such men contributed to the cause of freedom, if it were only by the legal skill, the love of system, and ability for organisation, which they infused into the party to which they adhered.

The opposition of the English clergy to the illegal aggressions of the crown in his father's reign taught Edward I a great lesson of policy. He at all events contrived to secure the services of the best of the prelates on the side of his government, and chose for his confidential servants men who were fit to be rewarded with high spiritual preferment. The career of Walter de Merton proves this: another of his great ministers, bishop William of March, was in popular esteem a candidate for canonisation and a faithful prime minister of the crown. Walter Langton, the minister of his later years, earned the gratitude of the nation by his faithful attempts to keep the prince of Wales in obedience to his father, and to prevent him taking the line which finally destroyed him. Of archbishop Winchelsey we have already seen reason to believe that he was an exceptional man, in a position the exceptional character of which must affect our judgments of both himself and the king. If the necessities of the case excuse the one, they excuse the other. He also was a man of learning, industry, and piety, and, if he did not play the part of a patriot as well as Stephen Langton had done, it must be remembered that he had Edward and not John for his opponent, Boniface and not Innocent for his pope. But on the whole perhaps the feeling of the English clergy in the great struggle should be estimated rather by the behaviour of the mass of the body than by the character of their leaders. The remonstrances of the diocesan and provincial councils are more outspoken than the letters of the bishops, and the faithfulness of the body of the clergy to the principles of freedom is more distinctly conspicuous than that of the episcopal politicians: the growing life of the Universities, which towards the end of the century were casting off the rule of the mendicant orders and influencing every class of the clergy both regular and secular, tended to the same end; and, although, in tracing the history of the following century, we shall have in many respects to acknowledge decline and retrogression, we cannot but see that in the quarrels between the crown and the papacy, and between the nation and the crown, the clergy for the most part took the right side. Archbishops Stratford and Arundel scarcely ever claim entire sympathy, but they gained no small advantages to the nation, and few kings had better ministers or more honest advisers than William of Wykeham.

If we ask, lastly, what was the share of the people, of the commons, of their leading members in town and shire, our review of the history furnishes a distinct if not very circumstantial answer. The action of the people is to some extent traceable in the acts of the popular leader. Simon de Montfort possessed the confidence of the commons: the knightly body threw itself into the arms of Edward in 1259 when it was necessary to counteract the oligarchic policy of the barons: the Londoners, the men of the Cinque Ports, the citizens of the great towns, the Universities under the guidance of the friars, were consistently on the side of liberty. But history has preserved no great names or programmes of great design proceeding from the third estate. Sir Robert Thwenge the leader of the anti-Roman league in 1232, and Thomas son of Thomas who led the plebeians of London against the magnates, scarcely rise beyond the reputation of local politicians. Brighter names, like that of Richard Sward, the follower of Richard Marshall, are eclipsed by the brilliance of their leaders. It was well that the barons and the bishops should furnish the schemes of reform, and most fortunate that barons and bishops were found to furnish such schemes as the people could safely accept. The jealousy of class privilege was avoided, and personal influence helped to promote a general sympathy. The real share of the commons in the reformed and remodelled constitution is proved by the success of its working, by the growth of the third estate into power and capacity for political action through the discipline of the parliamentary system; and the growth of the parliamentary system itself is due to the faithful adhesion and the growing intelligence of the third estate.

Let then the honour be given where it is due. If the result is a compromise, it is one made between parties which by honesty and patriotism are entitled to make with one another terms which do not give to each all that he might ask; and justly so, for the subjects on which the compromise turns, the relations of Church and State, land and commerce, tenure and citizenship, homage and allegiance, social freedom and civil obligation, are matters on which different ages and different nations have differed in theory, and on which even statesmen and philosophers have failed to come to a general conclusion alike applicable to all ages and nations as the ideal of good government. [CHE, II: 303–318]

VI

THE PRESERVATION OF
THE CONSTITUTION
(1307–1485)

The Character of Late Medieval Government
and Civilization in England

❧ Between the despotism of the Plantagenets and the despotism of the Tudors lies a period of three eventful centuries. The first of these we have now traversed; we have traced the course of the struggle between the crown and the nation, as represented by its leaders in parliament, which runs on through the thirteenth century, and the growth of the parliamentary constitution into theoretical completeness under Edward I. Another century lies before us, as full of incident and interest as the last, although the incident is of a different sort, and the men around whom the interest gathers are of very different stature and dissimilar aims. We pass from the age of heroism to the age of chivalry, from a century ennobled by devotion and self-sacrifice to one in which the gloss of superficial refinement fails to hide the reality of heartless selfishness and moral degradation—an age of luxury and cruelty. This age has its struggles, but they are contests of personal and family faction, not of great causes; it has its great constitutional results, but they seem to emerge from a confused mass of unconscious agencies rather than from the direct action of great lawgivers or from the victory of acknowledged principles. It has however its place in the history of the Constitution; for the variety and the variations of the transient struggles serve to develop and exercise the strength of the permanent mechanism of the system; and the result is sufficiently distinct to show which way the balance of the political forces, working in and through that mechanism, will ultimately incline. It is a period of private and political faction, of foreign wars, of treason laws and judicial murders, of social rebellion, of religious division, and it ends with a revolution which seems to be only the determination of one bloody quarrel and the beginning of another.

But this revolution marks the growth of the permanent institutions. It is not in itself a victory of constitutional life, but it places on the throne a dynasty which reigns by a parliamentary title, and which ceases to reign when it has lost the confidence of the commons. The constitutional result of the three reigns that fill the fourteenth century is the growth of the House of Commons into its full share of political power; the recognition of its full right as the representative of the mass and body of the nation, and the vindication of its claim to exercise the powers which in the preceding century had been possessed by the baronage only. The barons of the thirteenth century had drawn the outline of the system by which parliament was to limit the autocracy of the king. Edward I had made his parliament the concentration of the three estates of his people; under Edward II, Edward III, and Richard II, the third estate claimed and won its place as the foremost of the three. The clergy had contented themselves with their great spiritual position, and had withdrawn from parliament; the barons were no longer feudal potentates with class interests and exclusive privileges that set them apart from king and commons alike. The legal reforms of Edward I and the family divisions which originated under Edward III changed the baronial attitude in more ways than one: in the constitutional struggle the great lords were content to act as leaders and allies of the commons or as followers of the court; in the dynastic struggles they ranged themselves on the side of the family to which they were attached by traditional or territorial ties; for the royal policy had placed the several branches of the divided house at the head of the great territorial parties which adopted and discarded constitutional principles as they chose.

In this aspect the fourteenth century anticipates some part of the history of the fifteenth; the party of change is only accidentally and occasionally the party of progress; constitutional truths are upheld now by one, now by another, of the dynastic factions; Edward II defines the right of parliament as against the aggressive Ordinances, and the party of the Red Rose asserts constitutional law as opposed to the indefeasible right of the legitimate heir, even when the cause of national growth seems to be involved in the success of the White Rose. Both sides look to the commons for help, and, while they employ the commons for their own ends, gradually place the decision of all great questions irrevocably in their hands. The dynastic factions may be able alternately to influence the elections, to make the house of commons now royalist now reforming, one year Yorkist and one year Lancastrian, but each change helps to register the stages of increasing power. The commons have now gained a consolidation, a permanence and a coherence which the baronage no longer possesses. The constitution of the house of commons, like that of the church, is independent of the divisions and contests that vary the surface of its history. A battle which destroys half the baronage takes away half the power of the house of lords: the house of commons is liable to no such collapse. But the battle that destroys half the baronage leaves the other half not so much victorious, as dependent on the support of the commons. The possession of power rests ultimately with that estate which by its constitution is least dependent on personal accident and change. It gains not so much because the party which asserts its right triumphs over that which denies it, as because it stands to some extent outside the circle of the factions whose contests it witnesses and between which it arbitrates. All that is won by the parliamentary opposition to the crown is won for the commons; what the baronage loses by the victory of the crown over one or other of its parties is lost to the baronage alone. The whole period witnesses no great struggle between the lords and the com-

mons, or the result might have been different. There was a point at
which the humiliation of the baronage was to end in such an exal-
tation of the royal power as left the other two estates powerless;
and with the baronage fell or seemed to fall the power of parliament. But the commons had a vitality which subsisted even when
the church, deprived of the support of united Christendom, lay at
the feet of Henry VIII, and a new baronage had to be created out
of the ruins of the two elder estates. And when under the Stewarts
the time came for the maturity of national organisation to stand
face to face with the senility of medieval royalty, the contest was
decided as all previous history pointed the way and subsequent history justified. But we do not aspire to lead on our narrative to so
distant a consummation, and the discussion for the present lies
within much narrower limits.

It was natural that a system thus gaining in power and capacity
should gain in definiteness of organisation. The growth of the
house of commons, as well as of the parliamentary machinery generally, during the fourteenth century, is marked by increased
clearness of detail. With its proceedings more carefully watched,
and more jealously recorded, more conscious of the importance of
order, rule, and precedent, it begins to possess what may be called
a literature of its own, and its history has no longer to be gleaned
from the incidental notices of writers whose eyes were fixed on
other matters of interest, or from documents that presume rather
than furnish a knowledge of the processes from which they result.
The vast body of Parliamentary Writs affords from henceforth a
sufficient account of the personal and constitutional composition
of each parliament: the Rolls of Parliament preserve a detailed
journal of the proceedings, from which both the mode and the
matter of business can be elucidated, and the increasing bulk of the
statute-book gives the permanent result.   [CHE, II: 319–322]

&§ It is usual to compare Richard II with Edward II, but it is
perhaps more germane to our subject to view him side by side
with Edward III, the magnanimous, chivalrous king who had left
him heir to difficulties which he could not overcome and a theory

of government which could never be realised. Edward II had no kingly aspirations, Richard had a very lofty idea of his dignity, a very distinct theory of the powers, of the functions, and of the duties of royalty. It is true that they were both stay-at-home kings in an age which would tolerate royal authority only in the person of a warrior; but while Edward from idleness or indisposition for war stopped abruptly in the career which his father had marked out for him, when all chances were in his favour and one success-ful campaign might have given him peace throughout his reign, Richard during the time that he was his own master was bound by truces which honour forbade him to break, and if he had broken them would have had to contend with the opposition of a parlia-ment always ready to agree that he should go to war, but never willing to furnish the means of waging war with a fair hope of vic-tory. The legislation again of the reign of Richard is marked by real policy and intelligible purpose: Edward II can scarcely be said to have legislated at all: everything that is distinctive in the statutes of his reign was forced upon him by the opposition. Nor, singu-larly parallel as the circumstances of the deposition in the two cases were, can we overlook the essential difference, that the one was the last act of a drama the interest of which depends on mere personal questions, the other the decision of a great struggle, a pitched battle between absolute government and the cause of na-tional right. The reign of Edward III was the period in which the forces gathered. The magnificence of an extravagant court, the shifty, untrustworthy statecraft of an unprincipled, lighthearted king, living for his own ends and recking not of what came after him, careless of popular sorrows unless they were forced upon him as national grievances, careless of royal obligation save when he was compelled to recognise it as giving him a claim for pecuniary support,—these formed the influences under which Richard was educated; and the restrictions of his early years caused him to give an exaggerated value to the theory which these influences had inculcated. Richard cannot be said to have been the victim of his grandfather's state policy, because he himself gave to the causes that destroyed him both their provocation and their opportunity; but he reduced to form and attempted to realise in their most definite form the principles upon which his grandfather had acted. Edward III was a great warrior and conqueror, the master of his own house and liable to no personal jealousies or rivalries in his own dominion; Richard was a peaceful king thwarted at every turn of his reign by ambitious kinsmen. But Edward was content with the substance of power, Richard aimed at the recognition of a theory of despotism, and, as has so often happened both before and since the assertion of principles brought on their maintainer a much severer doom than befell the popular autocrat who had practised them, however little he was loved or trusted.   [CHE, II: 534-536]

⤢ The struggle between royal prerogative and parliamentary authority does not work out its own issue in the fate of Richard II; the decision is taken for the moment on a side issue,—the wrongs of Henry of Lancaster; the judicial condemnation of Richard is a statement not of the actual causes of his deposition, but of the offences by which such a measure was justified. Prematurely Richard had challenged the rights of the nation, and the victory of the nation was premature. The royal position was founded on assumptions that had not even prescription in their favour; the victory of the house of Lancaster was won by the maintenance of rights which were claimed rather than established. The growth of the commons, and of the parliament itself in that constitution of which the commons were becoming the strongest part, must not be estimated by the rights which they had actually secured, but by those which they were strong enough to claim, and wise enough to appreciate. If the course of history had run otherwise, England might possibly have been spared three centuries of political difficulties; for the most superficial reading of history is sufficient to show that the series of events which form the crises of the Great Rebellion and the Revolution might link themselves on to the theory of Richard II as readily as to that of James I. In that case we might have seen the forces of liberty growing by regular stages as the pretensions of tyranny took higher and higher flights, until the struggle was fought out in favour of a nation uneducated and untrained for the use of the rights that fell to it, or in favour of a king who should know no limit to the aspirations of his ambition or to the exercise of his revenge. The failure of the house of Lancaster, the tyranny of the house of York, the statecraft of Henry VII, the apparent extinction of the constitution under the dictatorship of Henry VIII, the political resurrection under Elizabeth, were all needed to prepare and equip England to cope successfully with the principles of Richard II, masked under legal, religious, philosophical embellishments in the theory of the Stewarts. Hence it is that in our short enumeration of the points at issue we are obliged to rest content with recording the claims of parliament rather than to pursue them to their absolute vindication: they were claimed under Edward III, they were won during the Rebellion, at the Restoration, or at the Revolution: some of them were never won at all in the sense in which they were first claimed; parliament does not at the present day elect the ministers, or obtain the royal assent to bills before granting supplies; but the practical responsibility of the ministers is not the less assured, and the crown cannot choose ministers unacceptable to the parliament, with the slightest probability of their continuing in office. If the development of the ministerial system had been the only point gained by the delay of the crisis for three centuries, from 1399 to 1688, England might perhaps have been content to accept the responsibility of becoming a republic in the fifteenth century. Had that been the case, the whole history of the nation, perhaps of Europe also, would have been changed in a way of which we can hardly conceive. Certainly the close of the fourteenth century was a moment at which monarchy might seem to be in extremis, France owning the rule of a madman, Germany nominally subject to a drunkard,—the victim, the tyrant, and the laughing-stock of his subjects,—and the apostolic see itself in dispute between two rival successions of popes. That the result was different may be attributed, for one at least out of several reasons, to the fact that the nations were not yet ready for self-government.

The fourteenth century had other aspects besides that in which we have here viewed it, aspects which seem paradoxical until they are viewed in connexion with the general course of human history, in which the ebb and flow of the life of nations is seen to depend on higher laws, more general purposes, the guidance of a Higher Hand. Viewed as a period of constitutional growth it has much to attract the sympathies and to interest the student who is content laboriously to trace out the links of causes and results. In literary history likewise it has a very distinct and significant place; and it is scarcely second to any age in its importance as a time of germination in religious history. In these aspects it might seem to furnish sufficient and more than sufficient matters of attractive disquisition. Yet it is on the whole unattractive, and in England especially so: the political heroes are, as we have seen, men who for some cause or other seem neither to demand nor to deserve admiration; the literature with few exceptions owes its interest either to purely philological causes or to its connexion with a state of society and thought which repels more than it attracts; the religious history read impartially is chilling and unedifying; its literature on both sides is a compound of elaborate dialectics and indiscriminate invective, alike devoid of high spiritual aspirations and of definite human sympathies. The national character, although it must be allowed to have grown into strength, has not grown into a knowledge how to use its strength. The political bloodshed of the fourteenth century is the prelude to the internecine warfare of the fifteenth: personal vindictiveness becomes, far more than it has ever yet been, a characteristic of political history. Public and private morality seem to fall lower and lower: at court splendid extravagance and coarse indulgence are seen hand in hand; John of Gaunt, the first lord of the land, claims the crown of Castille in the right of his wife, and lives in adultery with one of her ladies; he is looked up to as the protector of a religious party, one of whose special claims to support lies in its assertion of a pure morality; his son, Henry Beaufort, soon to become a bishop, a crusader, and by and by a cardinal, is the father of an illegitimate daughter, whose

mother is sister to the earl of Arundel and the archbishop of
Canterbury. If we look lower down we are tempted to question
whether the growth of religious thought and literary facility has as
yet done more good or harm. Neither the lamentations nor the
confessions of Gower, nor the sterner parables of Langland, nor
the brighter pictures of Chaucer, nor the tracts and sermons of
Wycliffe, reveal to us anything that shows the national character
to be growing in the more precious qualities of truthfulness and
tenderness. There is much misery and much indignation; much
luxury and little sympathy. The lighter stories of Chaucer recall
the novels of Boccaccio, not merely in their borrowed plot but in
the tone which runs through them; vice taken for granted, revelry
and indulgence accepted as the enjoyment and charm of life; if it
be intended as satire it is a satire too far removed from sympathy
for that which is better, too much impregnated with the spirit of
that which it would deride. Edward III, celebrating his great feast
on the institution of the order of the Garter in the midst of the
Black Death, seems a typical illustration of this side of the life of
the century. The disintegration of the older forms of society has
been noted already as accounting for much of the political history
of a period which notwithstanding is fruitful in result. There is no
unity of public interest, no singleness of political aim, no heroism
of self-sacrifice. The baronage is divided against itself, one part
maintaining the popular liberties but retarding their progress by
bitter personal antipathies, the other maintaining royal autocracy,
and although less guilty as aggressors still more guilty by way of
revenge. The clergy are neither intelligent enough to guide education nor strong enough to repress heresy; the heretics have neither
skill to defend nor courage to die for their doctrines; the universities are ready to maintain liberty but not powerful enough to lead
public opinion; the best prelates, even such as Courtenay and
Wykeham, are conservative rather than progressive in their religious policy, and the lower type, which is represented by Arundel,
seems to combine political liberality with religious intolerance in a

way that resembles, though with different aspect and attitude, the policy of the later puritans.

The transition is scarcely less marked in the region of art; in architecture the unmeaning symmetry of the Perpendicular style is an outgrowth but a decline from the graceful and affluent diversity of the Decorated. The change in the penmanship is analogous; the writing of the fourteenth century is coarse and blurred compared with the exquisite elegance of the thirteenth, and yet even that is preferable to the vulgar neatness and deceptive regularity of the fifteenth. The chain of historical writers becomes slighter and slighter until it ceases altogether, except so far as the continuators of the Polychronicon preserve a broken and unimpressive series of isolated facts.

It may seem strange that the training of the thirteenth century, the examples of the patriot barons, the policy of the constitutional king, organiser and legislator, should have had so lame results; that, whilst constitutionally the age is one of progress, morally it should be one of decline, and intellectually one of blossom rather than fruit. But the historian has not yet arisen who can account on the principles of progress, or of reaction, or of alternation, for the tides in the affairs of men. How it was we can read in the pages of the annalists, the poets, the theologians: how it became so we can but guess; why it was suffered we can only understand when we see it overruled for good. It may be that the glories of the thirteenth century conceal the working of internal evils which are not new, but come into stronger relief when the brighter aspects fade away; and that the change of characters from Edward I to Edward II, Edward III and Richard II, does but take away the light that has dazzled the eye of the historian, and so reveals the hollowness and meanness that may have existed all along. It may be that the strength, the tension, the aspirations of the earlier produced the weakness, the relaxation, the grovelling degradation of the later. But it is perhaps still too early to draw a confident conclusion. Weak as is the fourteenth century, the fifteenth is weaker still;

more futile, more bloody, more immoral; yet out of it emerges, in spite of all, the truer and brighter day, the season of more general conscious life, higher longings, more forbearing, more sympathetic, purer, riper liberty.   [CHE, II: 652–656]

&§ If the only object of Constitutional History were the investigation of the origin and powers of Parliament, the study of the subject might be suspended at the deposition of Richard II, to be resumed under the Tudors. During a good portion of the intervening period the history of England contains little else than the details of foreign wars and domestic struggles, in which parliamentary institutions play no prominent part; and, upon a superficial view, their continued existence may seem to be a result of their insignificance among the ruder expedients of arms, the more stormy and spontaneous forces of personal, political, and religious passion. Yet the parliament has a history of its own throughout the period of turmoil. It does not indeed develope any new powers, or invent any new mechanism; its special history is either a monotonous detail of formal proceedings, or a record of asserted privilege. Under the monotonous detail there is going on a process of hardening and sharpening, a second almost imperceptible stage of definition, which, when new life is infused into the mechanism, will have no small effect in determining the ways in which that new life will work. In the record of asserted privilege may be traced the flashes of a consciousness that show the forms of national action to be no mere forms, and illustrate the continuity of a sense of earlier greatness and of an instinctive looking towards a greater destiny. And this is nearly all. The parliamentary constitution lives through the epoch, but its machinery and its functions do not much expand; the weapons which are used by the politicians of the sixteenth and seventeenth centuries are taken, with little attempt at improvement or adaptation, from the armoury of the fourteenth. The intervening age has rather conserved than multiplied them or extended their usefulness.

Yet the interval witnessed a series of changes in national life, mind, and character, in the relations of classes, and in the balance of political forces, far greater than the English race has gone through since the Norman conquest, greater in some respects than it has experienced since it became a consolidated, Christian nation. Of these changes the Reformation, with its attendant measures, was the greatest; but there were others which led to and resulted from the religious change. Such was that recovered strength of the monarchic principle, which, in England as on the Continent, marked the opening of a new era, and which, although in England it resulted from causes peculiar to England, from the exhaustion of all energies except those of the crown, whilst abroad it resulted from the concentration of great territorial possessions in the hands of a few great kings, seemed almost a necessary antecedent to the new conformation of European politics, and to the share which England was to take in them. Such again was the liberation of internal forces, political as well as religious, which followed the disruption of ecclesiastical unity, and which is perhaps the most important of all the phenomena which distinguish modern from medieval history. Such was the transformation of the baronage of early England into the nobility of later times, a transformation attended by changes in personal and political relations which make it more difficult to trace the identity of the peerage than the continuous life of clergy or commons. The altered position of the church, apart from Reformation influences, is another mark of a new period; the estate of the clergy, deprived of the help of the older baronage, which is now almost extinguished, and set in antagonism to the new nobility that is founded upon the spoils of the church, tends ever more and more to lean upon the royal power, which tends ever more and more to use the church for its own ends, and to weaken the hold of the church upon the commons, whenever the interests of the commons and of the crown are seen to be in opposition. Partly parallel to these, partly resulting from them, partly also arising from a fresh impulse of its own liberated and directed by these causes, is the changed position of the commons: the third estate now crushed, now flattered; now consolidated, now divided; now encouraged, now repressed; but escaping the internecine enmities that destroy the baronage, learning wisdom by their mistakes and gaining freedom when it is rid of their leadership, rising by its own growing strength from the prostration in which it has lain, with the other two estates, at the feet of the Tudors, all the stronger because it has itself only to rely upon and has springs of independence in itself, which are not in either clergy or baronage;—the estate of the commons is prepared to enter on the inheritance, towards which the two elder estates have led it on. The crisis to which these changes tend is to determine in that struggle between the crown and the commons which the last two centuries have decided.   [CHE, III: 2–4]

⊸§ The historian turns his back on the middle ages with a brighter hope for the future, but not without regrets for what he is leaving. He recognises the law of the progress of this world, in which the evil and debased elements are so closely intermingled with the noble and the beautiful, that, in the assured march of good, much that is noble and beautiful must needs share the fate of the evil and debased. If it were not for the conviction that, however prolific and progressive the evil may have been, the power of good is more progressive and more prolific, the chronicler of a system that seems to be vanishing might lay down his pen with a heavy heart. The most enthusiastic admirer of medieval life must grant that all that was good and great in it was languishing even to death; and the firmest believer in progress must admit that as yet there were few signs of returning health. The sun of the Plantagenets went down in clouds and thick darkness; the coming of the Tudors gave as yet no promise of light; it was 'as the morning spread upon the mountains,' darkest before the dawn.

The natural inquiry, how the fifteenth century affected the development of national character, deserves an attempt at an answer; but it can be little more than an attempt; for very little light is thrown upon it by the life and genius of great men. With the exception of Henry V, English history can show throughout the age no man who even aspires to greatness; and the greatness of Henry V is not of a sort that is peculiar to the age or distinctive of a stage of national life. His personal idiosyncrasy was that of a hero in no heroic age. Of the best of the minor workers none rises beyond mediocrity of character or achievement. Bedford was a wise and noble statesman, but his whole career was a hopeless failure. Gloucester's character had no element of greatness at all. Beaufort, by his long life, high rank, wealth, experience and ability, held a position almost unrivalled in Europe, but he was neither successful nor disinterested; fair and honest and enlightened as his policy may have been, neither at the time nor ever since has the world looked upon him as a benefactor; he appears in history as a lesser Wolsey,—a hard sentence perhaps, but one which is justified by the general condition of the world in which the two cardinals had to play their part; Beaufort was the great minister of an expiring system, Wolsey of an age of grand transitions. Among the other clerical administrators of the age, Kemp and Waynflete were faithful, honest, enlightened, but quite unequal to the difficulties of their position; and besides them there are absolutely none that come within even the second class of greatness as useful men. It is the same with the barons; such greatness as there is amongst them, —and the greatness of Warwick is the climax and type of it,—is more conspicuous in evil than in good. In the classes beneath the baronage, as we have them portrayed in the Paston Letters, we see more of violence, chicanery and greed, than of anything else. Faithful attachment to the faction which, from hereditary or personal liking, they have determined to maintain, is the one redeeming feature, and it is one which by itself may produce as much evil as good; that nation is in an evil plight in which the sole redeeming quality is one that owes its existence to a deadly disease. All else is languishing: literature has reached the lowest depths of dulness; religion, so far as its chief results are traceable, has sunk, on the one hand into a dogma fenced about with walls which its defenders cannot pass either inward or outward, on the other hand into a mere warcry of the cause of destruction. Between the two lies a narrow borderland of pious and cultivated mysticism, far too fastidious to do much for the world around. Yet here, as everywhere else, the dawn is approaching. Here, as everywhere else, the evil is destroying itself, and the remaining good, lying deep down and having yet to wait long before it reaches the surface, is already striving toward the sunlight that is to come. The good is to come out of the evil; the evil is to compel its own remedy; the good does not spring from it, but is drawn up through it. In the history of nations, as of men, every good and perfect gift is from above; the new life strikes down in the old root; there is no generation from corruption. [CHE, III: 632–634]

The Lancastrian Constitution

⏀ Any attempt to balance or to contrast the constitutional claims and position of the houses of Lancaster and York, is embarrassed by the complications of moral, legal, and personal questions which intrude at every point. The most earnest supporter of the constitutional right of the Lancastrian kings cannot deny the utter incompetency of Henry VI; the most ardent champion of the divine right of hereditary succession must allow that the rule of Edward IV and Richard III was unconstitutional, arbitrary, and sanguinary. Henry VI was not deposed for incompetency; and the unconstitutional rule of the house of York was but a minor cause of its difficulties and final fall. England learned a lesson from both, and owes a sort of debt to both: the rule of the house of Lancaster proved that the nation was not ready for the efficient use of the liberties it had won, and that of the house of York proved that the nation was too full grown to be fettered again with the bonds from which it had escaped. The circumstances too by which the legal position of the two dynasties was determined, have points of likeness and unlikeness which have struck and continue to strike the readers of history in different ways. It may fairly be asked what there was in the usurpation of Edward IV that made it differ in kind from the usurpation of Henry IV; whether the misgovernment of Richard II and the misgovernment of Henry VI differed in nature or only in degree; what force the legal weakness of the Lancastrian title gave to the allegation of its incompetency, to what extent the dynastic position of the house of York may be made to palliate the charges of cruelty and tyranny from which it cannot be cleared.

Such questions will be answered differently by men who approach the subject from different points. . . . The student who approaches the story from the point of view at which these pages have been written, will recognise the constitutional claim of the house of Lancaster, as based on a solemn national act, strengthened by the adherence of three generations to a constitutional form of government, and not forfeited by any distinct breach of the understanding upon which Henry IV originally received the crown. He will recognise in the successful claim of the house of York a retrogressive step, which was made possible by the weakness of Henry VI, but could be justified constitutionally only by a theory of succession which neither on the principles of law nor on the precedents of history could be consistently maintained.

But he may accept these conclusions generally without shutting his eyes to the reality of the difficulties which from almost every side beset the subject—difficulties which were recognised by the wisest men of the time, and knots which could be untied only by the sword. There are personal questions of allegiance and fealty, broken faith and stained honour; allegations and denials of incapacity and misgovernment; a national voice possessing strength that makes it decisive for the moment, but not enough to enable it to resist the dictation of the stronger; giving an uncertain sound from year to year; attainting and rehabilitating in alternate parliaments; claiming a cogency and infallibility which every change of policy belies. The baronage is divided so narrowly that the summons or exclusion of half a dozen members changes the fate of a ministry or of a dynasty; the representation of the commons is liable to the manipulation of local agencies with which constitutional right weighs little in comparison with territorial partisanship: the clergy are either, like the baronage, narrowly divided, or, in the earnest desire of peace, ready to acquiesce in the supremacy of the party which is for the moment the stronger. Even the great mass of the nation does not know its own mind: the northern counties are strong on one side, the southern on the other: a weak government can bring a great force into the field, and a strong government cannot be secured against a bewildering surprise: the weakness of Henry VI and the strength of Richard III alike succumb to a single defeat: the people are weary of both, and yet fight for either. The history contains paradoxes which confused the steadiest heads of the time, and strained the strongest consciences. Hence every house was divided against itself, and few except the chief actors in the drama sustained their part with honesty and consistency. Oaths too were taken only to be broken; reconciliations concluded only that time might be gained to prepare for new battles. The older laws of religion and honour are waning away before the newer laws are strong enough to take their place. Even the material prosperity and growth of the nation are complicated in the same way; rapid exhaustion and rapid development seem to go on side by side; the old order changes, the inherent forces of national life renew themselves in divers ways; and the man who chooses to place himself in the position of a judge must, under the confusion of testimony, and the impossibility of comparing incommensurable influences, allow that on many, perhaps most, of the disputed points, no absolute decision can be attempted.

Without then trying to estimate the exact debt which England owes to either, it will be enough, as it is perhaps indispensable, to compare the two dynasties on the level ground of constitutional practice, and to collect the points on which is based the conclusion, already more than sufficiently indicated, that the rule of the house of Lancaster was in the main constitutional, and that of the house of York in the main unconstitutional. It might be sufficient to say that the rule of the house of Lancaster was most constitutional when it was strongest; and that of the house of York when it was weakest: that the former contravened the constitution only when it was itself in its decrepitude, the latter did so when in its fullest vigour. Such a generalisation may be misconstrued; the administration of Henry V may be regarded as constitutional because he was strong enough to use the constitutional machinery in his own way, and that of Edward IV as unconstitutional because he was strong enough to dispense with it. If however it be granted, as for our purpose and from our point of view it must, that the decision of the quarrel was not directly affected by constitutional questions at all,—if it be admitted, that is, that the claim of York and the Nevilles to deliver the king and kingdom from evil counsellors was neither raised nor prosecuted in a constitutional way, and was in reality both raised and resisted on grounds of dynastic right,—there is no great difficulty in forming a general conclusion. Nor need any misgivings be suggested by the mere forensic difficulty that the claim of the house of York, based on hereditary right of succession, is in itself incompatible with the claim of the baronage, or of the nation which it represented, to use force in order to compel the king to dismiss his unpopular advisers.

[CHE, III: 240–243]

The Winning of English Liberty

❧ And now let us in conclusion ask our question again, how was English liberty won? It was not won all at once; it was not a paper constitution written out at the will of a liberal sovereign, or extorted from a needy one according to the will and pleasure of a school of theorists. It was the growth of two hundred and thirty years of labour and sorrow [1066–1297]; it was not designed by any one master mind; it is in its best aspect a bundle of expedients devised by their authors to meet cases which they never did meet, but which in the process of time were found to answer purposes for which they were never designed. It is a work of very fallible men, a result brought out of weakness by the strength of the Wise Ruler, King of kings. We are proud of it, and rightly: no other nation in the world has its like to compare with it. We may be prouder still when we see how our fathers won it. There was no foreign intervention here: no foreign liberator fought our battles. The thought of invasion had and has, at any moment of our history, the effect of uniting every contending element in the realm in defence. It was not done by secret conspiracy. . . . Conspiring is not an English characteristic, and we may be thankful that tyranny has never forced us to learn it. It was not won by any one man's ambition, making his countrymen believe him a liberator while on the way to make a tyrant; step by step, line by line, it was written by men who had no personal ambition, but abundant patriotic honour and moderation. Their works abide, while the flimsy edifices of men who have had but their own aggrandisement at heart perish. It was not won by one class at the expense or to the loss of another; the nobles and the church won it, but not for themselves only: their cause was the people's cause, and by them the people was freed. It was not won by rebellion or cemented by perjury; it was a gradual limitation of oppression and oppressive power that was indeed in itself a usurpation, but was a discipline needed to bring strength out of weakness; and as it was won in moderation, and unselfishly and truly, it was stained by no great crimes or excesses. The men who earned it were not likely to sully it with disgrace; the people for whom it was earned were gradually trained for it before it came. There was nothing in the full growth of it to turn a people from despair to extravagant excesses. We thank God that it was so; we hope and pray that as it was won and balanced, so it may be maintained, confirmed, and extended. By the light that it gives us we can read and grieve over the abortive efforts of foreign races to win what was won for us. We cannot have much hope of freedom forced upon an unwilling people, undisciplined, unprepared to receive it. We cannot hope for lasting freedom founded upon personal ambition, maintained by perjury and cruelty. We can grieve over the oppressed, but there are worse things even than oppression, things more precious even than liberty—truth and honour and honesty. By these our rights were won: when these are lost, we are slaves indeed. [LEEH, 351–352]